P9-BIX-800

Jewish Theology and Process Thought

SUNY SERIES IN
CONSTRUCTIVE POSTMODERN THOUGHT
DAVID RAY GRIFFIN, EDITOR

Jewish Theology and Process Thought

Edited by

Sandra B. Lubarsky
and
David Ray Griffin

State University of New York Press

Hans Jonas, "The Concept of God after Auschwitz: A Jewish Voice." *Journal of Religion*, Vol. 67, No. 1, Jan. 1987, 1–13. Permission granted by the University of Chicago Press. Chicago, IL © 1987 by The University of Chicago. All rights reserved.

Peter Ochs, "Rabbinic Text Process Theology." *Journal of Jewish Thought and Philosophy*, 1991, Vol. 1, No. 1, 141–177. Permission granted by Harwood Academic Publishers GmbH. Reading, Berkshire, United Kingdom.

Levi Olan, "The Prophetic Faith in a Secular Age," *Journal of Reform Judaism*, Spring, 1979, 1–9. Permission granted by *Journal of Reform Judaism/CCAR Journal*.

Published by
State University of New York Press, Albany

© 1996 State University of New York

All rights reserved.

Printed in the United States of America

No part of this book may be used or reproduced in any manner whatsoever without written permission.
No part of this book may be stored in a retrieval system or transmitted in any form or by any means including electronic, electrostatic, magnetic tape, mechanical, photocopying, recording, or otherwise without the prior permission in writing of the publisher.

For information, address State University of New York Press,
State University Plaza, Albany, N.Y., 12246

Production by Cynthia Tenace Lassonde
Marketing by Dana Yanulavich

Library of Congress Cataloging-in-Publication Data

Jewish theology and process thought / edited by Sandra B. Lubarsky and David Ray Griffin.
    p.   cm. — (SUNY series in constructive postmodern thought)
    Includes bibliographical references and index.
    ISBN 0-7914-2809-5 (hc : alk. paper). — ISBN 0-7914-2810-9 (pbk.
    : alk. paper)
    1. Judaism—Doctrines.   2. Process philosophy.   3. Process
theology.   4. Judaism—Relations—Christianity.   5. Christianity and
other religions—Judaism.   I. Lubarsky, Sandra B., 1954–
II. Griffin, David Ray, 1939–   , III. Series.
BM601.J48   1996
296.3′01—dc20   95-22274
                                           CIP

10 9 8 7 6 5 4 3 2 1

In memory of two of our contributors,

Hans Jonas and Levi A. Olan

Introduction to SUNY Series in Constructive Postmodern Thought

The rapid spread of the term *postmodern* in recent years witnesses to a growing dissatisfaction with modernity and to an increasing sense that the modern age not only had a beginning but can have an end as well. Whereas the word *modern* was almost always used until quite recently as a word of praise and as a synonym for *contemporary*, a growing sense is now evidenced that we can and should leave modernity behind—in fact, that we *must* if we are to avoid destroying ourselves and most of the life on our planet.

Modernity, rather than being regarded as the norm for human society toward which all history has been aiming and into which all societies should be ushered—forcibly if necessary—is instead increasingly seen as an aberration. A new respect for the wisdom of traditional societies is growing as we realize that they have endured for thousands of years and that, by contrast, the existence of modern society for even another century seems doubtful. Likewise, *modernism* as a worldview is less and less seen as The Final Truth, in comparison with which all divergent worldviews are automatically regarded as "superstitious." The modern worldview is increasingly relativized to the status of one among many, useful for some purposes, inadequate for others.

Although there have been antimodern movements before, beginning perhaps near the outset of the nineteenth century with the Romanticists and the Luddites, the rapidity with which the term *postmodern* has become widespread in our time suggests that the antimodern sentiment is more extensive and intense than before, and also that it includes the sense that modernity can be successfully overcome only by going beyond it, not by attempting to return to a premodern form of existence. Insofar as a common element is found in the various ways in which the term is used, *postmodernism* refers to a diffuse sentiment rather than to any common set of doctrines— the sentiment that humanity can and must go beyond the modern.

Beyond connoting this sentiment, the term *postmodern* is used in a confusing variety of ways, some of them contradictory to others.

In artistic and literary circles, for example, postmodernism shares in this general sentiment but also involves a specific reaction against "modernism" in the narrow sense of a movement in artistic-literary circles in the late nineteenth and early twentieth centuries. Postmodern architecture is very different from postmodern literary criticism. In some circles, the term *postmodern* is used in reference to that potpourri of ideas and systems sometimes called *new age metaphysics*, although many of these ideas and systems are more premodern than postmodern. Even in philosophical and theological circles, the term *postmodern* refers to two quite different positions, one of which is reflected in this series. Each position seeks to transcend both *modernism* in the sense of the worldview that has developed out of the seventeenth-century Galilean-Cartesian-Baconian-Newtonian science, and *modernity* in the sense of the world order that both conditioned and was conditioned by this worldview. But the two positions seek to transcend the modern in different ways.

Closely related to literary-artistic postmodernism is a philosophical postmodernism inspired variously by pragmatism, physicalism, Ludwig Wittgenstein, Martin Heidegger, and Jacques Derrida and other recent French thinkers. By the use of terms that arise out of particular segments of this movement, it can be called *deconstructive* or *eliminative postmodernism*. It overcomes the modern worldview through an antiworldview: it deconstructs or eliminates the ingredients necessary for a worldview, such as God, self, purpose, meaning, a real world, and truth as correspondence. While motivated in some cases by the ethical concern to forestall totalitarian systems, this type of postmodern thought issues in relativism, even nihilism. It could also be called *ultramodernism*, in that its eliminations result from carrying modern premises to their logical conclusions.

The postmodernism of this series can, by contrast, be called *constructive* or *revisionary*. It seeks to overcome the modern worldview not by eliminating the possibility of worldviews as such, but by constructing a postmodern worldview through a revision of modern premises and traditional concepts. This constructive or revisionary postmodernism involves a new unity of scientific, ethical, aesthetic, and religious intuitions. It rejects not science as such but only that scientism in which the data of the modern natural sciences are alone allowed to contribute to the construction of our worldview.

The constructive activity of this type of postmodern thought is not limited to a revised worldview; it is equally concerned with a postmodern world that will support and be supported by the new worldview. A postmodern world will involve postmodern persons, with a postmodern spirituality on the one hand, and a postmodern society, ultimately a postmodern global order, on the other. Going beyond the modern world will involve transcending its individualism, anthropocentrism, patriarchy, mechanization, economism, consumerism, nationalism, and militarism. Constructive postmodern thought provides support for the ecology, peace, feminist, and other emancipatory movements of our time, while stressing that the inclusive emancipation must be from modernity itself. The term *postmodern*, however, by contrast with *premodern*, emphasizes that the modern world has produced unparalleled advances that must not be lost in a general revulsion against its negative features.

From the point of view of deconstructive postmodernists, this constructive postmodernism is still hopelessly wedded to outdated concepts, because it wishes to salvage a positive meaning not only for the notions of the human self, historical meaning, and truth as correspondence, which were central to modernity, but also for premodern notions of a divine reality, cosmic meaning, and an enchanted nature. From the point of view of its advocates, however, this revisionary postmodernism is not only more adequate to our experience but also more genuinely postmodern. It does not simply carry the premises of modernity through to their logical conclusions, but criticizes and revises those premises. Through its return to organicism and its acceptance of nonsensory perception, it opens itself to the recovery of truths and values from various forms of premodern thought and practice that had been dogmatically rejected by modernity. This constructive, revisionary postmodernism involves a creative synthesis of modern and premodern truths and values.

This series does not seek to create a movement so much as to help shape and support an already existing movement convinced that modernity can and must be transcended. But those antimodern movements which arose in the past failed to deflect or even retard the onslaught of modernity. What reasons can we have to expect the current movement to be more successful? First, the previous antimodern movements were primarily calls to return to a premodern form of life and thought rather than calls to advance, and the human spirit does not rally to calls to turn back. Second, the previous antimodern movements either rejected modern science, reduced it to a description of mere appearances, or assumed its adequacy in principle; therefore, they could base their calls only on the negative social and spiritual effects of modernity. The current movement draws on natural science itself as a witness against the adequacy of the modern worldview. In the third place, the present movement has even more evidence than did previous movements of the ways in which modernity and its worldview *are* socially and spiritually destructive. The fourth and probably most decisive difference is that the present movement is based on the awareness that *the continuation of modernity threatens the very survival of life on our planet*. This awareness, combined with the growing knowledge of the interdependence of the modern world-view and the militarism, nuclearism, and ecological devastation of the modern world, is providing an unprecedented impetus for people to see the evidence for a postmodern worldview and to envisage postmodern ways of relating to each other, the rest of nature, and the cosmos as a whole. For these reasons, the failure of the previous antimodern movements says little about the possible success of the current movement.

Advocates of this movement do not hold the naively utopian belief that the success of this movement would bring about a global society of universal and lasting peace, harmony, and happiness, in which all spiritual problems, social conflicts, ecological destruction, and hard choices would vanish. There is, after all, surely a deep truth in the testimony of the world's religions to the presence of a trans-cultural proclivity to evil deep within the human heart, which no new paradigm, combined with a new economic order, new child-rearing practices, or any other social arrangements, will suddenly eliminate. Furthermore, it has correctly been said that "life is robbery": a strong element of competition is inherent within finite existence, which no social-political-economic-ecological order can overcome. These two truths, especially when contemplated together, should caution us against unrealistic hopes.

However, no such appeal to "universal constants" should reconcile us to the present order, as if this order were thereby uniquely legitimated. The human proclivity to evil in general, and to conflictual competition and ecological destruction in particular, can be greatly exacerbated or greatly mitigated by a world order and its worldview. Modernity exacerbates it about as much as imaginable. We can therefore envision, without being naively utopian, a far better world order, with a far less dangerous trajectory, than the one we now have.

This series, making no pretense of neutrality, is dedicated to the success of this movement toward a postmodern world.

David Ray Griffin
Series Editor

Contents

Introduction

Sandra B. Lubarsky

The purpose of this collection of essays is to promote a serious encounter between Jewish theology and the process thought that is based on the philosophies of Alfred North Whitehead and Charles Hartshorne. Process thought has been explored and employed by theologians and philosophers of religion virtually since its inception in the 1920s, but for most of this period almost all these thinkers were Christian. In recent years, however, a number of Jewish theologians and philosophers of religion have become interested in process thought. This book constitutes the first extended discussion of the relationships, both positive and negative, that might ensue between Judaism and process thought. It functions in a number of ways:

(1) as a brief introduction to process thought;
(2) as a collection of pioneering essays on Judaism and process thought;
(3) as an appraisal by Jewish and Christian thinkers of the appropriateness of process metaphysics for their respective religious traditions; and
(4) as a catalyst for a Jewish process vision.

I. Early Jewish Responses to Process Thought

The term *process thought* refers in this volume to the metaphysical cosmology developed primarily by Alfred North Whitehead and, somewhat independently and with some significant differences, by Charles Hartshorne. It is a way of understanding reality that emphasizes the changes in the nature of the universe and that interprets such change as the natural consequence of real and essential freedom, novelty, purpose, and experience.

This volume is not intended as an extended exploration of the roots of process thought, but it is important to recognize that process

1

thought is a family with many members whose *paterfamilias* is historically neither Whitehead nor Hartshorne. There is an impressive and influential consortium of intellectuals who promoted ideas that Whitehead and Hartshorne share, and who deserve to be credited as well. Hegel, Bergson, Alexander, Peirce, and James, among others, developed in their own ways the ideas that change is systemic, that individuals are radically related, and that creativity is the energy of life. There are important differences between them, but their individual commitments to the image of reality as processive make them philosophical "family." The expansion, systematic development, and application of these familial ideas to questions of science and religion in the twentieth century is most clearly represented by Whitehead and Hartshorne and their now three generations of students. Hence, the term "process philosophy" has become linked, in the last several decades, primarily to these two figures.

As a school of thought, process philosophy gained prominence and a geographical home in the years between 1930 and 1955 at the University of Chicago Divinity School. People there, such as Henry Nelson Wieman, Bernard Loomer, Bernard Meland, and Charles Hartshorne, encouraged students to consider the relationship of process thought and Christian theology. The consequence has been the development of several forms of Christian process theology, now represented by such individuals as John B. Cobb, Jr., David Ray Griffin, Clark M. Williamson (all included in this volume), Delwin Brown, Catherine Keller, Jay McDaniel, Schubert M. Ogden, and Marjorie Hewitt Suchocki.

During this same period and earlier, there was some engagement with process philosophy by several Jewish thinkers. Max Kadushin, in his book *Organic Thinking: A Study in Rabbinic Thought* (1938), directly addressed the relationship of his notion of rabbinic theology as "organic or organismic" and "the most comprehensive philosophy of organism . . ., that developed by Whitehead."[1] He found important overlap between Whitehead's metaphysics and rabbinic theology— "many of his [Whitehead's] metaphysical concepts can be taken as generalizations of the characteristics of rabbinic theology"—but finally was suspicious of Whitehead's commitment to organicity because of the latter's doctrine of "eternal objects."[2] (In this volume, Peter Ochs provides a critical comparison of Kadushin's organic thought with Whitehead's.)

In addition to Kadushin's participation in the philosophical movement identified as process or organic philosophy and his criticisms of Whitehead's thought, it is important to note in this introduction the fact that Kadushin did not consider Whitehead's thought to be distinctly Christian. He discussed the metaphysical importance of Whitehead's ideas for religion in general and tested their adequacy against his own interpretation of rabbinic thought. But he did not see any necessary or intimate connection between process philosophy and Christianity.

The historical context, as well, freed Kadushin from making an association between process philosophy and Christianity. When Kadushin wrote, process philosophies were in their vigorous years of development and occupied centerstage in significant portions of the philosophical world. Whitehead's thought was part of the new intellectual framework that galvanized the intellectual community. It was only later, in the late 1940s and largely by way of the Divinity School of the University of Chicago, that Whitehead's thought garnered sustained influence in American Christian theology.[3] Even then, those Christian theologians who attempted to "restate the insights of the Christian faith within a philosophical framework" that was specifically Whiteheadian found themselves having to make a case for the appropriateness of process philosophy for expounding Christian faith.[4]

One measure of their success in relating the two is the assumption today by many Jewish thinkers that process philosophy is markedly Christian in orientation. For example, a recent essay on current trends in liberal Jewish thought referred to "Protestant 'process theology.'"[5] The reference here was not to a position that was distinctly Protestant, but rather to the general theological notion that there is an "intimate relationship between the human realm and the divine" such that God is somehow present in human consciousness.[6] The fact that such a broad theological concept, which the author admits is central to (Jewish) Lurianic thought, is nonetheless linked with Protestantism tells us more about the theological success of certain Protestant theologians than about the affinity between Judaism and process theology. At the outset of this volume, then, it seems important to stress that process philosophy presents a general metaphysical scheme for understanding reality as a whole. It has relevance to particular religious configurations but to no one in particular. In Whitehead's own words:

> The useful function of philosophy is to promote the most general systematization of civilized thought.[7]

It provides "generic notions" to be assayed by the actual instances that are the measure of life.

We are wiser today regarding the conditionedness of all speculative schemes. Among the cultural facts of Whitehead's lifestory are that he was white, middle-class, English, male, and the son of an Anglican priest (although in his late, metaphysical period he evidently felt the greatest affinity with Unitarianism). Certainly, any claims for the generality of his system must be weighed against these features and our methodological analyses need to include attention to the philosopher's personal history. But the more significant issue remains the actual usefulness of Whitehead's system for contemporary Jewish theologians.

Among Jewish thinkers in the 1950s who found process philosophy inviting, Milton Steinberg is notable. Above all, Steinberg was concerned that an adequate theology for American Judaism be formulated. In Arthur A. Cohen's estimation,

> No other contemporary Jewish thinker had examined with comparable care and concern the relevance of contemporary metaphysical theory to the problem of Jewish theism. He alone among his contemporaries sustained a concern for the relevance of reasoned inquiry to the task of faith.[8]

Steinberg described himself as a "traditionalist," yet joined the Reconstructionist ranks because of its commitment to "essential tradition and . . . to the demands of contemporary conditions."[9] On a number of important issues, however, Steinberg diverged from Kaplan. Unlike Kaplan, Steinberg believed that theological and philosophical issues are central to a reconstruction of Judaism, legitimate in and of themselves, and not simply derivatives of psychology and sociology. Most significantly, Steinberg differed with Kaplan on the nature of God. Opposed to supernaturalism, he nonetheless argued for the reality of God as a being and not simply as a process or force that makes for good in the world. He explained his differences from Kaplan on the nature of God as follows:

> Because Dr. Kaplan has refused any description of his God as that God is not in his implications but in Himself; because he speaks so generally of the God-idea rather than of God; because, furthermore, he shrinks God to the sum of those aspects of reality which enhance man's life, these being all of God which he regards as mattering to man, because of all this, the following has resulted:

a) The actuality of God is brought under question. It is asked: does God really exist or is He only man's notion?

b) The universe is left unexplained. To say of God that He is a power within the scheme of things leaves the scheme altogether unaccounted for.

c) A need arises for another God beyond and in addition to Dr. Kaplan's who shall account for the world in which they find themselves . . . .

d) Something alarmingly close to tribalism in religion is revived. A God possessed of metaphysical standing, a Being who is also a principle of explanation for reality, must be beyond the parochialism of time and space, of nation and creed. But a God who is all relativist, especially such a God as Kaplan's who tends to be a function of social life, an aspect of a particular civilization, is in imminent peril of breaking down into a plurality of deities, each civilization possessing and being informed by its own.[10]

In the same paper, Steinberg cited with approval Peirce, Whitehead, and Hartshorne, with particular reference to the idea of a transcendent-immanent God who is neither immutable nor omnipotent. Elsewhere, he acknowledged his debt to Hartshorne's neo-classical image of God, which he said freed him from:

servitude to the classical metaphysicians and their God, who in His rigid eternal sameness is no God at all, certainly not the God of whom Scripture maketh proclamation nor whom the human heart requires.[11]

Regrettably, Steinberg did not live long enough to develop these ideas into a Jewish form of process naturalistic theism. Whether he would have is an inference that some reject. Arthur A. Cohen, for example, held that Steinberg was moving more and more toward religious existentialism. But it seems at least equally plausible that Steinberg's lifelong commitment to rational philosophy, modified though it was by a deepened recognition of human imperfection, would have led him to develop a Jewish process theology.

Steinberg is regarded as a transitional figure whose importance in the history of American Jewish theology lies in his recognition of the debilitating effects of Kaplan's sociological approach on religious liberalism and his subsequent call for a renewal of Jewish theology. Those who responded to his call were, on the whole, influenced not by Whitehead and Hartshorne but by neo-orthodox and existentialist thinkers, both Jewish and Christian.[12] Beginning in 1960 and extending until very recently, forms of Judaism that emphasized naturalism and/or rationalism were eclipsed by forms that emphasized the theologically transcendent, the biblical, and, to a lesser extent, the mystical. Central to this shift has been the need to develop Holocaust theologies and to respond to related issues of identity, both of which were often worked out in terms of a "modernistic" particularism. Those like Levi Olan (included in this volume), who maintained the naturalist orientation, have been characterized as pursuing "an extreme Jewish rationalism based on science, nature, and logic."[13]

II. Modernity, Postmodernity, and Process Thought

The "theological issues of the hour" (to use Steinberg's phrase) have changed since neo-orthodoxy became influential in theological circles. Three issues in particular draw our attention. Chief among them is the environmental crisis and the theological obligation to address the relationship of religious traditions and philosophical systems to nature. It has become apparent that all sorts of dualisms, including the dualism between nature and God promoted by neo-orthodoxy, have contributed to the adversarial relationship of humanity to nature. Second, there is the cluster of issues connected with religious and cultural pluralism, including the relationship of one tradition to another, one gender to another, and one culture to another. The "other" argues for an acknowledgment of their inner lives and the reality and legitimacy of their particular perspectives (and consequently the limitations of other perspectives). Subject-object dualism again is indicted, and also absolutism, objectivism, and sexism, all of which call for theological response. How we negotiate between different perspectives and truth-claims is deeply related to how we understand God's nature and the principles of reality. Thirdly, there is the issue of spirituality, often described as the search for transcendent meaning and value distinct from the religious enterprise. That religion has become, for many, disconnected from spirituality is a profound indicator of its failure in the modern world. Liberal forms of Judaism, which have been most willing to submit to the arbitration of the modern, scientific worldview, share in this failure. As Rodger Kamenetz acknowledges in his recent book on Jewish-Buddhist dialogue, "The house of Judaism in North America has not been satisfactorily built—it does not have a spiritual dimension for many Jews."[14]

In broad terms, the issue before us is modernity itself. David Griffin's introduction to the SUNY Series in Constructive Postmodern Thought, which precedes this essay, outlines the matter. Based as it is on dualism or materialism, or a confused mixture thereof, the modern worldview has left us spiritually disenfranchised, alienated from both natural (including human) and transcendent forms of life. The structure of existence built by modernity is incongruous with a religious vision, except for perhaps a greatly attenuated vision. Living between a past tragedy of unspeakable dimensions and a possible future of universal catastrophes, contemporary Jewish thinkers must respond to the crisis of belief raised by both the Holocaust and modernity. Towards this end, Holocaust theology must be placed within a larger religious and metaphysical setting; indeed any discussion of evil requires an ecological setting, else it risks abstraction, trivialization, or glorification. But in addition to the need to address the Holocaust, contemporary Jewish thinkers face an audience of Jews who are neither fully comfortable with Judaism nor thoroughly at home in the secular world. For many, the modern scientific worldview cannot be correlated with Judaism (or any other religious tradition). A Judaism that has nonetheless attempted to comply with its materialism and dualism offers at best meager, temporary shelter. A contemporary *Guide of the Perplexed* requires first a revisioning of the whole conceptual scheme, the worldview, in which Judaism abides.

In describing the role of Jewish philosophers, Neil Gillman writes that historically their task has been

> to provide a coherent, internally consistent and sophisticated defense of Judaism in terms of the conceptual scheme and vocabulary of the particular age; in short, to make the case for Judaism, precisely at a time when such a case has to be made.[15]

As two particularly good examples of Jewish philosophers, he cites Saadya, who raised philosophical inquiry to the level of mitzvah and relied on the Islamic Kalam for his structure, and Maimonides, who used the language of medieval Aristotelianism to address those who sought to follow their intellects and yet remain Jewish.

Many of the Jewish thinkers included in this book seek to make a case for Judaism in terms of a conceptual scheme that is described as postmodern. Process philosophy is a form of postmodern thought in that it supersedes many of the philosophical assumptions of modernity, including, especially, late modernity's rejection of theism. Like deconstructive postmodernism, it rejects supernaturalism, the idea of a totally independent, absolutely powerful God who transcends the world. But unlike the deconstructionists who proclaim the death of God and hence of all authority and truth, process thought affirms that God, the soul of the universe, is alive. And whereas deconstruction calls for a "closing of the past," postmodernist process thought uses the past in a process of reconstruction and renewal.

In brief, a process metaphysics embraces both the finite world and divinity; defends freedom, purpose, and reason as inherent in the structure of reality; insists that reality is "out there"; argues against both pure objectivity and pure subjectivity; and upholds the goals of truth, beauty, and goodness. In taking these positions, process thought rejects philosophical materialism, dualism, and sense-empiricism.

As process thinkers understand it, reality is organic and social, creative and communal—change and interrelatedness are part of its nature—and God is intimately involved in all the events of reality. God's involvement is revealed in the ongoing process itself, although God is not the process per se. God's activity is in one sense natural, like that of all other actual entities, as "there is only one genus of actual entities."[16] There is no metaphysical dualism in the process worldview. But God is not simply another finite being. God exemplifies the metaphysical principles but, at the same time, as the "chief exemplification" of these principles, qualitatively surpasses the abilities of all other beings. God is described as "perfect," both in God's "primordial aspect"—as the one who envisages all possibilities and who offers them, in graded form, to each arising occasion—and in God's "consequent nature"—as the one who experiences and responds to the creative advance as it is actualized in each moment, in each individual. (But perfection in the sense of completion and immutability in all respects is denied. If God were "perfect" in this sense, nothing that happened anywhere would mean anything to God.)

For Whitehead, genuine creativity and community require the existence of God. All individuals are understood to be radically related so that the world is alive in every individual and every individual is felt by every other individual. There are no solitary selves for whom relationships are accidental. Thus, the unceasing change that occurs affects the entirety. God is the being who infuses creativity with order. Apart from God, creativity—the principle of novelty—is simply an abstraction; God is that actuality who provides novel forms based on an appetitive valuation of the eternal possibilities, thereby rescuing the process from being a perpetual rehash of old forms. Moreover, God is the chief stimulus behind the drive for community and the virtues that make it possible.

Although God is logically required by a process metaphysics, God is not simply a logical concept. Whitehead speaks of God as companion, and Hartshorne describes God as "the Holy One, the ethical Absolute, the literally all-loving Father," assertions based not only on logic but on the "felt" experience of God.[17] Experiential knowledge, it is argued, is not limited to that which we acquire through our sensory organs. If it were, we could at most speak of God, with Kant, as a logical construct or, with many contemporary thinkers, as an important part of our cultural heritage. For process thinkers, sensory experience is very important but it is itself dependent on a primordial feeling, called a *prehension*, which is unmediated by consciousness, culture, or developed physiology. Direct access to the world is given by the very process of coming-to-be. The past is not a datum received through sensory organs, nor are causality or values smelled, tasted, touched, seen or heard. Yet memory, connection, and value are undeniably part of our experience, as even sensory empiricists admit by their daily practice, if not verbally. God, too, is part of our basic prehension of experience: God is felt as with us, within us, and also other than us, just as the world is so felt.

Process thought affirms, with Jewish tradition, that God is both present in and transcendent to the world. It is not a form of pantheism, but is, rather, "pan*en*theistic." Hartshorne has defined panentheism as the view that:

> deity is in some real aspect distinguishable from and independent of any and all relative items, and yet, taken as an actual whole, includes all relative items. . . . Panentheism agrees with traditional theism on the important point that the divine individuality, that without which God would not be God, must be logically independent, that is, must not involve any particular world.[18]

This understanding of God's relation to the world is clearly not pantheistic. God is not the world, nor is nature God. Here process thought parallels Rosenzweig's contention that God and World and Individual cannot be dissolved into one another and yet are intimately related.

> God *and* the world *and* man! This "and" was the beginning of experience and so it must recur in the ultimate aspect of truth. For there must be an "and" within truth itself, within ultimate truth that can only be *one*.[19]

A similar insight is celebrated by a number of Kabbalists, who cite Midrash (Gen. R. 68) in support of their understanding of the Godhead:

> The Holy One blessed be He is the place of the world but the world is not His place.

The distinction between pantheism and panentheism is crucial and, although the Kabbalists did not always maintain this distinction, it is vigilantly maintained by process thinkers.[20]

Although the process view is sympathetic to the naturalism of Mordecai Kaplan and others, it is nevertheless a different form of religious naturalism. (This issue is discussed more fully in my essay later in this volume.) Kaplan's naturalism makes religion compatible with the modern scientific worldview by equating God with the process of life. Process theology rejects the mechanism, determinism, and materialism of that worldview in favor of an organic worldview that allows God as a personal being to be active in the process of life, without simply being the process itself. Because God is not the process itself, this form of religious naturalism, unlike Kaplan's, can account for moral value.

III. Whitehead on Religion

Whitehead's description of religion as "what an individual does with his own solitariness"[21] is often quoted as if it were his complete definition of religion. Were this so, there would be reason to be skeptical about the benefits of a Jewish-process exchange, for Judaism is not a religion of the individual but of the individual-in-community. Later in the same book, however, Whitehead clarifies his earlier statement. Having commented that "the world is a scene of solitariness in community," Whitehead says:

> The topic of religion is individuality in community.[22]

In *Science and the Modern World* the role of religion is described more fully:

> Religion is the vision of something which stands beyond, behind, and within, the passing flux of immediate things; something which is real, and yet waiting to be realised; something which is a remote possibility, and yet the greatest of present facts; something that gives meaning to all that passes, and yet eludes

apprehension; something whose possession is the final good, and yet is beyond all reach; something which is the ultimate ideal, and the hopeless quest.

    ... The fact of the religious vision, and its history of persistent expansion, is our one ground for optimism. Apart from it, human life is a flash of occasional enjoyments lighting up a mass of pain and misery, a bagatelle of transient experience.

    ... Evil is the brute motive force of fragmentary purpose, disregarding the eternal vision. Evil is overruling, retarding, hurting. The power of God is the worship He inspires. That religion is strong which in its ritual and its modes of thought evokes an apprehension of the commanding vision.[23]

In *Process and Reality*, Whitehead describes the relationship between philosophy and religion in this way:

> Philosophy ... attains its chief importance by fusing the two, namely, religion and science, into one rational scheme of thought. Religion should connect the rational generality of philosophy with the emotions and purposes springing out of existence in a particular society, in a particular epoch, and conditioned by particular antecedents. Religion is the translation of general ideas into particular thoughts, particular emotions, and particular purposes; it is directed to the end of stretching individual interest beyond its self-defeating particularity. Philosophy finds religion, and modifies it; and conversely religion is among the data of experience which philosophy must weave into its own scheme. Religion is an ultimate craving to infuse into the insistent particularity of emotion that non-temporal generality which primarily belongs to conceptual thought alone.
> ... The two sides of the organism require a reconciliation in which emotional experiences illustrate a conceptual justification, and conceptual experiences find an emotional illustration.[24]

In Whitehead's view, religion and science and philosophy form a coherent whole. Philosophy is not superior to religion or science; rather, they are mutually interdependent.

IV. A Brief Overview of the Essays

Many of the Jewish thinkers who have been directly influenced by process thought in their struggle with modernity are included in this volume. Part I consists of essays by Jewish thinkers who have found process thought to be a useful way to explore Judaism and its theology. The issues discussed are primarily theological: God's transcendence and immanence, the problem of evil, and the idea of revelation. Among the authors in this first section there is general agreement with Levi Olan's statement:

> The metaphysics which most satisfactorily accounts for the nature of the universe . . . was formulated by Whitehead.

According to Olan, we are at an *axial point* in time, precipitated by atomic fission and requiring a "re-evaluation of our basic understanding of man's place in the universe." Neither classical supernaturalism nor the "empirical-rational epistemology" of the sciences that explained away supernaturalism is satisfactory. Rather the *neo-classical* picture of the divine as transcendent-immanent, relational, personal, mutable, and persuasive (not coercive) is both more adequate to what we now know about reality and "readily appropriated by the prophetic faith" of Judaism.

William Kaufman draws on Hartshorne's notion of God as dipolar as a way to navigate between images in Jewish literature of God as wholly transcendent and immutable, on the one hand, and images of God as wholly immanent and mutable, on the other. Likewise, it is Hartshorne's distinction between God's necessary and contingent aspects and his neo-classical notion of perfection that my essay employs in delineating a form of Judaism that is neither dualistic nor pantheistic. Sol Tanenzapf suggests that the ideas of divine dipolarity and internal relatedness to the world enable the construction of a more adequate theory of revelation and philosophy of Mitzvot than can be derived from a dualistic, substance metaphysics.

The issue of divine power is addressed in several essays. In this first section, Harold Kushner gives us a personal account of how he found philosophical support from process thought for his own moral intuitions about divine power. Later, the notion that God's power is persuasive rather than coercive is addressed in more detail by David Griffin, Norbert Samuelson, and Hans Jonas.

Lori Krafte-Jacobs offers a critique of efforts to define *an* essence of Judaism. Her argument is grounded in process metaphysics and its emphasis on freedom, change, internal relatedness, and the character of actual entities. In this light, such terms as *Judaism* and *the Jews* are shown to be ontological abstractions; their referents are, as Jewish history makes clear, complex and mutable individuals. Krafte-Jacobs proposes speaking of continuity rather than essence, suggesting both pragmatic and metaphysical benefits.

Part II consists of a dialogue between Jewish and Christian thinkers on the appropriateness of process thought for Judaism. Three of the originating essays were written by Jewish thinkers—Peter Ochs, Hans Jonas, and Alvin Reines—and three by Christian thinkers—David Griffin, Clark Williamson, and William Beardslee.

Peter Ochs offers a "rabbinic text process theology," based on the thought of Max Kadushin, as an alternative to "Jewish natural process theology." He assumes Kadushin's critique of Whitehead and elaborates on the differences between the two. After raising a number of criticisms, he nonetheless concludes that "text process and natural metaontologies . . . represent mutually-irreducible but complementary forms of inquiry." John Cobb responds to Kadushin and Ochs with a positive appraisal of the "harmonious fit" between text process theology and his own natural process theology. When fully understood, Cobb believes, Whitehead's conception of God as an *actual entity* is quite compatible with rabbinic thought; many of the most important differences raised by Ochs are reduced to a matter of emphasis.

Further compatibility between Ochs' rabbinic text process theology and a Whiteheadian/Hartshornean approach is evidenced in William Beardslee's essay on process hermeneutics. Ochs says:

> Revelation . . . displays its meaning to a potentially indefinite series of symbolizing interpretants: in rabbinic theology, these constitute the revelation's text process.

Beardslee reaches a similar conclusion:

> Each reading of a biblical text invokes a different group of propositions . . . . We always deal with Scripture-and-interpretation.

For both thinkers, the text is foundational but its interpretation is unfixed. From Beardslee we again hear a critique of the search for *essence,* in this case the essence of the biblical message or text, for such a search denies the process of creative transformation that takes place between the reader, the text, and God's presence in our lives. With Ochs, furthermore, Beardslee believes that an encounter with the text should positively transform the reader. In his response to Beardslee's essay, Nahum Ward also affirms the criterion of transformation. The Torah, Ward asserts, "is about transformation," confronting us "with a reality that breaks into and challenges our own."

Ward connects this way of thinking about the text with classic rabbinic hermeneutics.

Four of the exchanges—between Griffin and Samuelson, Jonas and Cobb, Williamson and Laytner, and Reines and Griffin—center on the concept of God as it appears in process and Jewish theologies, with particular emphasis on the issue of God's power.

In "Process Theodicy, Christology, and the *Imitatio Dei*," Griffin details the benefits of conceiving of God's power as persuasive rather than coercive. In addition to offering a more benevolent divine image for human imitation, "persuasive omnipotence," Griffin argues, is the only possible kind of omnipotence in relation to a world in which nondivine beings inherently have some degree of freedom. Once freedom is extended to beings other than divinity, as it is in both the process and Jewish perspectives, God's activity necessarily takes the form of persuasion. Griffin understands power to be inherent in every created being, not simply a divine gift which could be revoked. When power or "creativity" is understood as ingredient in the world, evil becomes a relational event and not a source of accusation against God. Griffin develops the further implications of persuasive omnipotence in an exposition of Christology and Jewish-Christian relations, ending with the entreaty that theologians recognize:

> the degree to which people's emotions and attitudes, and therefore their behavior, are determined by their "intoxication" with their perception of the Holy.

Norbert Samuelson, through the medieval rabbinic authority Gersonides, tests Griffin's assertion that process theology is compatible with Jewish thought. He summarizes Gersonides' positions on creation out of nothing, divine omnipotence and omniscience, human freedom, and divine revelation. In general, Samuelson finds much agreement between Gersonides' positions on creation and revelation and that of process thought. On the issue of God's power, however, Samuelson points out that Gersonides affirms both coercive and persuasive power for divinity.

> Insofar as the laws of nature are an expression of divine power, it is coercive. Similarly, insofar as the moral ideals that function as the end toward which all of history moves are an expression of divine goodness, and insofar as that goodness is identical with God's power, it is persuasive.

The theological revisioning that is entailed by the process position of divine persuasive omnipotence is thus not foreshadowed in classical rabbinic philosophy. Neither, however, is coercive action seen as the only form of divine activity.

Hans Jonas offers a concept of God and a theodicy that is in concert with the process vision. The voice of Auschwitz, he asserts, calls us again to Job's question: "What is the matter" with God? If, as Jews understand things, God is "eminently the Lord of *History*" and this world is "the locus of divine creation, justice, and redemption," then Auschwitz cannot be the last word.

> [O]ne who will not thereupon just give up the concept of God altogether . . . must rethink it so that it still remains thinkable; and that means seeking a new answer to the old question of (and about) Job.

Jonas draws for us a speculative myth about how the world came to be and by what sort of creator. God is described as "suffering," "becoming," "caring," and, "the most critical point in our speculative, theological venture," as "not *all*-powerful." Instead, Jonas proposes that God willingly divested Godself of coercive omnipotence in order to create a world in which there were other beings. He argues that the very concept of omnipotence is paradoxical because it is a relational term in which all relations (such as resistence to the omnipotent one) are negated. Omnipotence is omnivorous, destroying the very beings who give its power meaning! Jonas urges us to consider the idea that God's power is not "power to interfere with the physical course of things" but instead "the mutely insistent appeal of His unfulfilled goal." In other words, God's power is persuasive power, working in the world as a divine lure.

The Christian theologian John Cobb sees much that is "virtually identical" in Jonas' thought and in process theology. There are differences, Cobb explains, but there is no great divide separating Jonas from Hartshorne and Whitehead. What Jonas offers is a form of Jewish process theology, drawing upon the Lurianic concept of *tzimtzum* (divine contraction) but modifying its sense of divine activity so that God is not responsible in full detail for the events of the world. Jonas' position that the heart of God's power lies in the "Hear, O Israel!" (the *Shema*), calling us to create a better home for God and the world, represents a process vision of theology.

Clark Williamson discusses the supersessionist ideology that has characterized much of the Christian discussion of covenant and election. He is deeply critical of this position and argues that the process theory of internal and external relations and the mutability of God can "intelligibly articulate" an alternative and "more appropriately Christian position" in which the Christian covenantal relation with God does not contravene the Jewish covenant but testifies to its truth. Anson Laytner affirms this approach and offers additional ways in which process thought can engender "interfaith reconciliation." In particular, the idea that reality is processive opens up a "spiritual space" in which a new and healthy relationship between Judaism and Christianity can develop.

> Christians ought to free themselves from viewing Judaism in only its Old Testament or even New Testament Pharisaic modes, and Jews need to stop seeing Christianity as a Jewish heresy and as an oppressor.

Laytner maintains that when the many theological commonalities of the two faiths are coupled with the insights of process thought, there is firm ground for understanding.

The final set of essays also centers on God and the proper conception of divinity, but the theological discussion gains wider purview as a discussion of the differences between modern and postmodern worldviews. Alvin Reines, well known for his liberal notion of Judaism as polydoxy,[25] presents a "theology of pure process," called *hylotheism*, which takes as its starting point the Enlightenment inheritance. In particular, he emphasizes freedom of thought, radical individuality, religious tolerance, and the epistemological view that truth about the extramental world is to be based entirely on sense data. On these bases, he argues for a concept of God as "the enduring possiblity of being." Such a God is empty of actuality and thus dependent upon the world for instantiation. The actual, the world, is, however, dependent upon the possible, God. But this necessary relationship between God and the world lacks intimacy because actuality involves finitude and is thus logically separated from that which endures. One consequence of this situation is that human knowledge of the divine is "muted": The only certain knowledge that we can have about God's will is that God wills to exist, and hence the world exists.

> [A] universe that has undergone value-death is equal in divine worth to a universe that is rich in value for human beings. The universe does not exist to fulfill some ideal and esteemed purpose

of its own. It possesses no ultimate and intrinsic value. Its sole function is to be an instrument of the godhead's existence.

Reines criticizes other forms of process philosophy for their inconsistent affirmation of change. Hylotheism, he asserts, is the only form of process theology that affirms the unadulterated mutability of God because it affirms God-as-possibility and not as limited actuality.

In response, David Griffin describes Reines' worldview as "substantively indistinguishable from scientistic secularism." Reines, says Griffin:

> continues to use the word "God,". . .but the meaning of the word has virtually nothing in common with widely accepted meanings.

Griffin offers a response to hylotheism and the "modern liberalism" on which it is based. He argues against the "sensationist epistemology" and "individualistic ontology" that Reines embraces and for the Whiteheadian epistemology of "prehensive" or nonsensory knowing and ontology of relationality. Griffin proposes that just as supernaturalism needed to be rejected, a point on which both he and Reines agree, so too must modernism and its attendant atheism (or "scientistic secularism") be rejected. Griffin concludes his essay, and this book, in support of the late Rabbi Levi Olan's witness that God who is Creator is also "Liberator from the modern to the postmodern world."

Like all metaphysical systems, process philosophy is "the tentative effort to seek coherence and consistency, the perspectival effort to seek relevant generality."[26] It is not a final model for theology or metaphysics; like all else it is limited, partial, and imperfect. Nonetheless, such understanding as can be gained from the process approach awaits us.

It is important to note that process thought is only one of several resources upon which today's Jewish thinkers can draw in seeking to coordinate the truths of Jewish tradition with contemporary insights. Some of what process theologies point to can be found in the Kabbalistic tradition, some in parts of Martin Buber's, Franz Rosenzweig's, and Abraham Heschel's works (for example), some in the renewal movements in contemporary Jewish circles. Some of it can also be found in a sustained dialogue with Eastern traditions, deep ecology and varieties of feminist thought. The dialogue with process philosophy is not the only dialogue that needs to be undertaken. We must seek theological insight wherever it is available.

It is also important to note that Judaism has something to contribute to all of these dialogues. Dialogue is an opportunity for teaching as well as learning. The long intimacy with God that Jews have felt and the texts and language in which this experience has been expressed can enrich and personalize theological discussion. Judaism's commitment to the historical realm and its mending, here and now, makes theological and philosophical discussion answerable to the actual world. At various times in the past, Judaism has been a ferment in the generation of new worldviews, not simply a respondant to an existing one. Judaism has much to gain in dialogue and much to offer to other ways of understanding.

Does process thought have a role to play in a contemporary understanding and development of Judaism? Does Judaism have a role to play in an understanding and development of process thought? My answer to both questions is affirmative. But this collection of essays does not exclude the contrary postion. What is important is not that the affirmative position be taken, but that an earnest encounter between Jewish thinkers and process thought occur, that the incipient dialogue of the recent decades receive a serious hearing by those who lovingly imagine a Judaism for the twenty-first century.

Notes

1. Max Kadushin, *Organic Thinking: A Study in Rabbinic Thought* (1938; New York: Bloch Publishing Co., no date on reissue), 247–50.

2. Ibid., 248, 250.

3. In their introductory essay, "The Development of Process Theology" (in *Process Philosophy and Christian Thought*, Delwin Brown, Ralph E. James, Jr., and Gene Reeves, eds. [Indianapolis: The Bobbs-Merrill Co., 1971]), Reeves and Brown note that "Whitehead's actual influence on American theology during the thirties was very limited. In 1939, some thirty-five participants in a 'How My Mind Has Changed In This Decade' series in *The Christian Century* gave scant mention of Whitehead. . . . A constructive approach to theology through the use of Whitheadian metaphysics is nowhere evident" (25).

4. Bernard M. Loomer, "Christian Faith and Process Philosophy," *The Journal of Religion*, XXIX/3 (July, 1949), reprinted in *Process Philosophy and Christian Thought*, Delwin Brown, Ralph E. James, Jr., and Gene Reeves, eds., 70–98. This essay has been described as an "early milestone in the develop-

ment of process theology." (John B. Cobb, Jr., and David Ray Griffin, *Process Theology: An Introductory Exposition* [Philadelphia: The Westminster Press, 1976], 178.)

5. Peter J. Haas, "The Making of a New American Jewish Theology," *CCAR Journal: A Reform Jewish Quarterly*, XXXIX/3 (Fall, 1992), 10.

6. Ibid. I believe that Haas is referring to the process perspective on God's consequent nature, though he does not name it as such.

7. Alfred North Whitehead, *Process and Reality: An Essay in Cosmology* (original edition, 1929), Corrected Edition, David Ray Griffin and Donald W. Sherburne, eds. (New York: Free Press, 1978), 17.

8. Arthur A. Cohen, *The Natural and the Supernatural Jew*, second edition (New York: Behrman House, 1979), 230–31.

9. Milton Steinberg, quoted in Simon Noveck, *Milton Steinberg: Portrait of a Rabbi* (New York: KTAV Publishing House Inc., 1978), 87.

10. Milton Steinberg, "The Theological Issues of the Hour," *Proceedings of Rabbinical Assembly*, 1949: 379–80, quoted in Noveck, *Milton Steinberg*, 259–60.

11. Steinberg, *Proceedings*, 377, cited in Noveck, *Milton Steinberg*, 262. See also, Steinberg, *Anatomy of Faith*, Arthur A. Cohen, ed. (New York: Harcourt, Brace & World, 1960), 177–79, 179–81, 270–71.

12. There are a few Jewish thinkers of the 1960s who continued to be influenced by the process perspective. Levi Olan, included in this volume, is one. Harold Schulweis is another; he was, to our regret, not able to contribute to this collection. Roland Gittelsohn, a Reform rabbi, has been described as having "wedded his naturalism to contemporary 'Process Philosophy' (deriving from the thought of A. N. Whitehead and Charles Hartshorne)" by Steven T. Katz in his book, *Jewish Philosophers* (New York: Bloch Publishing Co., 1975), 254. Katz goes on to summarize Gittelsohn as follows:

> The traditional transcendent referents of Judaism, e.g., God and Torah, are re-defined in immanentist naturalistic terms which translate, for example, the term "God" from meaning "the transcendent Creator of the world" to a natural process within the universe: "God is to nature what energy is to matter. He is *within* nature. He is not supernatural."

In this brief gloss, Katz errs in two important ways. First, he does not acknowledge the important fact that the description of God given by Whitehead and Hartshorne is much more sophisticated than this. He is therefore not able to make any distinction between Kaplan's naturalism and that of process philosophy. Second, Gittelsohn does not place himself with the process school of thought, nor does he refer to Whitehead or Hartshorne

in the book cited by Katz, *Man's Best Hope* (New York: Random House, 1961).
Gittelsohn specifically rejects the notion of God as a "Cosmic Person" and
affirms the use of the term "personal" in reference to God only if it means
that God "functions in our lives *personally.*" This is clearly Kaplanian
naturalism and not Whiteheadian/Hartshornean theology. Moreover, Gittelsohn describes God as one not conscious of individual actions and as fully
immanent in nature, never transcendent; he interprets "God's will" to mean
"the nature of the universe and myself," "God wants me to" to "refer to my
inescapable responsibility to conform to the nature of the universe and myself,"
and "God watches over me" to refer to "the laws of nature which are changeless
and dependable" (121–22). Such a theology is much removed from that of
Whitehead and Hartshorne and needs to be so recognized.

13. Steven T. Katz, *Jewish Philosophers* (New York: Block Publishing
Co., 1975), 254.

14. Rodger Kamenetz, *The Jew in the Lotus: A Poet's Rediscovery of
Jewish Identity in Buddhist India* (San Francisco: Harper, 1994), 282.

15. Neil Gillman, "The Jewish Philosopher in Search of a Role,"
Judaism 34/4 (Fall, 1985), 477.

16. Whitehead, *Process and Reality*, 28, 168.

17. Whitehead, *Religion in the Making* (Cleveland: World Publishing
Co., 1960), 16; Charles Hartshorne, "The Formally Possible Doctrines of God,"
in Delwin Brown, Ralph E. James, Jr., and Gene Reeves, eds., *Process
Philosophy and Christian Thought*, 213.

18. Hartshorne, *The Divine Relativity: A Social Conception of God*
(New Haven: Yale University Press, 1948), 89–90.

19. Quoted in Nahum N. Glatzer, *Franz Rosenzweig: His Life and
Thought* (New York: Schocken Books, 1961), 205.

20. The failure to differentiate between pantheism and panentheism,
incidentally, goes far beyond the confusion about process thought. Louis
Jacobs, for example, conflates Elizabeth Barrett Browning's panentheistic
exclamation with R. Levi Yitzhak of Berditchev's pantheistic song. Barrett
Browning writes:

Earth's crammed with heaven,
And every common bush afire with God;
But only he who sees, takes off his shoes.

R. Levi Yitzhak writes:

Where I wander—You!
Where I ponder—You!

Only You, You again, always You!
You! You! You!
When I am gladdened—You!
When I am saddened—You!
Only You, You again, always You!
You! You! You!
Sky is You! Earth is You!
You above! You Below!
In every trend, at every end,
Only You, You again, always You!
You! You! You!

The difference between "Earth's crammed with heaven" and "Sky is You! Earth is You!" is the difference between panentheism and pantheism; it is the difference between the-world-in-God-and-God-in-the-world, on the one hand, and the-world-is-God, on the other.

21. A.N. Whitehead, *Religion in the Making*, 16.

22. Ibid., 86.

23. Whitehead, *Science and the Modern World* (New York: Free Press, 1967), 191–92.

24. Whitehead, *Process and Reality*, 15–16.

25. See especially Alvin Reines, "Birth Dogma and Philosophic Religious Faith: A Philosophic Inquiry," *Hebrew Union College Annual*, 46 (1975), 297–329, and "God and Jewish Theology," in *Contemporary Reform Jewish Thought*, ed. Bernard Martin (Chicago: Quadrangle Books, 1968), 62–86.

26. Delwin Brown, "Thinking About the God of the Poor: Questions for Liberation Theology From Process Thought," *Journal of the American Academy of Religion*, LVII/ 2 (Summer 1989), 277.

Part I

Jewish Theology
and Process Thought

Chapter 1

The Prophetic Faith in a Secular Age

Levi A. Olan

Every age asks the religious question in terms of its own culture and must seek an answer within those terms. There is, of course, a logical continuity with the understanding of previous ages. The Hebrew prophets lived in an era which Karl Jaspers calls "the axial period of history," a time when radical questions were being asked and non-traditional answers were proposed. Confucius, Buddha, and the philosophers were engaged in a similar enterprise which set history upon a new cultural road. The religious question, which is the same for all ages, i.e., what is the meaning of human existence?, was answered by primitive man in terms of the culture of his time, and the pantheon of the ancients mirrored the life-style of the Greeks. The classical view of God as a supernatural, omnipotent, and omniscient being was acceptable to the cultural milieu of the western world until the twentieth century. "Culture," says Malinowski, "is the artificial secondary environment which man super-imposes on the natural. It comprises language, habits, ideas, beliefs, customs, social organization, inherited artifacts, technical processes, values."[1] As these vary and change, man's response takes on innovative and different expressions. Man cannot be said to lose faith when the current formulae no longer inform his life. The religious response to the meaning of human existence must be intelligible within the culture to which it addresses itself. Religion disappears as an active phenomenon when it fails to heed the demands of cultural development.

The present cultural climate is not receptive to the classical view of the universe. It rejects the idea that there is an ultimate, perfect, unchanging, supernatural being who is self-sufficient, adequate to himself without need of all else, an uncompromising absolute. The atheist pays his respect to this classical view of God by asserting that his denial of its truth is the rejection of all theism. "Whenever it abandons a system of thought," says Lubac, "humanity imagines it has lost God. The God of 'classical ontology' is dead, you say? It may be so: but it does not worry over much . . . and if classical ontology disappeared, it was surely because it did not correspond adequately with being. Nor was its idea of God adequate for God. The mind is alive, and so is the God who makes himself known to it."[2]

It is becoming increasingly clear that the liberalism which characterized the culture of the modern world was naive in its view of human nature and innocent about the dynamics of human history. It committed a very critical error when it applied the rational-empirical epistemology to the entire cognitive sphere, and the logical positivists enshrined this error into dogma. There are dimensions of human experience that the scientific-rational method can neither investigate nor explain. Aesthetic reality, for example, is for physicists "mere appearance," thus consigning an important segment of human experience to unreality. Religion suffered similarly when its claim to truth was tested by a method alien to its nature. The question of the meaning of human existence is not the subject matter of either science or morals. Stephen Toulmin suggests that there are "limiting questions" which arise at the limit of our moral and scientific inquiry. After all the conventional answers to our moral questions have been given, we are still confronted with the limiting question: Why should I be moral at all? "Ethics provides the reason for choosing the right course, religion helps us to put our hearts into it."[3] Erich Fromm supports this view in psychological terms:

> All men need a frame of orientation which is a more fundamental need than sexuality, social power, and possessions. Man has a craving for knowledge of the right direction.[4]

Religion's primary function is to satisfy that craving.

As the modern age passes into the postmodern it is evident that the remarkable success of the empirical-rational epistemology in the physical and social sciences left unexplained important areas of human experience. Religion is one of these. The protest which arose against this embarrassing failure came from Neo-Orthodoxy (Barth) and Existentialism (Kierkegaard). These have proved themselves inadequate to answer the religious question as modern secular man asks it. A tragically staggering price has been paid for this failure. Man finds himself today living in a crisis which, in Whitehead's words, is all "foreground with no background."

The event that, more than any other, separates the modern world from the postmodern is the fission of the atom. It ushered in an axial point in human history which calls for a re-evaluation of our basic understanding of man's place in the universe. Matter is no longer material; the atom is formed of protons, neutrons, electrons, and twenty or more other particles. We cannot ask what these particles are "made of," since they are not "substances." We may speak of energy, waves, particles, but we are actually dealing with fleeting episodes in the microcosm that are not permanent. Our picture of reality, then, is not yesterday's matter but today's relationships, processes, and events. Instead of an edifice of hard building blocks, ultimate reality is relational.

Along with relationality, indeterminacy is an integral character of matter. Alternatives and chance are inherently part of reality. Quantum physics demonstrates that there are several possible states a system may occupy. Only in large numbers of identical systems does predictable behavior arrive and become more determinate in a statistically significant sense, as the number and frequencies of occurrences increase. The universe could have had many histories other than the one it has had. Something else could have been and was not. For five or ten billion years each stage of history has been a springboard for the next, with many possible directions in which the jump could be made. These basic characters of reality—relationality and indeterminacy—comprise a unitary, integrated whole of systemic interdependence, solidarity, and common destiny for all of its inhabitants and components.

The metaphysics that most satisfactorily accounts for the nature of the universe as disclosed by this scientific revolution was formulated by Whitehead. Basically, this metaphysics rejects the "sensationalist" doctrine of Descartes, and the "world sensa" of the Enlightenment. Instead, it begins with the experience of the self which is aware of past bodily and mental states, as well as of the world beyond itself. It asks a critically new question: What is the dominating insight whereby we suppose ourselves as actualities within a world of actualities? The answer begins with a nonsensuous perception—a mode of awareness more basic than sensation—so that we know ourselves as creatures in a world of creatures. The metaphysics that supports this advances the proposition that "at the base of our existence is the sense of worth . . . it is the sense of existence for its own sake, of existence which is its own justification, of existence with its own character."[5] Here, then, is something that matters, which is to say that reality is something that matters.

Cognition in this case begins not with substance, but with self-enfolding fellow creatures as well as the infinite whole in which we are, somehow, included as one. The *One* is compelled in experience which is relational and monistic at the same time. Whitehead implies that reality comprised of ourselves, others, and the whole is the sense of deity, or, as he describes it, "the intuition of holiness," which is the foundation of religion. The reality of God is inescapable as long as we experience that whole of which we are a part and which we trust. Schubert Ogden defines it concisely:

> "God" is the very meaning of "reality" when this word is defined in terms of our basic confidence in the significance of life and the kind of questions and answers such confidence make possible.[6]

The secularist and atheist protestations against the role of God in nature and history do not, in themselves, constitute a denial of his existence. They represent, in most instances, a rejection of a particular scheme common to a different cultural era. What is dead today, in an age dominated by science, is the classical view of God who is "up there" or "out there," someone who manages the world as he wills. History records many reformulations of man's view of God. The prophets did not reject God when they discarded the priestly view of him. The theism of the prophets was rooted in a theology that conceived of God as supernatural, omnipotent, and a being who acted directly to move the course of history. The mood of our postmodern culture is inhospitable to this classical theology in which God can either cause a holocaust or prevent it. The idea of "the God of the gaps" does not pass muster with men informed by the new scientific revolution. The neo-classical theology based on Whiteheadian metaphysics seems adequate for the present. It is, however, not the final and unchangeable view of God. The future will probably look back upon it as a step forward in the ongoing process of history.

The central meaning of the prophetic faith is best described as "ethical monotheism" and is based upon the covenant that God made with Israel at Sinai. The prophets did not invent it; they interpreted it and re-interpreted it as changing historical situations demanded. But they never discarded the spirit of the original covenant in which the fundamental principles were spelled out. They employed the language and form of their age, describing God as a being of stern moral will, and the omnipotent Lord of history.

> Shall the horn be blown in a city, / And the people not tremble? / Shall evil befall a city, / And the Lord hath not done it?[7]

> I form the light, and create the darkness: / I make peace and create evil; / I am the Lord that doeth all these things.[8]

No matter how appealing the ethical dimension of the prophetic faith is to modern secular man, the theological form in which it is framed is unacceptable.

A principle of openness characterizes the prophets' approach to the covenant. They were free to criticize the popular view of God which tradition had preserved and jealously protected. This freedom introduces the possibility that their own theological formulation, as well as any other, may be critically examined and, if found wanting, discarded. This openness allows men to question and to alter every theism, so long as the meaning of the original covenant is preserved. But it also rules out every form of atheism, since ethics without God violates the essence of the covenant to which God is a partner with man. The neo-classical view of God which is presented here is readily appropriated by the prophetic faith. The essence of the covenant is retained and postmodern culture accepts it; in fact, it strongly supports it. Relationality is the heart of the prophetic faith. "The prophetic idea of God," wrote Martin Buber, "is an expression of man's longing for unity, and for rescue from his own inner duality."[9] The biblical command "Thou shalt love the Lord thy God" is meaningless unless there is in man a desire to be reunited with his origins. Love can never be demanded, even the love of God, unless it is directed toward finding oneself in unity with the *One* who is the unity of all that exists.

The reality of God is inescapable once we begin our thinking with the self as part of the organic nature which is visible to everyone. What is not immediately self-evident is God's nature and how he functions. There are intimations that help us in our search for possible answers. The first is that reality is a unified whole which supports the prophetic claim for the truth of monotheism. Within this one reality, it is clear today, there exist elements of chance, mind, creative freedom, and cosmic purpose. There are intimations that God is supreme and ultimate, but never beyond. He is part of reality, not apart from it. He is best described as transcendent-immanent. A second intimation arises from the proposition that all known reality, including God, is relational, not absolute. The universe seems to be an ecosystem in which all parts are interrelated, interdependent, and interpenetrating. No one part exists in isolation; it is affected by, and itself affects, all others and the system as a whole. God's being, then, depends upon what happens in the uncertainty of time: What God will be is contingent, in large measure, upon what man does. God is the "eminently" relative *One*, and, being relative to all others, is himself relative to nothing. God is the absolute ground of any and all relationships, his own and all others. God, being the most relative, is, therefore, the most absolute.

A third intimation points to the view that God is personal, not abstract. God, like a human person, is self-identical. Although he changes, unity in continuity persists. He prehends all; he is aware of what is going on in our inmost mind; he can feel for us and sympathize with us. He is the fellow-sufferer who loves and is loved. The proposal that God is a person raises the spectre of anthropomorphism. Why not use the term "reality" instead of "God"? Heschel suggests that the biblical idea of man made in the image of God points to a theomorphic anthropology. In the charge "Holy shall ye be, for I the Lord your God am holy," the character of the God described includes intelligence, valuation, and volition, which Tennant says constitute the essence of personality as we know it, in addition to the subjecthood it presupposes.[10]

A fourth proposition inherent in the worldview derived from the new sciences is the extended nature of man's freedom. Unlike Aristotle, who assigned man the role of unfolding what had been enfolded by fate, nature, or God, the new *Weltanschauung* imposes upon him the task of selecting goals as well as creating the means for achieving them. Men are, thus, evaluating beings free to choose their course. Man is free to choose among alternatives and is guided by the experience of the whole and the *One*. In classical theism, God's power is coercive, even though he grants man the freedom to rebel. The idea of an omnipotent being possessing both coercive and unlimited power is disabused in history. Power, however, need not be coercive; it can be persuasive and unlimited. God creates by persuading the world to create itself. This is effective only as men choose and confirm the purposes which are urged upon them. That there has been an evolutionary movement from the simple to the complex is undeniable. It is no more to be explained by chance than by coercive power. The existence of a power directing this process over billions of years, a power "introducing richer possibilities of order for the world to actualize," is inescapable.

It follows from this view that tragedy is an inseparable ingredient of freedom, which, along with chance, is bound together with law and design. The root of tragedy lies in free activity, since creatures can choose not to be persuaded. All free creatures are more or less dangerous, and the most free is man. Born to freedom, man is born to tragedy; but he is born, also, to opportunity. The role of God, the Supreme Creativity, is to inspire lesser creative action, and to take it up into his own unsurpassable actuality. In this process, opportunities for existence outweigh its risks, and life becomes, essentially, good. In a poetic passage toward the end of his *Process and Reality*, Whitehead writes:

> The wisdom of the divine subjective aim prehends every actuality for what it can be in such a perfected system—its sufferings, its sorrows, its failures, its triumphs, its immediacies of joy— woven by rightness of feeling into the harmony of universal feeling. . . . The revolts of destructive evil, purely self-regarding, are dismissed into their triviality of merely individual facts; and yet the good they did achieve in individual joy, in individual sorrow, in the introduction of needed contrast, is yet saved by its relation to the completed whole. The image—and it is but an image—the image under which this operative growth of God's nature is best conceived is that of a tender care that nothing be lost. The consequent nature of God is his judgment on the world. He saves the world as it passes into the immediacy of his own life. It is the judgment of a tenderness which loses nothing that can be saved. It is also the judgment of a wisdom which uses what in the temporal world is mere wreckage.[11]

The unknown prophet of the Babylonian exile understood God in a similar way:

> And a bruised reed he will not break, / And a dimly burning wick he will not quench; / He will faithfully bring forth justice.[12]

Freed from the theological framework of the biblical age, the prophetic faith's primary interest is God's concern for man. The power to coerce is present, but the divine effort to persuade men to do good and not evil is dominant. That men do not heed, that they disregard God's pleading, awakens within God a profound feeling of pathos. "Not self-sufficiency but concern and involvement," says Heschel, "characterizes his relation to the world. . . . [W]hat the prophet proclaims is not his silence but his pathos."[13] God is never presented by the prophets as a metaphysical entity beyond change. "If that nation, concerning which I have spoken, turns from its evil, I will repent of the evil I have intended to do it."[14] The reality of God is sensed in pathos rather than in power. Heschel suggests that divine ethics does not operate without pathos; indeed ethics and pathos are one. The prophets proclaim not God's justice, but his pathos; they speak not for justice, but for the God of justice. Concern for the world is the ethics of God.[15] No word of God is the final word; his judgments are conditional. A change in man's response brings about a change in God's judgment. "Love is the ultimate principle of justice," wrote Paul Tillich. "Love reunites; justice preserves what is united. It is the form in which and through which love performs its work. Justice in its ultimate meaning is creative justice, and creative justice is the form of reuniting love."[16] The prophets sought the reunion of the separated parts which neo-classical theism defines as God's primary goal. He is the ultimate source of values in an ongoing, dynamic activity.

Western civilization today, it seems, is not in harmony with the basic character of the universe as the new science describes it. Materialism dominates our culture at a time when the universe is disclosed to be non-material. Fragmentation is increasingly the mode of human organization, while the universe is revealed to be an integrative unity. Fierce competition among men and nations takes place in a setting of nature which acts as a co-operative whole. Rugged individualism is extolled as a high virtue in a universe that emphasizes individuality in community. The major drive of western culture aims at separating the part from the whole. Alongside materialism and fragmentation there is persuasive evidence that man is being transformed into a machine at the very time when the universe seems to reflect qualities of personhood. The rise of technology in the service of sophisticated science threatens the very existence of man on earth. Nature is described as organic, while man increasingly behaves as a mechanism. The brutality of the Nazis fell far below the savagery of animals. Only a lifeless machine can operate an Auschwitz. In this moment men possess the power to destroy the unity of the planet and ultimately the planet itself.

The paradox that baffles modern man is that he finds himself in a life-or-death crisis at the very time when his secular endeavors have succeeded brilliantly. The evils that threatened human existence in the past—hunger, disease, natural calamities—are today, in increasing measure, subject to control, and even disappearance. The advances made through science and technology are truly wonderful, and by an earlier generation would have been described as miracles. And yet, the crisis in which man finds himself today is far more threatening than ever before in history. The tragic irony of it is that the instruments that promised man's liberation have themselves become the source of the possible, some believe probable, threat to his existence on earth. Prophecies of doom today are not proclaimed in the name of God; they come from scientific laboratories, the writings of social scientists, and the works of modern creative artists.

This bizarre development of the promise of liberation turning into the spectre of total annihilation is attributed to a variety of causes and is not pertinent to our concern here. What is important to our thesis is that all of this is happening as one *Weltanschauung* is fading and being succeeded by another. Theism is giving way to secularism, and what men believe about the universe, sooner or later, determines what they do. The prophetic faith in the neo-classical frame is not only acceptable to our postmodern culture; it is enriched by it and becomes more meaningful. Ethical monotheism takes on added significance in a universe that is basically one, whole, relational, and purposive. God, the untiring persuader and prehender, can help men actualize the novel opportunities he presents to advance history toward the divine goal.

Notes

1. B. Malinowski, "Culture," *Encyclopedia of the Social Sciences*, Edwin R.A. Seligman, ed. (New York: Macmillan, 1931), IV: 621–45, at 621.

2. Henri De Lubac, *The Discovery of God* (New York: P.J. Kennedy, 1960), 167.

3. Stephen Toulmin, *An Examination of the Place of Reason in Ethics* (Cambridge: Cambridge University Press, 1950), 219.

4. Quoted by Huston Smith, "The Death and Rebirth of Metaphysics," in *Process and Divinity: The Hartshorne Festschrift*, William L. Reese and Eugene Freeman, eds. (La Salle: Open Court, 1964), 37–47, at 41.

5. A. N. Whitehead, *Modes of Thought* (New York: Macmillan, 1938), 146.

6. Schubert Ogden, *The Reality of God* (New York: Harper & Row, 1963), 29.

7. Amos 3:6.

8. Isaiah 45:7.

9. Quoted in review of Martin Buber's *On Judaism*, in *Saturday Review of Literature*, February 10, 1968: 34.

10. F. R. Tennant, *Philosophical Theology*, II (Cambridge: Cambridge University Press, 1930), 166.

11. A. N. Whitehead, *Process and Reality*, Corrected Edition (New York: Free Press, 1978), 346.

12. Isaiah 47:3.

13. A. J. Heschel, *The Prophets* (Philadelphia: Jewish Publication Society of America, 1962), 260.

14. Jeremiah 18:8.

15. Heschel, *The Prophets*. The chapter on pathos is especially important.

16. Paul Tillich, *Love, Power, and Justice* (New York: Oxford University Press, 1954), 70–72.

Chapter 2

A Process Theory of Torah and Mitzvot

Sol Tanenzapf

It is widely held among Jewish theologians that process philosophy is unavailable for Jewish theological reflection. Some doubt whether a theory of revelation that is adequate to the authoritative sources of the Jewish tradition—biblical and rabbinic—can be formulated using the concepts of process philosophy. Others object that there can be no place in process theology for the life of Mitzvot (literally, God's commandments) and the practice of Halakhah (the discipline of sacred deeds). The second line of objection is, I think, especially important. Jewish theology must be tested for its capacity to make intelligible the liturgical life of the Jew and the practice of Halakhah. While the Halakhah is not the whole of Judaism, it is its most distinctive feature. If the life of Mitzvot is to make sense—and countless Jews through the generations have testified that the life of Mitzvot and the halakhic discipline is a path to God—then there must be a theory of revelation in which God is distinct from nature and humanity and in which human beings can know what God's will is for them. I will argue that the objections of these critics can be met, and that a theory of revelation and a philosophy of Mitzvot that is adequate to the faith of Judaism can be formulated within the conceptual framework of process philosophy.

To formulate a process theory of revelation, one must first separate two questions:

(1) Is God's revelation at Sinai and to the prophets possible given process theology's metaphysical account of reality?

(2) Did such revelatory events actually occur?

35

It is clear, I think, that within the metaphysics of process theology revelatory events are possible. However, I also think that it is largely a matter of historical investigation to determine whether the events attested to by a religious community did in fact occur, and a matter of existential commitment to decide that the events are indeed revelatory. I will focus attention, therefore, on the first question: if the revelatory events did occur, can they be described using the metaphysical categories of process philosophy? Surely, a process theory of revelation is, at first sight, more promising than a theory of revelation formulated within the conceptual framework of a dualistic, substance-accident metaphysics, in which God is conceived to be independent and apart from the world, immutable and impassible, externally related to and unaffected by human beings.

I. The Possibility of Revelation in Process Theology and Maimonides

In process theology, ultimate reality is God-with-the-world; there is no ontological gap that must be bridged by God's self-disclosure. God is the all-inclusive actuality, who at once transcends the world and is immanent within each actual entity in the world.[1] In process theology, God is conceived as unsurpassable by any other actuality and, consequently, eminently worthy of worship. However, God is also thought of as capable of surpassing any previous state of Himself. Because God is unsurpassably knowing, powerful, and loving, and endures everlastingly, no other entity is as great as God and no other entity is worthy of worship. Because God can surpass previous states of God's own actuality, God can change and grow in response to events in the world of nature and of human history. God includes in His knowledge all that happens as it happens and responds lovingly to everything that does happen.[2] This divine responsiveness or relativity does not detract from God's worshipfulness. A God who in His consequent nature can change and who is affected by the acts of other entities, a God who has physical as well as conceptual feelings, is a God who can meaningfully be described as personal. God who in His primordial nature can lure human beings to creative transformation, to higher and higher stages of human development, is a God who can meaningfully be said to act in history. God can make His will known to humankind, and can do so in a persuasive, noncoercive way, in a way that respects the autonomy of persons. Such is the God proclaimed by Jewish tradition, and such is the God conceived by process theologians.

Of course, if we assume that revelation must occur in one particular way, namely, in a supernaturalistic way, then a process theory of revelation is condemned as inadequate from the start. But we ought not to assume that God acts only by special intervention into the natural course of events, or that God disclosed His will for humanity only by direct or verbal communication to the prophets. Nor should we assume that what is known through revelation cannot be known in any other way. Maimonides' theory of revelation, for example, makes none of these assumptions.

Critics of process theology often take biblical imagery in the most literal way possible and interpret the biblical account of God's self-disclosure in history, and in the lives of the prophets, in terms of miraculous intervention. These critics have long ago rejected any notion of miracles on grounds that such a view is incompatible with scientific method and theory, and with our commonsense observations. To demand that process theology provide a defense of supernaturalistic views of God's revelation and of literalistic interpretations of the biblical text is disingenuous on the part of these critics. The great classics in Jewish theology, such as Maimonides' *The Guide of the Perplexed*, also abandoned supernaturalistic accounts of divine revelation and literalistic textual interpretations, and for the same reasons.

It will be instructive, therefore, briefly to examine Maimonides' theory of revelation. In his conception of God, Maimonides insists on God's unity and simplicity, in contrast to Whitehead's and Hartshorne's conceptions of God's dipolar nature. He also stresses God's complete transcendence and ontological self-sufficiency, while they do not. Nevertheless, he finds a way to speak of divine immanence. The theory that God's essential attributes are negative, without positive content, implies that God is transcendent, distinct from the world, and unlike anything in it. The theory that God's other (nonessential) attributes are attributes of action implies that God is immanent in the world, that we can know God by studying the world of nature and human experience, that is, by studying the sciences and history. For Maimonides, then, God is not totally distinct from the world. Indeed, the flow or emanation from God through the Active Intellect provides purposeful order to the world of nature and providential direction to human beings who have cultivated the intellectual and spiritual life.[3]

It is in his theory of revelation that Maimonides' immanentalism is most evident. For Maimonides, the *act* of revelation is in the end a mystery: the divine act is beyond human comprehension. However, the human side—the prophets' reception of the divine disclosure—

can be studied. Moreover, the content of revelation can be comprehended and explained by human beings; in particular, the reasons for
the Mitzvot can be understood and delineated.

Opponents of Maimonides long ago pointed out that Maimonides'
account of prophecy is almost naturalistic. The prophet, according
to Maimonides, is like the philosopher in aspiring to the perfection
or realization of the intellectual capacities, and like the statesman
in cultivating the imaginative faculties. Studying the human side of
the revelatory event, Maimonides emphasizes the similarities between
the prophet's acquisition of knowledge and that of other persons. The
acquisition of knowledge by all human beings is the joint result of
divine initiative through the Active Intellect and of human response.
Sometimes the influence of the Active Intellect is just sufficient for
the perfection of the individual; sometimes it is so abundant that the
recipient seeks to impart the newly acquired knowledge to others and,
consequently, takes the role of prophet. There are different grades or
classes of prophecy. These gradations are due to differences in the
development of the reason, the imagination, and the moral character
of the individual prophet. Prophecy can be withheld by God, but most
often the differences among human beings in this regard reflect
differences in aptitude, preparation, and study that qualify individuals
for prophetic insight.[4]

A process theological account of revelation would also compare
the prophet's acquisition of knowledge and of moral insight to the
acquisition of knowledge and moral insight by human beings generally. It would stress God's immanence in the efforts of all persons (not
just prophets) to attain knowledge and spiritual awareness. The differences between prophets and others would not be absolute, but
matters of degree. John Cobb and David Griffin point out that in
process theology there is no sharp distinction between general revelation (God's revelation in nature and in human experience as a whole)
and special revelation (God's revelation in the decisive insights that
arose through extraordinary historical occurrences).[5]

If we stress the similarity of revelation to other quests for
knowledge and moral insight, it is not because process theology cannot
accommodate the notion of a special source of knowledge supple-
menting what human reason can attain on its own and whose content
might conflict with the results of natural methods of inquiry. It is
because such claims to a special source of knowledge are already
problematic for reasons recognized by philosophers and theologians
long before Whitehead and Hartshorne began to write. One cannot
reflectively believe in revelation unless one has some notion of how

revelation is possible, and unless the content of revelation is coherent with other things we know to be true. If revelation is taken to involve a miraculous intervention of God into the course of events, then we have a discordance between the belief in revelation and the fundamental principles of a worldview compatible with scientific theory and method. The critical study of the Bible provides evidence of the cultural influences acting on the biblical authors. The morally objectionable passages in the biblical texts can only be explained, like the literary history of the texts, as the products of human authorship, although the fact of human authorship does not, by itself, rule out the possibility of divine inspiration. The conflicting claims made by different religious communities do, however, rule out any account of revelation as a unique or final act of God. Otherwise, we would have to explain how it is that God made Himself known to one people and not to other peoples, and how other people can be so mistaken in thinking that their scriptures are revelations of God.

A process theory of revelation will affirm God's immanence without denying God's transcendence. As the all-inclusive reality, God is necessarily related to each actual occasion (and thus immanent), and as the all-inclusive reality, God is radically different from every other entity in the universe (and thus transcendent). All actual occasions prehend God, as well as all other actual occasions that constitute their environment. In conceptually prehending relevant possibilities (eternal objects) for novel actualization, the emerging occasion of experience prehends God. It follows from process theology's theory of real internal relations that the God who is prehended is present in the actual occasion.[6] All actual occasions experience God-relatedness, but only some are consciously aware of what is unconsciously experienced by all others. While each occasion must take account of God, this prehension can be excluded from the later phases of a moment of experience in which consciousness may arise. Only in some persons is the prehension of God raised to the level of conscious awareness, and expecially in prophets is this awareness made the focus of attention.

From its prehension of God, the actual occasion derives its initial aim toward the most intense enjoyment possible for itself and for the future occasions it will affect. God's primordial nature is the source of novelty and order, drawing the actual occasion on to creative transformation, but also setting limits to the extent to which an actual occasion may go beyond its past. God envisages all possibilities (the eternal objects) and presents them to each actual occasion. God's vision leads each occasion toward novel possibilities that might add richness and intensity to the experience of that occasion and of future occasions. There is a divine call forward to actualize new possibilities in an orderly and harmonious way.[7] It is in the personal series of higher-grade actual occasions that constitute themselves as the mind of the prophet that God's persuasive call is most clearly heard. The prophet deliberately chooses to work toward the achievement of God's purposes for the world.

The initial aim is toward the actualization of the greatest enjoyment both for the occasion and for the subsequent occasions that it will affect. Because there is most likely a tension between the present enjoyment of the occasion and the novel possibilities that are known by God, the occasion will not only prehend God's will for it; it will prehend it as other than its own.[8]

For revelation to occur at all, there must be a human reception of, and response to, God's call. Because each actual occasion is partially self-creative, as well as partially determined, different actual occasions will not respond to the divine call in the same way. God does not compel them to act in accordance with His vision for the whole of reality. An actual occasion has real freedom and is, therefore, responsible for selecting from what is presented to it, what will become part of its subjective aim.

By providing the initial aim of each actual occasion God is immanent in the quest for knowledge and for moral insight in all persons. The pursuit of knowledge and of moral insight in the prophet is not essentially different from similar pursuits by other persons; the differences are only matters of degree. Some persons respond more fully to God's call than do others. The limitations arise from the prior history of the actual occasions in a personal series, from environmental conditions, and from the self-determination of the occasions of experience in the process of becoming concrete actualities.

II. Revelation in Louis Jacobs and Abraham Heschel

I propose to cite from the writings of two contemporary Jewish theologians—Louis Jacobs and Abraham Heschel—whose views of revelation and philosophies of Mitzvot are compatible with the theory of revelation presented here.

Louis Jacobs has wrestled with the objections to the traditional accounts of revelation and has formulated a theory of revelation that attempts to meet those objections and still provide a justification for the life of Mitzvot and halakhic practice. Professor Jacobs is not a process theologian; indeed, he is critical of process theology.[9] However, it is my contention that his is a theory of revelation that is both consistent with Jewish tradition and with a process theory of the God-world relation. Jacobs insists that revelation includes a human as well as a divine side, that it includes both human response and divine act. Like Franz Rosenzweig and Martin Buber, Jacobs describes revelation as the prophet's response to an encounter with God. Revelation, he says, is an event in which a person is confronted by God. Prophets experience God's presence in the history of Israel and in the events of their own lives; they do not hear words. The actual words of the Torah are those of the prophets, not of God. Prophets express their understanding of God's will in the words and images of their time and place. Yet God does speak to human beings, not directly, but through the prophets and through the larger community of Israel, which appropriated and interpreted the prophets' words.

The Mitzvot are binding on the Jew because, writes Jacobs, they bring him or her nearer to God. They make worship possible and enable the Jew to relive the initial revelatory experiences. God's will is expressed in the Mitzvot, not because God directly spoke in these very words, but because the Mitzvot are Israel's response to God's self-disclosure. The Mitzvot continue to be experienced as sources of spiritual exaltation, leading people into the presence of God. Moreover, they commend themselves to reasoned understanding: the Mitzvot, with very few exceptions (and Jacobs is prepared to specify these exceptions), are consistent with our best ethical thinking. This is the justification of the claim that they come from God.[10]

Abraham Heschel's philosophy of Mitzvot has much in common with that of Louis Jacobs. Like Jacob's theory of Jewish practice, Heschel's theory is part of a comprehensive philosophy of Judaism, which includes an account of revelation that is responsive to the challenges posed by literary and historical criticism of the Bible and scientific, moral, and philosophical objections to the belief in revelation. Heschel seeks to avoid rational justifications of the life of Mitzvot that are reductionistic. He writes:

> The problem of ethics is, what is the ideal or principle of conduct that is *rationally* justifiable? To religion the problem of living is, what is the ideal or principle of living that is *spiritually* justifiable? The legitimate question concerning the forms of Jewish observance is the question: *Are they spiritually meaningful?*[11]

To ask whether the Mitzvot are spiritually meaningful is to ask whether they add holiness to the life of the individual.

Heschel characterizes his philosophy of Mitzvot as synoptic and comprehensive. He insists that sociological, aesthetic, moral, and dogmatic reasons for the practice of the Mitzvot are all pertinent. Practice of the Mitzvot identifies the practitioner as a Jew and promotes group cohesiveness. Keeping the traditional rituals adds a dimension of beauty to the commonplace activities of one's life and a dimension of significance to life-cycle events. The ethical Mitzvot directly, and the ritual Mitzvot indirectly, transmit values and habituate individuals to their actualization. Furthermore, the practice of Mitzvot enables one to obey God's will. However, Heschel insists on subordinating the useful, the right, and the beautiful to the holy. The happiness of the individual, and the survival of Israel, are legitimate goals of religious living only when they derive from the pursuit of the holy. He writes:

> Judaism is concerned with the happiness of the individual as well as the survival of the Jewish people, with the redemption of all men and with the will of one God. It claims, however, that happiness is contingent upon faithfulness to God; that the unique importance of the survival of the people is in its being a partner to a covenant with God; that the redemption of all men depends upon their serving His will.[12]

The Mitzvot, according to Heschel, have three purposes: the achievement of one purpose leads to the achievement of the next, culminating in the sanctification of life. First, doing the Mitzvot evokes in the individual a sense of wonder and an awareness of the sublimity of the world, points to a meaning beyond the mystery of existence, and makes one aware of God's presence in the universe. Second, doing the Mitzvot transforms the person who does them. Finally, doing the Mitzvot contributes to the redemption of humankind.

Consider the first purpose of the Mitzvot. The sense of wonder and feelings of awe and reverence need to be kept alive. The liturgy reminds one of the "miracles which are daily with us," of "continual marvels" that one would otherwise take for granted because they are so familiar. One is trained in experiencing wonder by uttering blessings before the enjoyment of food, before performing both significant and commonplace actions. The practice of Mitzvot can lead to "radical amazement," to surprise that there is a world at all, and that one is alive and aware of living in such a wondrous world. Radical amazement can prompt one to ask ultimate questions, questions to which the Jewish tradition provides answers, but whose answers are pointless unless one first asks the appropriate questions.[13] Heschel calls for a leap of action rather than a leap of faith. He proposes an experiment and claims that such an adventure of the soul can be a path back to God. Heschel thinks that contemporary humanity's most pressing problem is its increasing secularity, its increasing tendency to live life as though God were absent from the world and unconcerned about human life. Heschel's aim is to enable persons to recapture those experiences in terms of which talk about God and God's will for humankind becomes meaningful again. He does, of course, believe that God addresses humankind, most discernibly in the Torah, in the preaching of the prophets, and in the interpretations of the sages. The commandments in the Torah, he says, and the sages' explication of those commandments, express God's will for humanity. Nevertheless, Heschel gives little emphasis to the "dogmatic approach" to the Mitzvot. Instead, he calls attention to the meaning of the Mitzvot and their values for the individual who observes them. Their primary value is that they enable the individual to recapture an awareness of God, to experience God's presence in nature and in the events of Israel's history. Heschel does not argue to a logically prescriptive conclusion. He calls for an existential decision on the part of his reader. What he does provide is a phenomenological description of the sense of wonder and radical amazement, and of the feelings of awe and reverence. In addition, he offers personal testimony, and the witness of saintly Jews of generations past, that the practice of the Mitzvot leads to spiritual exaltation and raises one to an awareness of the divine dimension of reality.

Heschel also contends that the Mitzvot have transforming power. He writes that the ecstasy of deeds done with proper devotion can take one out of oneself, enable one to rise above one's selfish needs and interests, to overcome one's demonic and evil impulses. For Heschel, the temptations to aggression and unrestrained acquisitiveness are real, the struggles with them, of utmost seriousness. Heschel's view of human nature is dark; it was forged out of his experience of the destruction of European Jewry during World War II. We know now, he says, that all people are capable of cruelty, complicity, indifference, or willed ignorance in the face of human suffering, and we know now how insidiously evil disguises itself with the cloak of noble ideals. In addressing a meeting of Quakers in Frankfurt in March of 1938, protesting the actions of the Nazi party, Heschel recalled the words of the Baal Shem Tov:

> If a man has beheld evil, he may know that it was shown to him in order that he learn his own guilt and repent; for what is shown to him is also within him.[14]

The Mitzvot, however, are an antidote to the poisons of the soul. Heschel writes:

> The Mitzvot are formative. The soul grows by noble deeds. The soul is illumined by sacred acts. Indeed, the purpose of all Mitzvot is to refine man: to protect and to ennoble him, to discipline and to inspire him.[15]

Heschel believes that not only do actions follow from intentions, but actions engender intentions. Since "God requires the heart," and overt behavior is the way one controls one's impulses and trains one's heart, sacred deeds will change one's character in line with God's will.

Finally, the purpose of the practice of the Mitzvot is to hasten the redemption of the world.[16] Heschel writes:

> It is within our power to mirror [God's] unending love in deeds of kindness . . . . He has delegated to man the power to act in His stead. We represent Him in relieving affliction and in granting joy.[17]

Heschel does not believe that humans by their own efforts can redeem the world, nor does he believe that the world will be redeemed by a sheer act of grace on God's part. What humans can do is make the world worthy of redemption. The initiative is ours; the consummation must be left to God. This account of the import of the Mitzvot is grounded firmly in Heschel's theology. It is compatible with Heschel's conception of God's "restrained omnipotence" and with Heschel's claim that God is in need of human beings. Heschel contends that God emerges out of His hiddenness through humanity and that humanity is God's proxy in the world. The Mitzvot are a constant reminder that God, too, has a stake in human affairs, that God is capable of pathos, that He is affected by what human beings do or fail to do, and that God suffers with all who suffer, and rejoices with all who rejoice. It is especially in the sacred deed that God and humanity meet, and humanity is reassured that it is not alone.

III. Conclusion

Both medieval and modern Jewish theologians, then, writing from within the community of faith and responding to the philosophical, moral, scientific, and critical objections raised against the tradition's claim to be grounded in God's revelation to Israel and to humankind,

have formulated theories of revelation that are neither supernaturalistic in their metaphysics nor literalistic in their hermeneutics, that
do not insist on miraculous intervention or on verbal inerrancy.
Moreover, contemporary Jewish thinkers, such as Louis Jacobs and
Abraham Heschel, have developed philosophical justifications of the
discipline of Halakhah and the life of Mitzvot that are compatible
with these accounts of revelation, accounts of revelation that are in
turn compatible with the worldview of process philosophy. The justifications put forward by Louis Jacobs and Abraham Heschel do not
depend on the claim that the Mitzvot derive their authority from the
explicit verbal disclosure of God's will to the prophets and people of
Israel. The justification of the life of Mitzvot is that putatively the
Mitzvot add holiness to the lives of individuals who practice them
with proper devotion and right intention, and consequently bring
those persons closer to God. It is claimed that in the past the Mitzvot
have led persons to a greater awareness of God's presence in the world,
have enabled them to control the darker impulses of their nature, and
have motivated them to serve God's purposes by acting to redeem the
world from hatred and oppression. It is further claimed that the
Mitzvot can do so again.

Notes

1. Alfred North Whitehead, *Religion in the Making* (London:
Cambridge University Press, 1926), 85; *Process and Reality* (New York: The
Free Press, 1978), 348.

2. Whitehead, *Process and Reality*, 344–46, 348–49. Charles
Hartshorne, *Man's Vision of God* (New York: Harper & Row, 1941), 35–40;
A Natural Theology For Our Time (La Salle, Illinois: Open Court, 1967), 72–76.

3. Moses Maimonides, *The Guide of the Perplexed*, I. 50–60; III. 17–18,
22–23.

4. Ibid., II. 32–48.

5. John B. Cobb, Jr., and David Ray Griffin, *Process Theology* (Philadelphia: The Westminister Press, 1976), 159.

6. Whitehead, *Religion in the Making*, 81; *Process and Reality*, 348.

7. Whitehead, *Process and Reality*, 343–44. Cobb and Griffin, *Process
Theology*, 28–29.

8. Whitehead, *Religion in the Making*, 87–89. Cobb and Griffin,
Process Theology, 105.

9. Louis Jacobs, *A Jewish Theology* (New York: Behrman House, 1973), 75–77, 122–23.

10. Ibid., chapters 14–15.

11. Abraham J. Heschel, *God in Search of Man* (New York: Farrar, Straus and Cudahy, 1955), 351 (italics added).

12. Ibid., 349.

13. Ibid., 48–49.

14. Heschel, *Between God and Man*, Fritz Rothschild, ed. (New York: Harper and Brothers, 1959), 255.

15. Heschel, *God in Search of Man*, 357–58.

16. Ibid., 296, 313.

17. Ibid., 290–91.

Chapter 3

Judaism and Process Thought: Between Naturalism and Supernaturalism

Sandra B. Lubarsky

Many of Judaism's best and most influential thinkers have deliberately come to terms with various non-Jewish philosophies: Philo came to terms with Plotinus, Maimonides with Aristotle, Cohen with Kant, Rosenzweig with Hegel, Kaplan with Dewey, and a whole host of Jews have come to terms with various non-Jewish existentialists. "Coming to terms with" has not meant uncritical adoption but it has involved serious regard for the non-Jewish philosopher. Whitehead's philosophy of organism would seem to be a likely contemporary candidate for such dialogue. There are several reasons why this has not yet happened on a large scale, not least of which is the current preference of Jewish thinkers for history and sociology rather than theology. But for those who have continued to speak theologically, I believe that Whitehead's thought has not received serious consideration primarily because it has been equated with the naturalistic theology of Mordecai Kaplan, which was rejected by those who now dominate Jewish theological discussion. The purpose of this essay is, first, to make clear the distinctions between a naturalism based on Whitehead and Hartshorne and one based on Kaplan, and then to suggest reasons why a process naturalistic theology is more compelling than either supernaturalism or Kaplan's type of naturalism.

I. From Naturalism to Neo-Orthodoxy

Robert Goldy, in *The Emergence of Jewish Theology in America*, chronicles the theological battle that was waged between "second-generation" Jewish thinkers (those who reached intellectual maturity between 1925 and 1930) and "third-generation" thinkers (those coming of age between 1950 and 1955).[1] In large part, the second generation accepted the naturalistic theology of John Dewey as adapted by Mordecai Kaplan, and theology became an enterprise that required justification. Thus, Samuel Cohon found that his chair in Jewish theology at Hebrew Union College had to be defended.

> Proposals were urged to alter its [the chair's] name to something more euphonious and less committed to theistic presuppositions. It therefore became necessary to demonstrate the religious nature of Judaism and the role of theology in its development, as well as to justify the place of theology in the curriculum of a rabbinical seminary.[2]

Here was a generation making sense of a world that seemed rapidly to be improving, and to be doing so as a consequence of human reason and hard work. Theism was tangential to the melioristic enterprise; speculation about the nature of God enfeebled it. And so, Mordecai Kaplan wrote:

> The only alternative to the traditional and supernaturalist conception of God's self-manifestation that can make a difference in people's lives is not the metaphysical approach but the social-behavioral one . . . . [R]eligion which aims to improve human nature and the conditions of human living cannot be based on the ultimate nature of God. Its field of operations must be the nature of man. . . . *It is the business of religion not to give a metaphysical conception of God, but to make clear what we mean by the belief in God, from the standpoint of the difference that belief makes in human conduct and striving.*[3]

The "business of religion" was to direct itself toward the betterment of human nature and human institutions. It was a task undertaken with confidence that life was inherently worthwhile, with optimism that human fulfillment would be achieved, and with the belief that the outcome would be universally good. Its fundamental theological doctrine was that God's presence in human history takes the form of human reason, freedom, and responsibility. When people acted reasonably, freely, and responsibly, they expressed the "self-conscious will to salvation" which is, according to Kaplan, "the immanent aspect of that cosmic reality for which no term can be more appropriate than 'God.' "5

What came to be known as the *New Jewish Theology* was a rejection of this type of religious naturalism. The rationalism of the second generation was criticized as excessive, the meliorism as naive, the focus on humanity as idolatrous, the concept of God as bourgeois. The leading figures of this "third generation" in American theology were Will Herberg, Abraham Heschel, Emil Fackenheim, and Joseph Soloveitchik (all influenced by Franz Rosenzweig and Martin Buber), and they described their approach as "neo-orthodox," "existential," and/or "biblical." Like certain of their Christian counterparts, they found naturalism to be incongruent with the history that they had experienced. In the light of the "unnatural" events of the two world wars, naturalistic theology seemed childish at best. Reasonable and responsible behavior had not been the order of the day; indeed, world events warranted a counter assumption—that human beings are naturally sinful. The years between 1918 and 1945 constituted more than enough evidence for the failure of the natural order as a means of salvation. And yet it was clear that salvation was needed.

In place of a human-centered vision, the third generation of Jewish thinkers promoted a God-centered vision. While the second generation had emphasized the prophetic message of ethics, the third generation renewed the prophetic method per se—criticism of human institutions, behavior, and reason itself. These thinkers debunked the notion that self-realization is equivalent to salvation, arguing instead that human nature rightly understood is hardly a source of promise.

[T]he twentieth century . . . demonstrates the fact that destructiveness is not merely something "unnatural," the product of sickness. . . . "Normal" men beyond suspicion of sickness, morbidity, and frustration "express themselves" in war, destruction, and wholesale murder.5

These third-generation thinkers called instead for a renewal of the divine-human relationship, where the divine and the human occupy different regions, where God's transcendence is crucial and we are reminded of the "unfathomable" aspects of God. Theonomy replaced autonomy. Human reason, freedom, and responsibility are not "natural" but are derived from God: only in relationship to what Fackenheim calls the "absolute, existential *apriori*" do people have the ability to use their reason and freedom responsibly.

If life is to find total integration, we must seek it in a Reality transcending our contradictory self and the ideals and standards relative to it.[6]

The Christian theologian Reinhold Niebuhr greatly inspired this third generation of Jewish theologians in America. Of Niebuhr, Abraham Heschel wrote:

Niebuhr not only helps many of his contemporaries to see through their delusions, deceptions, and pretensions; he also succeeds in recovering some of the insights of prophetic thinking that are of tremendous aid in understanding the central issues of existence from a religious perspective.[7]

Many Jewish thinkers of the naturalistic bent deplored this new perspective on Judaism. They accused such thinkers as Will Herberg—who publically affirmed his theological debt to Niebuhr—of concocting a model of theology that was essentially un-Jewish. Herberg's thought was condemned as a "Judaism cross-fertilized with Christian existentialism" and as "a Jewish version of Christian theology."[8] According to Mordecai Kaplan:

The Apostle Paul started this cult, which may be called the Religion of Unreason; Tertullian institutionalized it; Kierkegaard revived it after a long period of suspended animation; Barth, Brunner, and Niebuhr have made it fashionable; and some Jewish theologians are now dancing to its tune.[9]

Jewish neo-orthodoxy was censured on two counts: for its "unreason" and for its supposedly Christian roots. The fact that theology was the mode for such thinking was considered to be additional evidence of alien influence.

Nonetheless, by the 1960s neo-orthodoxy was victorious in its battle against naturalism and its attendant secularism. Since then, naturalism in any form has not been given a serious hearing by those thinkers who embraced neo-orthodoxy. Surely the acrimony that characterized the early relations between neo-orthodox and naturalistic thinkers is a partial explanation for this disregard. But the fuller reason is that no distinctions have been drawn between the various forms of naturalism; indeed, naturalism has been understood as shorthand for "Deweyan religion" or Kaplan's "Judaism without supernaturalism." And so it is that the process theology of Whitehead and Hartshorne has been neglected as a possible direction for future Jewish thought, at a time when Jewish thinkers are faced with a new round of historical events that seem rather too heavy for the footings of religious existentialism.

II. Whiteheadian Naturalism

The naturalism that follows from a Whiteheadian metaphysics is very different from the naturalism of John Dewey, although there are some important similarities. Likewise, the naturalism of this form of process thought has affinities with both neo-orthodoxy and liberalism and some important differences.

The most important difference between the naturalism of Whitehead and Hartshorne, and that of Dewey and Kaplan, is that the former affirms the existence of a divine *being*, very much like the God of the Hebrew Bible. Dewey, of course, rejects the notion of a divine being, per se, and his primary motivation for doing so is his belief that life is relational and processive. That life is relational and processive is fundamental to the process metaphysics of Whitehead and Hartshorne as well, but for them this affirmation does not entail the rejection of theism. By affirming "being" and "becoming" as two aspects of God's nature, they avoid Dewey's either/or—either an eternal, self-sufficient supernatural being or an ever-changing process that naturally promotes growth.

For Dewey, traditional theism in which God is unaffected by events, in particular by the event of being known, undercuts the whole of human experience. Supernaturalism supports a "spectator theory" of knowledge, where humans *see* the truth but are in no way partners in its making. All human activity is thus eviscerated, because, if the ideal is already actual and unaffected by what we do, then our action is insignificant. To make sense of human experience, Dewey rejects classical theism.

However, as the neo-orthodox thinkers noted, Dewey's alternative is highly unsatisfying. Supernaturalism remained the more fulfilling option, in spite of its problems. In 1982, Seymour Siegel reported that:

> [E]ven the Columbia University campus, where John Dewey taught, does not want Deweyan religion; it prefers the Baal Shem Tov . . . . Kaplan taught a God who is totally understood. It turns out that such a God is irrelevant. God is real and concrete only when He is beyond our grasp and understanding—when He is,

in the words of Kaplan's Seminary colleague, the late Abraham J. Heschel, ineffable.[10]

Clearly, the naturalism of Dewey and Kaplan has been rejected by many. What is not clear is the sort of supernaturalism that is thus affirmed.

For most people, a turn away from Kaplan and Dewey has not entailed a return to traditional supernaturalism with its miracles, censorship of science, and authoritarianism. Instead, the ineffability of God's nature and the transcendence of God over the world have been affirmed along with the blessings of philosophy, science, and the autonomy of reason. This has resulted in some ambivalence. One of the most telling theological examples of the ambivalence of "modern supernaturalism" is the notion of "contentless revelation," a notion promoted by a host of third-generation Jewish thinkers. Not comfortable with accepting Torah as the literal word of God's revelation, and yet wanting to speak of the encounter between God and the world, the notion of contentless revelation reflects a compromise between traditional supernaturalism and the truisms of the age of biblical criticism, historical consciousness, and pluralism, which had brought forth naturalistic religion in the second generation. God's presence is disconnected from God's word: there is revelation but no spoken truth.

Such is the ambivalence of liberal Jews who cannot return to the assumptions of premodern thought and yet cannot settle with Kaplan's naturalism. The solution has been a return to Kantian-based dualism by which they have simultaneously cultivated reason and nurtured a religion that is beyond reason.[11]

Whitehead and Hartshorne have, however, suggested a middle way between naturalism and supernaturalism. Their position is that "being" and "becoming" are equally aspects of God's nature. They have proposed that God's nature be thought of in "dipolar" terms. Whitehead uses the language of *primordial* and *consequent* to distinguish between God's eternal nature and God's responsive nature. Hartshorne speaks in terms of God's *necessary nature* and *contingent states*. In both cases, being is considered to be an abstraction, while becoming is the most concrete mode of reality. In neither case is it sufficient to speak of God either as pure being or pure becoming.

Crucial to Whitehead's philosophy of organism is the notion of creativity, the process that characterizes the universe. Creativity is the ongoing, novel configuring of the world in which the disparate elements become a unity and the new unity itself becomes, at another point, an element to be included in a new whole. "The many become one, and are increased by one"—this is the journey of the world. Aristotle's category of "primary substance" is replaced by the "Category of the Ultimate," which is the triad of creativity-many-one.[12] Beginning with the principle that the preeminent character of the universe is its processive nature, thus rejecting the substance metaphysics that has dominated Western thought, Whitehead and Hartshorne develop a conception of God that is compatible with the "ultimate metaphysical principle"—the "advance from disjunction to conjunction."[13]

In God's primordial nature, God is unchanging, transcendent, unsurpassable, infinite, independent, and necessary. These qualities, reflecting the Greek notion of perfection, were ascribed to God by classical theism but were lacking in Kaplan's description of God. God for Whitehead embodies the "eternal objects," or "pure potentials," which correspond to Plato's eternal forms. God is, thereby, that being in whom the general potentiality of the universe finds its place. Pure potentials exist in God and are "graded" by God according to their relevance to the process of creation. In this way, God serves as the one who initially orders the universe with a view to enhancing creativity and experience.

The ideal order that God conceives for the world is unconditioned by the events of the world—"the *particularities* of the actual world presuppose *it*."[14] In this sense the primordial nature of God is complete and immutable. Nonetheless, God viewed in this way is also the "principle of concretion"—that being upon whom the processive advance depends—*concrescence* being another name for the process of the many becoming one. The primordial nature of God, "free, complete, primordial, eternal"[15] though it be, is also a necessary part of the creative process of the universe. It is both transcendent over the world and immanent in it.

But the primordial aspect of God—God as the "unlimited conceptual realization of the absolute wealth of potentiality"—is "deficiently actual."[16] It is only an abstraction from God as a whole. Finally, God is not God except as primordial *and* consequent, as eternal being *and* responsive becoming, and thus God is not deficient in any possible way.

God is truly perfect, but perfection in this model requires the ability to change in response to an ever-changing world. The consequent or contingent nature of God is that dimension of God that is "consequent upon the creative advance of the world."[17] It is the aspect of God that is affected by particular events. It is, in fact, not simply an aspect of God, but God as a whole, because this aspect of God includes the eternal aspect. This is God as personal being, as the one who feels with all of creation, who consoles, who urges, who enjoys, who sorrows, who is "with us." This is the aspect of God that moves us to speak of God as father, mother, parent, and of ourselves as daughters or sons. And yet, this aspect of God, so much a part of the biblical tradition, was highly problematic for classical theism, informed as it was by Aristotle and Plotinus.

Classical theism denies that God is affected by events because it accepts the Greek notion that change is evidence of deficiency: a being who changes was either imperfect before the change or has become imperfect as a consequence of the change. In this way of thinking, perfection entails completion, finality, invulnerability, impassibility, eternality, fixity, and absolute independence in all respects. As we have seen, for Whitehead and Hartshorne these are characteristics of the primordial nature of God, of that aspect of God that envisions the world in all its possibilities. But this description of God by itself is limiting of both God and human life. It limits God to providing value to the world, not allowing God then to enjoy the value realized. The reality of human life (indeed, all life) is thus utterly mundane, and human effort of every sort is unconditionally ephemeral; it contributes nothing to God, and therefore achieves nothing everlasting. Truly in this model we are simply spectators to the really real, an audience whose admiration goes unacknowledged. On this point, Dewey was certainly right. If God is unaffected by human action, then all our efforts to "be holy" or to "establish God's kingdom on earth" or to "do God's will" have no real significance to the one who matters most. Dewey's solution to this dilemma was to reject classical theism in favor of a nontheistic naturalism. The Whiteheadian response is to amend the notion of perfection, producing thereby a dipolar theism.

III. The Neo-Classical Idea of Perfection

It is Hartshorne who develops the "neo-classical" notion of perfection and, in doing so, makes it clear that dipolarity in reference to God's nature is not just a clever dodge for getting around modernity's challenge to theism, but the only way of making sense of God's perfect nature. He distinguishes between "absolute perfection" and "relative perfection," and argues that God is best understood as that being who is in some respects absolutely perfect and in other respects relatively perfect.[18] This is the essence of dipolarity. Absolute perfection refers to those aspects of being that are "unsurpassable in conception or possibility" by any other being or even by the "perfect" being itself in a subsequent state.[19] God is "absolutely perfect . . . in those things that depend by their nature upon one's own excellence alone."[20] So, for example, God is absolutely loving and, in this quality, immutable. Relative perfection, by contrast, refers to those aspects of the divine being that are unsurpassable *except by the divine being itself in a later state.* It concerns the "social" aspects of deity, which are matters of relationships. So, while God's loving nature is immutable, God's love for the world is always contingent on what there is to love, on the concrete particulars of the world. Likewise, God's knowledge of the past grows as the present moves to the past, as the past increases. Since the creative process is the ultimate reality, time is real because new things come into existence. God's knowledge of the past must change in order to "be complete." In this sense, God's knowledge is ever-increasing and God is self-surpassable.

According to the process model, then, perfection is not simply another name for self-sufficiency and immutability. To define perfection in this way only is to limit God to the realm of abstraction and to lose the God with whom the biblical authors were convinced we interact, the God who is not an unmoved mover, but who is (in Fritz Rothschild's words, describing Heschel's God) "the most moved mover," the God who is perfectly *related to each of us.*[21] In this regard, Hartshorne notes that:

> [T]he only sense in which "perfection" is used biblically is the ethical sense. "Be ye perfect" does not mean, "be ye immutable!" Nor is any immutability attributed to deity in the Scriptures save what the context implies is purely ethical. *A fixity of ethical principles is one thing, a fixity of a being's whole perceptive-conscious reality is another,* and worlds apart from the first.[22]

A theism that does not distinguish the personhood of God from the divine principles falls into the same error as a naturalism that does not distinguish between God and the process of nature: God is conceived as an impersonal force, active in the world in an indifferent and undifferentiated way. Such a God is clearly imperfect. To love such a God as this—who loves not or who at least loves no one in particular—would be pitiable; to be commanded to love such a God "with all one's heart" would be an outright abuse of power. If we are to maintain that part of the biblical and talmudic traditions that reflects much of the intuition of the ages, then it seems that the idea of perfection must be reinterpreted as Hartshorne has done and God's nature be understood as in all ways perfect, but in one way complete, in another way "becoming."

Process theology offers a form of naturalism that is neither pantheistic nor atheistic. It presents, instead, a pan*en*theistic option— God is in the world and the world is in God (as felt), yet God is *not* the world and the world is not God. God is greater than the world, yet God is always *with* a world. The world exists as naturally as does God. To be sure, our particular world—the one scientists tell us began some twelve to twenty billion years ago—with its particular forms of order (electrons, protons, the inverse square law, and so on) exists contingently, due to God's free creative activity. But *some* world or other has always existed, and exists necessarily or naturally, and therefore our world has types of relationships that are beyond divine decision, and therefore cannot be interrupted by divine will. The God-world relation is a fully *natural* relation.

The panentheistic option for describing God's relationship to the world is incumbent on the notion of dipolarity. Panentheism is a form of naturalism that affirms the existence of a transcendent being but without belittling or violating the natural order. God acts within the natural order in "natural" ways, not because God is nature or nature is God, but because God is not "an exception to all metaphysical principles, invoked to save their collapse. He is their chief exemplification."[23]

Although God acts naturally, we often experience God as "wholly other."[24] God is, of course, *numerically* other, a being distinct from each of us. But God is also felt as *qualitatively* other and, in our encounter with God, we are struck by the contrast between God and ourselves. What this feeling acknowledges is not God's utter transcendence or absolute difference, but God's perfection. For example, God is perfectly present to us. In contrast, we have a terribly hard time being truly present, even to those we love most. "Being present" is something that takes conscious effort from human beings. Clearly, this is a human imperfection. It is wonderfully "other-wise" with God. "[T]he otherness of God expresses itself, paradoxically if you will, in his absolute nearness."[25] God's perfect nearness is part of God's "otherness." We differ from God not in being "natural" while God is "supernatural," but in our degree of perfection. God is a perfectly natural being. We are in no way perfect; God is perfect in every conceivable sense.

Recognition of God's dipolar nature makes it possible for us to affirm a transcendent being and the worth of ourselves and the natural order. As Rabbi Meir counseled with regard to the teachings of the heretical master, Elisha Ben Abuyah, so we might approach both modern and premodern insights:

> As with a pomegranate, one eats the seeds and throws the rind away.

In neoclassical theism the seeds of theism are separated from the supernatural rind. A process approach, as articulated by Whitehead and Hartshorne in particular, can help us to move beyond the old antitheses of classical theism and atheism, supernaturalism and secularism, transcendence and pantheism, so that we might coordinate the truths reflected in these several ways of speaking about God.

Notes

1. Robert Goldy, *The Emergence of Jewish Theology in America* (Bloomington: Indiana University Press, 1990), 2.

2. Ibid., 7–8.

3. Mordecai Kaplan, *Judaism Without Supernaturalism* (New York: The Reconstructionist Press, 1967), 26–27.

4. Ibid., 27.

5. Emil Fackenheim, *Quest for Past and Future: Essays in Jewish Theology* (Boston: Beacon Press, 1970), 31.

6. Ibid., 43, 34.

7. Quoted in Goldy, 37.

8. Goldy, 33.

9. Quoted in Goldy, 30.

10. Quoted in Goldy, 46.

11. Eugene Borowitz, for example, in his *Choices in Modern Jewish Thought: A Partisan Guide* (New York: Behrman House, 1983), 279, writes:

> Classic liberal theology was mainly concerned with accommodating religion to science and a culture which largely accepted the naturalistic world view. While affirming the continuing importance of science to our sense of things, I do not see it as the dominant challenge to our human self-understanding. Rather, the accomplishments of

science have themselves (by their threats to our personhood) raised to primary concern the problem of being a person (socially as well as individually understood). Unfortunately there seems no satisfactory way to bridge the person-science dichotomy.

12. A.N. Whitehead, *Process and Reality,* Corrected Edition, David Ray Griffin and Donald W. Sherburne, eds. (1929; New York: Free Press, 1978), 21.

13. Ibid., 21.

14. Ibid., 344.

15. Ibid., 345.

16. Ibid., 343.

17. Ibid., 345.

18. Charles Hartshorne, "The Formally Possible Doctrines of God," in John Hick, ed., *Classical and Contemporary Readings in the Philosophy of Religion,* second edition (Englewood Cliffs: Prentice-Hall, 1970), 340–43.

19. Ibid., 340.

20. Ibid., 345.

21. Rothschild's phrase, coined in his introduction to Martin Buber's *Between Man and Man,* is pointed out by John Merkle in *The Genesis of Faith: The Depth Theology of Abraham Joshua Heschel* (New York: Macmillan, 1985), 9, 253.

22. Charles Hartshorne, "Philosophical and Religious Uses of 'God,' " in Ewert H. Cousins, ed., *Process Theology: Basic Writings* (New York: Newman Press, 1971), 111–12, emphasis added.

23. Whitehead, *Process and Reality,* 343.

24. John B. Cobb, Jr., *A Christian Natural Theology: Based on the Thought of Alfred North Whitehead* (Philadelphia: Westminster Press, 1965), 238.

25. Ibid., 243.

Chapter 4

Judaism and Process Theology: Parallel Concerns and Challenging Tensions

William E. Kaufman

"The major contribution of process theology to the doctrine of God," write John Cobb and David Griffin, "is its enrichment and clarification of thought about the divine nature."[1] The application of the conceptualities of process philosophy toward this enrichment and clarification of thought about the divine nature constitutes process theology. Process theology, generally speaking, refers to the theological account of God, based on the philosophies of Whitehead and Hartshorne, that envisages the Deity as undergoing real change and development.

Whitehead and Hartshorne place the accent on divine immanence. Whitehead, for example, maintains:

> God is *in* the world, or nowhere, creating continually in us and around us.[2]

And Hartshorne writes:

> Basic ideas derive somehow from direct experience or intuition, life as concretely lived. Moreover, it is demonstrable from almost any classical conception of God that He cannot be known in any merely indirect way, by inference only, but must somehow be present in all experience. No theist can without qualification deny the universal immanence of God.[3]

This is not to say that process philosophy lacks a doctrine of divine transcendence. In Whitehead's philosophy, for example, God is transcendent in the sense that, in William Christian's words:

his relative independence of the world follows from God's primordial character and is part of the meaning of his transcendence of the world.[4]

And according to Hartshorne's panentheism, in the words of Santiago Sia:

> in one sense God depends on the world and is therefore inclusive of it; in another sense, he is independent of it and consequently transcends it.[5]

What is to be noted here is that the process theologian can conceive of God's transcendence and at the same time emphasize God's actual, and not merely accidental, immanence.

Now, in classical Jewish theology, God is conceived of as essentially transcendent and only accidentally immanent. Thus, in the classical interpretation of the biblical verse, "Holy, holy, holy is the Lord of hosts, the whole earth is full of His glory,"[6] God is conceived of as the Supreme Subject who is holy or transcendent. To be sure, traces of His glory or immanence pervade the earth, but the being of God is radically transcendent. Accordingly, Fritz Rothschild, in explicating the biblical philosophy of Abraham Heschel, writes:

> The experience of God as revealing himself in and through the facts of life and nature, and yet infinitely surpassing all reality, is embodied in the biblical doctrine of God as essentially transcendent and only accidentally immanent.[7]

In medieval Jewish philosophy, the essential transcendence of God is combined with His immutability. Thus, for example, Maimonides writes of God in his *Guide of the Perplexed* as:

> the stable One who undergoes no manner of change, neither a change in His essence—as He has no modes beside His essence with respect to which He might change—nor a change in His relation to what is other than Himself, since, as shall be explained later, there does not exist a relation to which He could change.[8]

Basing himself on the biblical verse from Malachi 3:6, Maimonides continues:

And herein His being wholly changeless in every respect achieves perfection, as He makes clear, saying "For I the Lord change not," meaning that He undergoes no change at all.[9]

Yet the Bible also witnesses to God's dynamic and passionate nature. Hence we are informed, for example, in the book of Genesis that when the Lord saw that the wickedness of man was great on the earth, and that every imagination of the thought of his heart was only evil continually, that "it repented the Lord that He had made man on the earth and it grieved Him in His heart."[10] Here, *contra* Maimonides, God is conceived of as a personal being who enters into *real* relations with His creatures.

It is the thesis of this essay that the process philosophical theology of Charles Hartshorne—in particular, his notion of the dipolar God—can help to resolve the immanence-transcendence dilemma and the mutability-immutability dilemma that seem to create insoluble tensions between biblical and medieval theological thought and tensions within the Bible itself. I shall also show how Whitehead's dipolar categories of the primordial and consequent natures of God can be helpful in this task. It is my contention that the Jewish theologian can learn from process theology new ways of understanding God's glory or immanence in the world process and new ways of conceiving of God's transcendence. In short, the possibility of a synthesis of process theology and Jewish modes of thought about God involves the willingness of the Jewish theologian to be open to the new understandings of transcendence and immanence in process theology.

I. The Tension in Heschel's Theory of Divine Pathos

The twentieth-century Jewish theologian Abraham J. Heschel has struggled with this tension between immanence and transcendence. Heschel draws a contrast between the dynamic Judaic idea of God and the static concept of God that had its origin in Greek philosophy. Heschel describes the "static" Eleatic concept as follows:

The Eleatics taught that whatever exists is unchangeable. The ontological view was very soon put to use to determine the nature of God. Xenophanes, Anaxagoras, Plato, and Aristotle followed in much the same line. The principle that mutability cannot be attributed to God is thus an ontological dogma, and as such, it has become the property of religious philosophers.

It is easy to see how on the basis of the ontological view of the Eleatics there emerged a static conception of God. According to Greek theology, impassivity and immobility are characteristic of the divine.[11]

In contrast to the static Eleatic view, Heschel asserts that according to the Judaic prophetic idea, God is "concerned with man and . . . related to His people. The basic feature of the divine *pathos* is God's transcendental attention to man."[12]

It is important to note carefully how Heschel characterizes the Divine pathos. Pathos, he warns us, is not to be understood as mere feeling.[13] Pathos is "an act formed with intention, depending on free will, the result of decision and determination."[14] Moreover, "the divine pathos is not felt as something objective, as a finality with which man is confronted, but as an expression of God's will; it is a functional rather than a substantial reality. The prophets never identify God's *pathos* with His essence, because it is for them not something absolute, but a form of relation."[15] Nevertheless, Heschel does insist "that God can actually suffer. At the heart of the prophetic affirmation is the certainty that God is concerned about the world to the point of suffering."[16]

A tension is manifested in Heschel's conception of the Divine pathos. On the one hand, Heschel is reluctant to attribute pathos to the essence or nature of God. On the other hand, he affirms that God can actually suffer. What is the significance of this tension?

One interpreter of Heschel, Arthur A. Cohen, is acutely perceptive on this point. Writing about Heschel's ambivalence on this issue, Cohen says of Heschel:

> He is still too much the disciple of the Jewish philosopher, Maimonides, whose strictures against anthropomorphism prevent him from imputing to God's essence the meaningful and instructive experience of anything which might, in the view of human finitude, compromise divine perfection. Both Alfred North Whitehead and Charles Hartshorne have done much to indicate that perfection is not compromised by richness of experience; that there is no reason why simplicity is any more to be desired in the divine nature than complexity and involvement. At the same time Heschel is profoundly aware that the biblical testimony to divine tears and repentance, sorrow and compassion, cannot be put aside, for the biblical authors ascribed these experiences to God really, and not merely as an inaccurate metaphor.[17]

Cohen is correct in his assertion that Heschel, despite his notion of divine pathos, is still wedded to the Aristotelian-Maimonidean notion of perfection. Hence, Heschel accepts the essence-accident distinction of Aristotle and sees relativity and change as accidental to the divine nature. To be more consistent, a Jewish theology that began with a process rather than a substance approach to reality would make relationship fundamental.

Moreover, Cohen is also correct in ascribing the tension in Heschel's theory of the divine pathos to his reluctance to attribute it to the divine essence or nature, which he deems to be radically transcendent and, hence, unknowable. Here the problem that faces the Jewish theologian is the conflict between biblical references to God as present within the world and, hence, knowable and mutable, and other Jewish sources, such as Maimonides and Philo, that emphasize God's radical transcendence, unknowability, and immutability.

Let us, therefore, explore how the process philosophical theology of Charles Hartshorne can be helpful in resolving the immanence-transcendence dilemma and the mutability-immutability issue.

II. Hartshorne's Notion of Dipolarity

The process philosophical theology of Charles Hartshorne provides a reasonable way to talk about God as immanent and as transcendent. The first point to note is Hartshorne's emphasis on *reason*.

Hartshorne is a rationalist; at the early age of seventeen, he reminisces, after reading Emerson's essays, he made up his mind to trust reason to the end.[18] Accordingly, in his philosophical theology, Hartshorne undertakes to find out "whether and how God . . . can be conceived without logical absurdity, and as having such a character that an enlightened person may worship and serve him with whole heart and mind."[19] To be sure, Hartshorne recognizes a core of mystery in what he calls the "divine actuality": the concrete states in which God's existence is actualized. With respect to the divine actuality, Hartshorne says that there is "much, in a sense infinitely much, that we cannot know about the universe and God."[20] But, he argues, this is no justification for using and applying concepts sloppily. Either a concept such as "absolute" is our own human idea, or we have no right to use the term; if it is our concept, it is our responsibility to fix its meaning. The same would hold of any concept we use, whether it be "relative," "immanent," or "transcendent."

What, then, is Hartshorne's reasonable way of dealing with "immanence" and "transcendence?" Hartshorne sees these terms as polar concepts. Utilizing Morris Cohen's principle of polarity, according to which "ultimate contraries are correlatives, mutually interdependent, so that nothing real can be described by the wholly one-sided assertion of simplicity, being, actuality, and the like, each in a pure form, devoid and independent of complexity, becoming, potentiality, and related contraries,"[21] Hartshorne develops a dipolar or neoclassical idea of God as the union of "supreme being and supreme becoming, the most strictly absolute and the most universally relative of all entities, actual or possible."[22]

Accordingly, Hartshorne holds that God's existence is necessary and constitutes His abstract essence. And he maintains that this abstract essence can be known by the human mind on the basis of Anselm's second ontological argument. The exclusion of contingency from the divine *existence* is what Hartshorne calls Anselm's discovery. But whereas God's *existence* is necessary and knowable by the human mind, God's concrete actuality or *how* He exists is contingent upon each new state of the world process; that is, there must be for each new state of the world process a new consequent state of deity by which the world totality in question is prehended or possessed. Hartshorne locates the mystery of God—God's transcendence of our understanding—in the concrete manner in which God knows or prehends the world:

> Every concrete thing is in its fullness and uniqueness an unfathomable mystery, and in God all mystery is compounded, since God knows and contains all things, including all mystery. The mystery of God, however, as we have already noted, is not in the mere concept or essence of divinity, but in God as an actuality—not the abstract principle of His knowing, but the actual knowing. Of this we know next to nothing. The mere essence of deity, however, is the principle of all principles, and is really the entirety of what we can know *a priori* about reality.[23]

(As we shall see, Hartshorne's location of the mystery in *how* God, in His concrete actuality, knows the world differs from Whitehead's location of the mystery in God's primordial nature.)

Thus, for Hartshorne, we can know *a priori* the essence or abstract principle of God as necessary existence. The unknowable *transcendent* mystery of God, for Hartshorne, lies in God's concrete actuality. This aspect we may call *epistemological* transcendence.

The major issue of transcendence-immanence, however, involves the relationship of God and world. Hartshorne distinguishes three views of the relationship between God and world:

(1) God is merely the cosmos, in all aspects inseparable from the sum or system of dependent things or effects;
(2) He is both the system and something independent of it;
(3) He is not the system, but is in all aspects independent.[24]

The first view, which identifies God and the world, is pantheism. The third is classical theism. Hartshorne adopts the second view, which he calls panentheism. Hartshorne compares the relationship between God and the world to the relationship between a person and his or her body. One is not simply identical with one's body. While one's body undergoes constant change, personal identity remains overwhelmingly consistent. Similarly, the cosmos, as God's body, is constantly changing, but God in His necessary aspect remains Himself. Thus, God includes the world, yet is more than the world, akin to the way in which human identity includes, but also transcends, its corporeal structure. Thus, Hartshorne speaks of God as "the self-identical individuality of the world somewhat as a man is the self-identical individuality of his ever changing system of atoms."[25]

To speak of God as including the world is not, thereby, to forfeit God's transcendence. Whitehead contends (and Hartshorne agrees) that:

Every actual entity, including God, is something individual for its own sake; and thereby transcends the rest of reality.[26]

This means that what Whitehead calls God's "consequent nature" transcends the world, even while being consequent (and thereby dependent) upon it.

Moreover, in God's "primordial nature," which is God's primordial envisagement of all pure possibilities ("eternal objects"), God is eternally the same, transcending this and every cosmic epoch. Hartshorne's notion of dipolarity, which is somewhat different from Whitehead's, says that God has an "abstract essence" and "concrete actuality." God, analogously to the human soul, is a serially-ordered society of divine occasions of experience. Each occasion includes the entire previous universe into itself, thereby transcending it—these occasions are the concrete actuality of God. At the same time, this everlasting series of divine experiences has an eternal abstract essence, which is always the same. For example, God is always perfectly loving and perfectly cognizant, no matter what happens. This provides the second sense in which God transcends the world. And yet, this dual transcendence of God in no way excludes divine immanence, because both aspects of God, for both Whitehead and Hartshorne, are prehended by worldly actualities and thereby—partially but really—included within them. Process theology thus offers us a reasonable way to talk about God as immanent and as transcendent.

III. Perfection and Change

We now examine how Hartshorne's logic of perfection helps us to resolve the mutability-immutability dilemma. The first point to note about Hartshorne's logic of perfection is his interesting idea that there is an inner logic to the idea of worship. Hartshorne defines worship as "the integrating of all one's thoughts and purposes, all valuations and meanings, all perceptions and conceptions."[27] And he holds that the conscious integrity or wholeness of the individual is correlative to "an inclusive wholeness in the world of which the individual is aware, and this wholeness is deity."[28] As cosmic wholeness, God is the inclusive reality, the all-inclusive Being. Following Anselm, Hartshorne identifies God as the "not conceivably surpassable being."[29] Only the greatest conceivable being, Hartshorne holds, could be the cosmic correlate of our quest for personal self-integration.

But Hartshorne differs from Anselm in his *conception* of perfection. The presupposition of Anselm was that the most worshipful being must be self-sufficient and perfect in the sense of complete, and that what is complete cannot change, change being a sign of weakness. "Perfection" in its biblical usage, however, did not mean immutability but rather connoted a steadfastness of moral purpose. It is Hartshorne's claim that this religious idea of God is most at home in a philosophy that considers the supreme metaphysical reality to be process:

> For the self-surpassing divinity is in process of surpassing itself, and if the supreme reality is thus a supreme process, lesser individual realities will be instances of an inferior form of process.[30]

Hartshorne's argument here is that becoming is a more inclusive category than being, for what becomes and what does not become (but simply is) together constitute a total reality which becomes.

Additionally, a novel factor together with a non-novel factor provide a novel togetherness of the two factors. Thus, following Whitehead, and in contradistinction to Anselm and Aquinas, Hartshorne holds that perfection is not compromised by richness of experience and that divine perfection is more coherently conceived as self-surpassing becoming than as simplicity, since becoming is the more inclusive category. Moreover, this notion is more in consonance with the biblical idea of divine pathos, according to which God is moved and affected, and hence *becomes*, in response to what happens in the world.

But if God were pure becoming alone, this would entail that God is contingent and, hence, not the final or ultimate source of explanation. Hence, Hartshorne sees becoming as *one* aspect of God, which he calls the divine actuality, and which Whitehead called the consequent nature, interpreted by Hartshorne as the principle "that there must always be for each new state of the world process a new Consequent State of deity by which the world totality in question is prehended or possessed."[31] But, utilizing Morris Cohen's principle of polarity, Hartshorne develops a dipolar or neo-classical idea of God as the union of "supreme being and supreme becoming, the most strictly absolute and the most universally relative of all entities, actual or possible."[32]

Hartshorne is thus able to resolve the mutability-immutability dilemma *conceptually* by his notion of a dipolar God: God in His concrete *actuality* is mutable and becoming; God in His necessary *existence* is immutable being.

But has Hartshorne here fallen prey to the very thing he wanted to avoid as a rationalist—namely, an internal paradox in the nature of God, which in more realistic terms is nothing but a contradiction? No, because Hartshorne's two aspects of God refer to differing ontological levels of God as the universal individual.

Thus, it appears that Hartshorne has resolved the mutability-immutability dilemma conceptually. For Hartshorne, our knowledge of God is *a priori* or conceptual. Against Hume and Kant, and following Anselm, he holds that we can know that the concept of the necessary existence of God implies His real existence, for divine perfection means that God cannot be conceived of as not existing. And against Anselm and Aquinas, and following Whitehead, he argues that, from a conceptual analysis of the idea of perfection, the actuality or concrete reality of God is more coherently conceived as becoming or process, rather than as being.

I emphasize that Hartshorne has resolved the mutability-immutability dilemma *conceptually*. The issue here is whether

Hartshorne's conceptual analysis actually refers to the divine reality. Hartshorne's resolution of this issue lies in the fact that he accepts the premise of Anselm's second ontological argument: that if God can be coherently conceived, God must be conceived of as existing. It is on the basis of Hartshorne's belief in the power of reason—more precisely, the power of the *a priori* and also the power of the *religious a priori* (the notion of an inner logic of worship)—that Hartshorne's claim to have rescued metaphysics from the strictures of Hume and Kant rests.

Hartshorne's emphasis on the conceptual is nicely supplemented by Whitehead's stress on the empirical. Hartshorne asserts that we can know the essence of God as necessary existence and that we can only know an infinitesimal aspect of God's concrete actuality. For Whitehead, the primordial aspect of God refers to God's envisagement of the realm of possibility in its abstraction from all particular matters of fact. It is the order or structure that characterizes the world so that it can be one determinate reality, but it is deficiently actual in itself, because it has no concrete determination of matters of fact within it: it is the realm of possibility. The consequent nature of God refers to God's concreteness as He is related to the world and as the world's events are objectified in Him. The consequent nature acts by being prehended or felt by God's creatures. Whitehead speaks of the love of God flooding back into the world.[33] Now, just as in psychotherapy, there is a transformative power in the knowledge that our feelings have entered into "the consequent" nature of another person, so in our relation to God. Whitehead provides an empirical analogy in the notion of "feeling of feeling"—in particular, our feeling of the "communicative immanence of God."[34] Here is a notion of divine immanence that is not only theologically but also emotionally powerful. It is also conceptually enlightening, since it enables us to make sense out of our experience and to interpret God's reality in our lives in a non-magical and meaningful way.

The central concept underlying the notion of divine "communicative" immanence is that not only the primordial structure, but also the concrete being of God in relation to the world, manifested to us as God's love, is communicated to the creatures. Just as in psychotherapy, healing takes place, in part, through the felt knowledge that the client's feelings are understood by the therapist (underscoring the importance of the therapist communicating to the client that he or she is understood), so religious redemption is, in part, our feeling of divine knowledge and concern for us. The sense that "I know not" but God knows—that God's understanding of us is more profound than our self-understanding—is inherent in the feeling of being redeemed by God.

IV. Toward a Jewish-Process Theology

We now reflect on how the Jewish theologian may utilize these process motifs in developing a contemporary theology. In *Process and Reality*, Whitehead wrote:

> It is as true to say that the world is immanent in God, as that God is immanent in the World.
> It is as true to say that God transcends the World, as that the World transcends God.[35]

Commenting on this passage, Elizabeth Kraus explains:

> In the opposition between God and the world, the strain between transcendence and immanence which is a universal theological problem is overcome in a duality of contrasted relations. Each pole of the opposition both transcends and is immanent in the other.[36]

How can this process insight illumine Jewish theology? According to the interpretation of classical Jewish theology, the prophetic words "Holy, holy, holy is the Lord of hosts, the whole earth is full of His glory" characterize a deity essentially transcendent but only accidentally immanent. It is understood to present a theological paradox which the human mind cannot fathom. Whiteheadian-Hartshornean process philosophical theology offers a different interpretation—Whitehead through his notions of the primordial and consequent natures, Hartshorne by means of his doctrine of panentheism—which avoids the theological paradox.

Elizabeth Kraus provides a brilliant dialectical analysis of how she thinks the strain between transcendence and immanence is overcome in Whitehead's *Process and Reality*. She explains:

> From the standpoint of God, transcendence is absolute to a degree unimaginable by the most ardent deist. In his primordial nature, God is so indifferent to the world that He is not even aware of its existence . . . .Contrasted with this absolute transcendence is the absolute immanence of the world in the consequent nature, which takes up all finite accomplishment in its "tender care that nothing be lost" (PR 525), in its "judgment of a wisdom which uses what in the temporal world is mere wreckage" (PR 525) . . . . For the conscious creature, particularly

one attaining the intensity of human consciousness, this implies that in a very Spinozistic sense, redeemed human consciousness is a modality of divine consciousness. Following the lead of Hegel: since no entity, God included, can be immediately self-conscious, it might be said that human consciousness as fragmented through time and space *is* God's consciousness of the content of his own concrescence, that human religious consciousness *is* God's self-awareness diffused through the eyes and ears and mind of humanity and reunited in the redemptive act. Might it be said that in redeeming the world from partiality God also redeems himself from self-alienation? Be that as it may, God's absolute transcendence and the world's absolute immanence render both poles fully actual, fully determinate.[37]

Now it is obvious that this is not what the prophet Isaiah literally meant by his doxology of God's holiness. But Kraus's comments on Whitehead surely can serve as a contemporary Midrash or hermeneutic of Isaiah's words, because her ideas invest the concepts of transcendence and immanence with a meaning more available for our time. Our dominant mode of thinking is processive and evolutionary. Why not apply this type of thinking to our highest concept—the idea of God? I find the notion of a growing, dynamic God more religiously illuminating because of its lure and impetus to spiritual growth than the classical idea of the static "unmoved" Mover. Surely, the process image of God is closer to Heschel's and what he holds to be Judaism's emphasis on God as the most-moved Mover: the divine pathos. Heschel's problem vis-à-vis process thought, as we have seen, is that he was still too wedded to classical substance-accident thinking to make the decisive conceptual shift to God as dynamic process and concrescence.

The notion that God's self-redemption parallels the world's and human salvation, as articulated by Kraus's comments on Whitehead, finds an echo in Jewish sources in the prayers for salvation on the Festival of Succoth. In the *Hoshanot*, Jewish prayers for salvation, we find the words, "As Thou didst save together God and nation, the people singled out for God's salvation; so save Thou us."[38] Two additional passages from traditional Jewish midrashic literature shed light on how Whitehead's vision of redemption can serve as a philosophical hermeneutic to the Judaic concept of the reciprocity of God and humanity. In one passage, humans are conceived of as partners with God in creation: "From the first day of creation, the Holy One, blessed be He, longed to enter into partnership with the terrestrial world, to dwell with His creatures within the terrestrial world" (Genesis Rabbah 3:9).

And in another midrashic passage we read: "When Israel performs the will of the Omnipresent, they add strength to the heavenly power. When, however, Israel does not perform the will of the Omnipresent, they weaken, if it is possible to say, the great power of Him who is above" (Pesikta, ed. Buber XXVI, 166b). In the midrashic passages, God and world, in general, and the people of Israel, in particular, are inextricably interwoven. Whitehead, too, maintains that "God and World" are correlative concepts: "It is as true to say that God creates the World, as that the World creates God."[39] Whitehead's philosophical theology thus represents a contemporary philosophical hermeneutic of the midrashic concept of the mutual redemption of God and the world.

Moreover, Hartshorne's panentheism, with its stress on God's fellowship in suffering with His creatures, is a moving midrash on the biblical word of God: "I will be with him in trouble."[40] Hartshorne's panentheism—that God includes but is "more" than the world—conceives of God's all-inclusiveness as the ever-growing supreme World-Mind:

> The inclusiveness of the world-mind means, not that it is exalted above all suffering, but that no pain and no joy is beneath its notice. All things make their immediate contribution to the one, but they contribute what they are and have, their sorrow as well as their joy.[41]

Hartshorne's interpretation of the meaning of life as the wish "to contribute every experience . . . to the One who alone is capable of accepting the gift in its fullness—the Holy One, Blessed be He"[42] is surely in consonance with the Judaic idea of the partnership of God and humankind.

Of course, in addition to the foregoing parallels, there also remain challenging tensions between process theology and Judaism. For instance, process theology relies heavily on the notion of the world as the body of God. Kraus, for example, writes:

> Good and evil, joy and sorrow, find their niche in the divinely perfected world, which quite literally becomes the Body of God. To speak of redemption without realizing that it means Transubstantiation is to miss the point entirely.[43]

Now, perhaps, just as the Jewish theologian Heschel was still too much the disciple of Maimonides to distance himself from subject-accident modes of thought, so, in my attempts to be faithful to the "spirit" of Jewish philosophical theology, perhaps I am too wedded to Maimonides' emphasis on the incorporeality of God. In addition to the significance of Maimonides and Heschel, however, I also find Mordecai M. Kaplan's thought important. Kaplan held that Jewish theological thought has always been, and must continue to be, reconstructed. I believe that Judaic modes of thought about God need to be reconstructed in the direction of a *Jewish* process theology. Clearly, a *Christian* process theology is at home with the notion of the body of God. Kaplan found this notion and also the notion of a God as person too anthropomorphic for his process notion of God as the dynamic power that makes for human salvation. Whether the future of reconstructed Jewish theology should be less anthropomorphic, as Kaplan's, or more anthropomorphic, as Heschel's, remains to be seen. But Heschel also was too much the disciple of Maimonides to add to his notion of divine pathos a concept of the divine body.

However, the parallel motifs and concerns of Judaism and process theology by far outweigh the tensions between them. Process theology is surely the contemporary mode of thought most fruitful to be utilized for a synthesis of Judaism and contemporary philosophical theology.

Notes

1. John B. Cobb, Jr., and David Ray Griffin, *Process Theology: An Introductory Exposition* (Philadelphia: The Westminster Press, 1976), 43.

2. *Dialogues of Alfred North Whitehead*, as recorded by Lucien Price (Boston: Little, Brown and Company, 1954), 370.

3. Charles Hartshorne, *A Natural Theology for Our Time* (LaSalle: Open Court Publishing Co., 1967), 2.

4. William A. Christian, *An Interpretation of Whitehead's Metaphysics* (New Haven: Yale, 1959), 375.

5. Santiago Sia, *God in Process Thought* (Dordrecht: Martinus Nijhoff, 1985), 85.

6. Isaiah 6:3.

7. Introduction to *Between God and Man*, from the writings of Abraham J. Heschel, selected, edited, and introduced by Fritz A. Rothschild (New York: Harper and Brothers, 1959), 16, 17.

8. Moses Maimonides, *The Guide of the Perplexed*, translated with an introduction and notes by Shlomo Pines (Chicago: University of Chicago Press, 1963), 37–38.

9. Ibid., 38.

10. Genesis 6:6.

11. Abraham J. Heschel, *Between God and Man*, edited and introduced by Fritz A. Rothschild (New York: Harper and Brothers, 1959), 121.

12. Ibid., 123, 124.

13. Ibid., 117.

14. Ibid.

15. Ibid., 118.

16. Ibid., 120.

17. Arthur A. Cohen, *The Natural and the Supernatural Jew*, Second Revised Edition (New York: Behrman House, 1979), 250.

18. Charles Hartshorne, *The Logic of Perfection* (La Salle: The Open Court Publishing Company, 1962), viii.

19. Charles Hartshorne, *The Divine Relativity* (New Haven: Yale University Press, 1948), 1.

20. Ibid., 5.

21. Charles Hartshorne and William L. Reese, ed., *Philosophers Speak of God* (Chicago: University of Chicago Press, 1953), 2.

22. Ibid., 14.

23. Hartshorne, *The Logic of Perfection*, 119.

24. Hartshorne, *The Divine Relativity*, 90.

25. Charles Hartshorne, *Man's Vision of God and the Logic of Theism* (Chicago: Willet, Clark Co., 1941), 230–31.

26. A.N. Whitehead, *Process and Reality*, Corrected Edition, David Ray Griffin and Donald W. Sherburne, eds. (1929; New York: Free Press, 1978), 88.

27. Charles Hartshorne, *A Natural Theology for Our Time* (LaSalle: Open Court, 1967), 4, 5.

28. Ibid., 5.

29. Ibid., 17.

30. Ibid., 25.

31. Interrogation of Hartshorne in *Philosophical Interrogations*, edited with an introduction by Sydney and Beatrice Rome (New York: Holt, Rinehart and Winston, 1964), 323.

32. *Philosophers Speak of God*, 14.

33. See Alfred North Whitehead, *Process and Reality*, 351.

34. The phrase is that of Robert J. Calhoun, cited in Daniel Day Williams, "How Does God Act? An Essay in Whitehead's Metaphysics," in *Process and Divinity: The Hartshorne Festschrift*, William L. Reese and Eugene Freeman, eds. (LaSalle: Open Court, 1964), 176. The therapeutic analogy is suggested by Williams.

35. Whitehead, *Process and Reality*, 348.

36. Elizabeth Kraus, *The Metaphysics of Experience: A Companion to Whitehead's Process and Reality* (New York: Fordham University Press, 1979), 171.

37. Ibid., 172. The parenthetical citations, which are to the Macmillan (1929) edition of *Process and Reality,* correspond to page 346 of the Free Press Corrected Edition of 1978.

38. *Sabbath and Festival Prayer Book* (Rabbinical Assembly of America and the United Synagogue of America, 1973), 190.

39. Whitehead, *Process and Reality*, 348.

40. Psalms 91:15.

41. *The Logic of Perfection*, 202, 203.

42. Ibid., 243.

43. Kraus, *The Metaphysics of Experience*, 171.

Chapter 5

The "Essence" of Judaism:
A Process-Relational Critique

Lori Krafte-Jacobs

Endemic to theological discussion seems to be the desire to locate and describe the "essence" of the religion under scrutiny, a longing to get to the heart of the thing, to behold finally that pure extract, that distillation of an entire history—in short, to know oneself to be in possession of that which is most fundamental and most enduring. With a firm grasp on the essence of Judaism, for example, one could swiftly and confidently make judgments regarding the authenticity of particular theological developments or ritual practices. Simply, if a group identifying itself as Jewish somehow embodies or exemplifies the recognized essence, then said group will be deemed to belong within the Jewish fold. If that group does not embody the essence, then claims of Jewishness are considered implausible and the group is excluded. (Exclusion of individuals or groups whose views and/or practices are considered deviant from the norm need not amount to a formal *herem;* the label "not really Jewish" or "not very Jewish" suffices to effect the exclusion.)

One can readily understand the attractiveness to Jews of the idea of a discernible essence, in an age in which the sociological issues surrounding Jewish identity are paramount. Unequivocal criteria for deciding "who is" and "who isn't" would free us for the theological task often put on hold while we wrangle about the boundaries of the community.

I. Baeck, Buber and Heschel on Essence

Unfortunately, there has hardly been anything like a consensus regarding the nature of this essence of Judaism. Leaving aside the many

75

centuries of religious development that saw great changes in the understanding of Judaism, we can look at the major contemporary varieties of Jewish thought and see that not only sequentially, but also simultaneously, there is much disagreement as to what constitutes Judaism's essence. Some examples will be instructive.

Of all Jewish thinkers, the one most associated with the phrase "the essence of Judaism" is Leo Baeck. In his book by that name, he writes:

> A rich variety of phenomena is found in [Jewish] history. Not all of these are of equal value or scope; for life, unable to maintain a constant level, has its rises and falls. What is most characteristic of a people is best found in the highest levels of its history, so long as these levels are reached again and again. In this undulating movement from historical peak to peak, the essence of a people's consciousness . . . is manifested. Such constancy, such essence, Judaism does possess despite the shifting phases of its long history . . . . However much the Jewish religion exposed itself to alien influences, it never changed its essential character . . . . For this contention there is no better evidence than the fact that Judaism has preserved its monotheism stern and pure.[1]

For Baeck, then, essence is what is highest and most noble in Jewish tradition, regardless of whether it is found in all historical periods (or even the earliest, formative periods), and the best in Jewish tradition is ethical monotheism.

For Martin Buber, the essence of Judaism means something else.

> The act that Judaism has always considered the essence and foundation of all religiosity is the act of decision as realization of divine freedom and unconditionality on earth . . . . Unconditionality is the specific religious content of Judaism. Jewish religiosity is built neither on doctrine nor on an ethical prescription, but on a fundamental perception that gives meaning to man: that one thing above all is needed.[2]

Buber rejects both dogma and unsanctified act in favor of being guided by the voice.

> It bids us work for what is most profoundly Jewish, more Jewish than all forms and all norms: realization, reconstruction of God's community, and a new beginning.[3]

The ultimate foundation of Jewish faith is the relationship of trust based on the encounter one has with the voice. This encounter reveals not a specific content, but rather the presence of the Divine.

Abraham Heschel sees Judaism's essence in yet another way. For him, Jewish faith:

> is an attitude, the joy of living a life in which God has a stake, or being involved with God . . . . Faith comes with the discovery of being needed, of having a vocation, of being commanded.[4]

For Heschel, it is not what we believe *about* God that is decisive; rather it is the realization of our being needed by God that matters.

> The central issue is not man's decision to extend formal recognition to God, to furnish God with a certificate that he exists, but the realization of our importance to God's design . . . . The purpose of faith is not to satisfy curiosity or to fulfill a human need, but to confront man with a sublime challenge, to satisfy a divine need.[5]

Heschel's emphasis on God's feelings and needs, as revealed through Torah, differs both from Baeck's affirmation of ethical monotheism and from Buber's emphasis upon encountering the Divine in an I-Thou relationship.

These are just three examples, among many, of the ways in which various Jewish theologians have characterized the essence or the timeless disposition of Judaism. Yet, while debate persists as to the exact nature of Judaism's essence, the logically prior question of whether the term "essence" is itself meaningful has been far less rigorously pursued. Accordingly, this essay will offer a critique of the concept of essence itself. This critique will be advanced from the standpoint of process-relational metaphysics, which I find particularly helpful in illumining the problems inherent in any discussion of "Judaism's essence."

II. Some Common Assumptions Concerning Essence

In spite of the great variety of opinion regarding the essence of Judaism, it is clear that the diversity masks some common assumptions, usually implicit.

First, that such an essence exists is rarely (not to say never) questioned. However involved or protracted the search, the investigator customarily assumes that there is permanence amid change, and that the inquiry into the nature of thirty-five or more centuries of Jewish life will eventually yield some positive, unalterable habit of mind or practice.

Second, this essence is considered to be strictly immutable. Whatever else may change in accordance with the vicissitudes of the day, that which constitutes the essence persists. This assumption is shared by both defenders and critics of a particular understanding of Judaism. The former see the permanent character of the essence as a source of strength and connectedness; the latter see it as a weight anchoring the Jewish people in an obsolete world. Both see it as unalterable.

Third, the essence is implicitly assumed to have an ontological reality independent of the Jewish people. Judaism is not a result of what those whom we call "Jews" do; the appellation "Jew" results when one conforms to the essence of Judaism. This can result both in calling someone Jewish who is not self-identified as such, and in denying the Jewishness of someone who does so identify herself and who participates in the life of the Jewish people. Examples of the former would be pre-Mosaic descendants of Abraham, who can hardly be said to have conformed to a Jewish essence when such is understood to be compliance with Halacha, and those who are "Jewish" by Nazi standards but not by their own. An example of those denied Jewish identity, who would themselves claim it, would be those who did or do worship Hebrew goddesses (both centuries ago and in some contemporary explorations of feminist Jewish spirituality) and who, therefore, would not conform to the essence of Judaism when such is understood to be belief in ethical monotheism.[6]

The above assumptions and the approach they characterize engender numerous problems—some practical, others theoretical. Turning first to the practical, we find that there is simply no agreement as to what constitutes Judaism's essence. Now a plurality of opinions is not necessarily a bad thing, but in this particular case it would seem to defeat the purpose, namely, understanding the basis of the bond that unites Jews, as well as finding a criterion for determining Jewish authenticity.

Further, it is abundantly clear that nothing approaching objectivity exists in the pursuit of Judaism's essence. I am not suggesting that absolute objectivity is possible. I am suggesting that an admission of conditioned perspective, along with an effort toward objectivity (or, a happier phrase, toward a more broadly inclusive viewpoint), might at least lend some credibility to the enterprise. As it stands, any theologian can—and does—simply impose her (or, more frequently, his) priorities on the data and draw the desired conclusion therefrom. Thus, for example, Baeck makes it clear that he is not even interested in making his search as objective as possible. He states outright that the evidence is not all to be accorded equal weight, but rather it must be examined in the light of what he calls the "highest levels of Judaism's history." The "highest levels," of course, are not themselves objectively discerned, but are imposed by the theologian. For to identify what is "highest" is already to make a value-judgment about the evidence in advance, and then one is no longer looking for essence but rather is identifying those periods of which one theologically most approves.

Additionally, the belief in and search for essence tends to frustrate change and distort history. It frustrates change by arbitrarily choosing a slice of a community's history to be somehow normative for all time. It distorts history by, among other things, ignoring historical development and diversity and frequently making anachronistic claims about the early community's beliefs and/or practices. One frequently encounters descriptions of Judaism that assume a uniformity of purpose, belief, or action. But the assertion of uniformity flies in the face of the reality of Jewish diversity. Hence, for example, those who maintain that Judaism is strictly monotheistic would, to be consistent, have to eliminate from the Jewish community all those to whom the prophets addressed their admonitions regarding what they considered idolatry but who did not repent (and then in what sense were they addressing their own community, as Jewish theologians wish to maintain against classical Christian claims to the contrary?), an elimination that would likely exclude most of the Jewish community for at least the first several centuries of its existence. It is unlikely that a Judaism defined by monotheism would have had very many more adherents than there were priests and prophets in the early years. Similarly, and more obviously, the idea that Jewish essence centers around obedience to Halacha simply does not account for the vast number of Jews who have not expressed their Jewishness halachically. The assumption that there is (and always has been) one kind of Judaism is historically ludicrous, and serves to tie the hands of those who want a different Judaism, but still a *Judaism* and not something else.

Finally, the claim that Judaism has an essence tends to make the group more exclusive than inclusive, and this exclusivity is especially harmful to women. Because women have historically been denied equal participation in the creative periods from which one or another view of Judaism's essence is derived, exaggerated reliance on such periods for Jewish identity will necessarily bias Judaism against women's experience and contributions.

These practical problems derive from serious flaws in the concept of essence itself. Let us turn, then, to an examination of these flaws.

III. A Process-Relational Critique of Essence

It is not my purpose here to argue the superiority of process metaphysics over some other metaphysical system. I accept as sensible and useful many of the insights of process thought, and suggest that some of these can be of great help in clarifying the problems of essence. Such clarification establishes the cost of continued search for, belief in, or defense of the essence of Judaism; that is to say, one cannot accept the following insights while yet maintaining that an essence of Judaism is possible.

Process metaphysics maintains that reality is composed of moments of experience, which Whitehead designates "actual occasions."

> "Actual entities"—also termed "actual occasions"—are the final real things of which the world is made up. There is no going behind actual entities to find anything more real . . . . The final acts are, all alike, actual entities; and these actual entities are drops of experience, complex, and interdependent.[7]

Whitehead's system allows no exceptions to this rule, which he calls the "ontological principle":

> every condition to which the process of becoming conforms in any particular instance has its reason *either* in the character of some actual entity in the actual world of that concrescence[8] *or* in the character of the subject which is in process of concrescence . . . . This ontological principle means that actual entities are the only *reasons*; so that to search for a *reason* is to search for one or more actual entities.[9]

Insufficient attention to the ontological principle can lead to the Fallacy of Misplaced Concreteness, Whitehead's designation for the "error of mistaking the abstract for the concrete."[10] Here the concrete is understood only in terms of some aspects that are abstracted from it.

As applied to the problem of Judaism's essence, this insight about the concreteness of reality calls into question the ontological status normally attributed to the essence of Judaism. For there is no such actual occasion, or nexus[11] of occasions, that is Judaism. Rather, there are complex individuals, internally related to a past actual world that includes certain events that carry extraordinary weight in the becoming of the present; we call these nexūs Jews, because of their appropriation of just that history; and the abstraction of certain of their behaviors, beliefs, sancta, and so forth, we call Judaism. Just as Whitehead held that there is no going behind actual entities to find anything more real, so there is no going behind Jews to find anything more Jewishly real, namely, an independent essence. There can be no essence of Judaism prior to or in any way apart from the Jewish people. To maintain the ontological reality of Judaism is to confuse some abstracted characteristics of those whom we call Jews with concrete reality. But abstraction is not the form reality takes, according to the process view.

Now this is not to belittle the practical advantages of being able to speak of Judaism *as if* it "exists"; hence "Judaism teaches," "Judaism believes," "Judaism is characterized by," and so on, sometimes can be useful ways to speak of an historical recurrence of certain typical features. Nevertheless, we must not lose sight of the fact that this is merely a shorthand way of speaking. Such abstractions can be useful, but they do not thereby earn that ontological status reserved for concrete reality. Above all, they must not stand in the way of the Jew who believes herself or himself to be authentically appropriating the Jewish heritage and living in conscious relationship to it and to the contemporary community of those who are similarly committed. Judaism can become concrete, and therefore real, only through the lives of the Jewish people, and the form Judaism takes depends on them and not vice versa.

The claim that Judaism's essence is unalterable similarly rests upon an untenable metaphysical assumption, which is that any stage of development can be final. Such an assumption threatens two cherished convictions of process thought: that all becoming is characterized by some degree of freedom, and that all becoming is partially constituted by its internal relations.

Let us grant, for the sake of argument, the point denied earlier: that the essence of Judaism possesses ontological reality such that we might call it "actual" independently of the Jewish people. Now all actuality, in the process view, has some measure of freedom in its becoming.

The doctrine of the philosophy of organism [Whitehead's own term for process philosophy] is that, however far the sphere of efficient causation be pushed in the determination of components of a concrescence—its data, its emotions, its appreciations, its purposes, its phases of subjective aim[12]—beyond the determination of these components there always remains the final reaction of the self-creative unity of the universe. This final reaction completes the self-creative act by putting the decisive stamp of creative emphasis upon the determinations of efficient cause.[13]

Hence, the very nature of reality—that the many become one and are increased by one—includes the everpresent possibility (likelihood, in most cases) that each successive drop of experience will exhibit a difference—great or small—in the manner in which it brings together the "many" that constitute its past actual world, the data for its experience. So even if we were to maintain the independent ontological reality of the essence of Judaism, we should have to subject it to the metaphysical categories applicable by definition to all becoming (or else forfeit the insights of those categories). But once we do this, we realize that we must affirm the freedom of each successive generation that is a component of the essence of Judaism. When this freedom is acknowledged, we cannot expect—certainly, we cannot presuppose—that the essence of Judaism will remain unchanged. When freedom exists, change occurs. The character of reality is such that "no static maintenance of perfection is possible. This axiom is rooted in the nature of things. Advance or Decadence are the only choices offered to mankind. The pure conservative is fighting against the essence of the universe."[14] That which has the greatest survival power is the least "free": "The art of persistence is to be dead. Only inorganic things persist for great lengths of time."[15] Hence, the notion of the unchangeable essence of Judaism is both metaphysically untenable (because freedom exists and all becoming, therefore, represents change), and religiously disagreeable (because we hardly wish to affirm an allegiance to that which is enduring but lifeless).

In addition to some measure of freedom, all becoming is characterized, in the process model, by internal relations. This doctrine also renders untenable the assumption of the immutability of the essence of Judaism.

Relations are not secondary, in this view. Rather, an actual entity is constituted by its relations. As Cobb and Griffin say:

[A] momentary experience is essentially related to previous experiences. In fact, it begins as a multiplicity of relations, and achieves its individuality through its reaction to and unification of these relations. It is not first something in itself, which only secondarily enters into relations with others. The relations are primary . . . . The present occasion is nothing but its process of unifying the particular prehensions with which it begins.[16]

Again we see that, even if we were to allow the concrete reality of the essence of Judaism, its immutability would be impossible. For each successive generation of occasions making up the nexus "Judaism" would have in its past actual world—its data for experience—new and different occasions of becoming. And, in Hartshorne's words, "A different object means a different subject."[17] So if the essence of Judaism has anything at all to do with the history of the Jewish people, certainly these relations have influenced it accordingly.

We know Judaism to be an eclectic civilization whose incorporation of external beliefs and practices has been vast. To hold that Judaism has changed only in accidental respects, while the essence persists unchanged, is to remove from that essence all the fundamental characteristics of reality—process and relativity chief among them.

In sum, what is real is by definition partially self-creative and partially determined by its relations. But both freedom and interconnectedness are finally incompatible with a view of Judaism's essence as unchanging, isolated, and enduring through time.

Perhaps more interesting than the assumption that Judaism's essence exists and can persist through time unchanged is the desire that this be so. Hence we see that for Baeck, ethical monotheism is not only the highest achievement of Judaism thus far; it is the highest possible, the peak reached again and again in the history of the Jews. For the Orthodox Jew, Halacha represents the same apex of religious achievement; Halacha may evolve, but the essence of Judaism will remain halachically defined. Although no one will deny the need for changes in the way Judaism is lived—changes that mediate between Judaism and modernity—these are never understood as challenging the superiority of the established essence of Judaism.

Such faith in an established good does violence to a view of reality based on fundamental process. Here process metaphysics can remind Jews of our historical aversion to idolatry, and can help us to see the idolatry of worshipping an unsurpassable essence. Process thought undergirds the ancient Jewish intuition that we are not to worship created goods, and this must be understood to include religion.

Critics often take process metaphysics to task for unwarranted faith in progress. This criticism, however, ignores process thought's central affirmation of the fact of freedom in all becoming. Freedom to evolve into a greater harmony and intensity is also freedom to fall back into chaos and triviality. But while the process view does not guarantee advance, it does insist that advance is possible. Consequently, the claim that an essence of Judaism derived from a stratum of past history cannot be surpassed today is both absurd from a metaphysical standpoint and idolatrous from a religious one.

IV. Conclusion

From the foregoing, we may conclude that the only way to affirm the existence of an essence of Judaism—with whatever content—is to forfeit the insights of process-relational metaphysics regarding the nature of becoming, freedom, and interconnectedness. This I am not willing to do. However, I do think it possible to find within the process model a more coherent manner in which to speak of continuity within Judaism, and that is to utilize Whitehead's concept of perception in the mode of causal efficacy. This will not guarantee anything like an unchanging core of Judaism, but it will provide a way in which we might reasonably expect enough continuity to maintain an identifiable Judaism through time.

Writes Whitehead:

> Perception in its primary form is consciousness of the causal efficacy of the external world by reason of which the percipient is a concrescence from a definitely constituted datum. The vector character of the datum is this causal efficacy. Thus perception, in this primary sense, is perception of the settled world in the past as constituted by its feeling-tones, and as efficacious by reason of those feeling-tones.[18]

The percipient *inherits* a given world, objectified for it by the latter's feelings. Hence, the most fundamental structure of experience is the subject-object relation, provided this is not understood in the highly abstract form of "knowledge," but rather along the lines of "concern."

> [T]he Quaker word "concern," divested of any suggestion of knowledge, is more fitted to express this fundamental structure. The occasion as subject has a "concern" for the object. And the concern at once places the object as a component in the experience of the subject, with an affective tone drawn from this object and directed towards it . . . . [A]nything is an object in respect to its provocation of some special activity within a

subject. Such a mode of activity is termed a "prehension." Thus a prehension involves three factors. There is the occasion of experience within which the prehension is a detail of activity; there is the datum whose relevance provokes the origination of this prehension; this datum is the prehended object; there is the subjective form, which is the affective tone determining the effectiveness of that prehension in that occasion of experience.[19]

Perception in the mode of causal efficacy "is perception of the settled world in the past as constituted by its feeling-tones, and as efficacious by reason of those feeling-tones."[20] The efficacy of the past, then, the driving force of its legacy, is the power of inherited feeling. It is apt that Whitehead cites, as an example of causal efficacy, memory. Memory is the key to an understanding of continuity that is able to do justice both to the desire for stability and to the need for a coherent metaphysics.

Applying the concept of causal efficacy to the issue at hand (mutatis mutandis), we find that, although we cannot plausibly speak of Judaism's essence, we can speak of the weight of the past and its influence on our own becoming. As Jews, the "past actual world," the total set of data for our experience, includes a rich and diverse legacy of language, story, ritual, theology, folk legend, geography, and so on. This legacy presses upon us in ways much more fundamental than the conscious appropriation that can come later. We are shaped in ways we cannot articulate. The past of our people persists in our present. Regarding this we have no choice. We are just *this* people with just precisely *this* history. However we may choose to cherish or ignore it, to celebrate or deny it, this is our legacy, these are our memories.

In keeping with the above account of freedom and necessity, it must be remembered that, although we have no choice regarding our past actual world, we do have control over the way in which we choose to synthesize this past into our own becoming. That is to say, causal efficacy is not the whole story. The manner of our reaction to our past will in turn constitute our contribution to the heritage of the next generation. In this way it can be seen both that Judaism will have a strong element of continuity, because a clean, total, and widespread break with the past is highly improbable, and that Judaism will develop and change in accordance with each generation of decisions regarding which aspects of Jewish heritage we shall highlight and which we shall relegate to the background.

The sheer weight of the Jewish past encourages, but can never mandate, a familiar Judaism in our present and future. Causal efficacy and freedom of subjective form go hand in hand. Memory and advance: both are vital. And so we cannot finally get to the heart of the thing, because the heart lives and grows and changes along with the rest. Consequently, we cannot know the face of Judaism in the next epoch, cannot know which aspects of Jewish identity will inspire our children and our children's children. The choices belong to them. It is not for us to immortalize some cherished belief or practice of the Jewish people, deeming it *the* essential, authentic characteristic of Judaism for all time and for all Jews. What we can do is live our Jewish lives with as much enthusiasm and imagination as possible, looking forward with hope to the ever-new Judaisms that unfold.

Notes

1. Leo Baeck, *The Essence of Judaism* (New York: Schocken Books, 1948), 9, 18.

2. Martin Buber, *On Judaism* (New York: Schocken Books, 1967), 81, 87.

3. Ibid., 138.

4. Abraham Joshua Heschel, *The Insecurity of Freedom* (New York: Schocken Books, 1959), 66.

5. Ibid., 67.

6. Of course, worshipping the goddess does not of itself entail polytheism. In fact, most (though not all) *contemporary* Hebrew goddess worship takes place within a strictly monotheistic framework. So it is especially interesting to note that most theologians who understand Judaism's essence to be ethical monotheism tend to dismiss *all* such worship as not being essentially Jewish.

7. Alfred North Whitehead, *Process and Reality*, Corrected Edition, David Ray Griffin and Donald W. Sherburne, eds. (New York: The Free Press, 1978), 18.

8. Concrescence: the process of an actual occasion's becoming.

9. *Process and Reality*, 24.

10. Alfred North Whitehead, *Science and the Modern World* (New York: The Macmillan Company, 1925), 51.

11. Nexus: any of a variety of groupings of actual occasions making up the macrocosmic entities we usually consider objects or individuals. Plural: nexūs.

12. Subjective aim: the actual entity's ideal for its own becoming.

13. *Process and Reality*, 47.

14. Alfred North Whitehead, *Adventures of Ideas* (New York: The Free Press, 1962), 274. Whitehead himself is either not cognizant of or not concerned with the apparent contradictions between the concept of essence and the fundamental insights of his work; he employs the word "essence" in several contexts. Still, it is sometimes difficult to know how carefully he has chosen this word. When he says, for example, that "the pure conservative is fighting against the essence of the universe," he is really suggesting that the only "essence" is that there is no essence! That is, the one who desires no change is fighting a universe characterized by change. In this case, at least, essence is akin to arguing that the universe is immutable because the fact of its mutability does not change. There is, of course, a sense in which this is true; but, certainly, by itself it obscures the larger truth.

It may be, then, that at least some of the ways in which Whitehead speaks of essence are simply poor choices of wording. Nevertheless, there are other contexts in which something else is operating; John Cobb, in a discussion of the human soul in *A Christian Natural Theology*, suggests that Whitehead was troubled by the ethical implications of "the lack of absolute self-identity through time." Cobb, however, rather than resorting to "essence," offers a much more suitable way of understanding personal and communal continuity: not commonness of character, but memory, determines self-identity through time. Although Cobb was writing with very different concerns than those reflected here, his proposal indicates how the deeper insights of process theology can be used to critique the notion of "essence," even if Whitehead did not himself employ the categories thus.

15. Alfred North Whitehead, *The Function of Reason* (Boston: The Beacon Press, 1958), 4.

16. John B. Cobb, Jr., and David Ray Griffin, *Process Theology: An Introductory Exposition* (Philadelphia: The Westminster Press, 1976), 19, 20.

17. Charles Hartshorne, *The Divine Relativity* (New Haven: Yale University Press, 1948), 64.

18. *Process and Reality*, 120.

19. *Adventures of Ideas*, 176.

20. *Process and Reality*, 155.

Chapter 6

Would an All-Powerful God Be Worthy of Worship?

Harold S. Kushner

I had never been aware of process theology until my book *When Bad Things Happen to Good People* became an unexpected best seller in 1982, and all of a sudden I began to receive phone calls inquiring about my relationship to process thought. In order to know how to reply, I began to read up on it, being baffled by Whitehead and reading David Griffin with much benefit. What I learned is that the process theologians and I came to very similar conclusions about God and God's role in human tragedy, but by different routes and from different starting points. Process theologians, it seemed to me, challenged the concept of divine omnipotence on theological grounds: What kind of God would create a world in which God had all the power? What kind of universe would result from such a God? I, on the other hand, challenged the concept of divine omnipotence on moral grounds, asking with Abraham, "Shall not the God of Justice practice what He preaches?" In this, it seems to me, I shared common ground with the Psalmist who, faced with human suffering, did not ask a theological question, "Why does God permit this?", but cried out "How long, O Lord?"

If I find myself forced to choose between an All-Powerful God who is not completely good, or else an All-Benevolent God who is not completely powerful, which is the more religious alternative? I would insist that the latter is. I came to believe in a Limited God, a God who could do great things but could not do all things, not because I found such a God-concept theologically required or Scripturally defensible, but because I found it morally necessary.

89

"What sort of God is worthy of worship?" I am not sure that the answer is: A God who controls the whole world and can do anything. In fact, I am fairly sure that that is not the answer. A God of Power extorts obedience but cannot command love. A God who could spare the life of the dying child, who could prevent the earthquake but chooses not to, may inspire our fear and our calculated obeisance but does not deserve our love. Perhaps, in a world of tyrants and despots, one had to insist that God was at least as potent as those earthly rulers who controlled life and death and whose will bore no challenge. But today why should we worship power as the highest good?

We recall the old trilemma: God is good. God is powerful. Evil is real. Most theologians, amateur and professional, solve the problem by denying the reality of evil. ("There was a good reason for what happened. God knows what He is doing. In the long run, you'll be better off for it.") Some deny that God is good as we have been taught to understand the meaning of that word. ("God cannot be limited by considerations of human need or morality. God's mind works in different ways than ours do.") I choose to solve the trilemma by asking, "What's so great about being all-powerful?" Some power is undoubtedly good, and utterly powerless people may become desperate. But total power is bad. Power isolates. I cannot imagine a God worthy of worship who thrives on a diet of groveling obedience. Recall those immensely moving passages in Hosea and Jeremiah, in which God is pictured as lonely because there is no one to love Him. Power and love may well be mutually exclusive. We can fear an all-powerful God, but we cannot love Him, because love exists between equals, entities who if not matched in power at least have a mutual need for each other. Power, like water, only flows downhill, from the higher to the lower.

Freud suggests that when we are children, we believe that we are all-powerful. The myth of infantile omnipotence lets us feel that we are responsible for whatever happens in our world. We grow up and come to acknowledge our limitations, so then we believe that our parents are all-powerful. If they refuse to fix a broken toy or buy us a new one, it's not because they cannot. It is because they do not want to. When we grow older still and learn that our parents have their limitations as well, we transfer this sense of omnipotence to our political and religious leaders. And then when we find out that they are only human, we project this sense of omnipotence onto God. But it was never God's idea to be omnipotent. It was our need to have an omnipotent God which lay behind the concept. And needless to say, God is not obliged to be what our psyches would prefer him to be.

In the first serious theological conversation I ever had with David Griffin, he said something wonderful that has remained with me ever since. He said, "Maybe God is all-powerful but God's power is not the power to coerce but the power to enable." In other words, God can do anything, but only through human and other instruments. I thought that was a remarkable insight, and responded by saying, "That's why, so often in the Bible and afterwards, God is portrayed by fire—at the Burning Bush, in the Eternal Flame before the Ark, etc." Fire is not an object: fire is a process, the process by which the latent energy in a lump of coal or a log of wood is turned into actual energy. God is like fire, liberating the potential energy in each of us.

The question was raised in an earlier discussion, "How can you say that God could not stop the Holocaust but human beings were able to? Are we more powerful than God?" Here, I think, is the answer. God did stop the Holocaust, and it could not have been stopped without God. Human beings without God will be selfish, timid, apathetic. What force except God could have inspired so many people to be so brave and self-sacrificing to defeat the satanic forces of Nazism? God is not found in the flood or the earthquake; God is found in the ability of people to transcend themselves, to risk their lives to save their neighbor from the flood, to rebuild their ravaged communities after the earthquake.

In sum, I have come to cherish and accept process theology, not because I am persuaded that it is philosophically more coherent than any other view, and not because I find it theologically more persuasive. It may be, or it may not be. I accept and cherish process theology because it tells me that what I *need* to believe about God and God's role in human affairs on moral grounds is philosophically plausible as well. And for that, I am grateful.

Part II

Jewish-Christian Dialogue
On Process Thought

Chapter 7

Process Theodicy, Christology, and the *Imitatio Dei*

David Ray Griffin

The central religious question is whether there is a Holy Reality, meaning a reality that is worthy of worship with one's entire being, to which one's life can rightfully be committed without reserve. According to the biblical perspective, there *is* a Holy Reality: a God who created the world and is providentially active in it. From this perspective, the apparent evil in the world can become a theological problem, because this apparent evil, if taken to be *genuinely* evil, can be regarded as falsifying God's total goodness and thereby God's worthiness of worship. For many people, the Holocaust was an evil that cannot be rationalized as merely apparent evil. It was, in fact, an evil so great as to provide the ultimate challenge to belief in a Holy Reality creative of and providentially active in the world. The task of theodicy for Jews and Christians (and other theists) is to try to meet that challenge. The question of this essay is whether the process theology based on the philosophy of Alfred North Whitehead and Charles Hartshorne can produce a theodicy that is adequate to the basic beliefs of Jewish and Christian faith and is credible in the light of the enormity of evil in the world, especially the Holocaust.

As well as intensifying this theoretical problem of evil, which theodicies try to solve, the Holocaust brings to consciousness another problem for Christian faith. Christianity teaches that God is loving and just, and that we are to worship God by developing the kinds of virtues befitting those who believe in such a Holy Reality. One of the best-known lists of these virtues includes love, peace, patience, kindness, goodness, gentleness, and self-control (Galations 5:22–23). When

95

one reads the history of the Christian treatment of Jews, however, these virtues hardly leap off the page. The way blacks and Native Americans have been treated by white Christians in the United States is also not a pretty tale. Whether or not one sees the Holocaust as exceeding previous atrocities qualitatively, it poignantly raises the question of Christian faith's practical value.[1] For, as has been pointed out many times, the Nazis could draw on Christian writings and precedent for much of their propaganda and practice. And, even if it could be maintained that the perpetrators of the Holocaust were no longer Christian, the fact remains that they were rather immediately *post*-Christian: One would expect that the virtues instilled by Christianity would still be quite dominant. From this perspective, the Holocaust constitutes an overwhelming indictment of Christianity, especially in the light of the prior and later atrocities committed by those in countries in which Christianity has been the dominant form of religion.

Sometimes indictments of Christianity in terms of its practical fruits seem to presuppose a view of the "natural goodness" of human nature prior to its being "corrupted" by "dogmatic religion." Such a view is naive. Human beings have thought in terms of "us" and "them" in every part of the earth, as far back as recorded history goes, and have often resorted to force to deal with "them," sometimes very brutally. This is a tendency of human nature. It would be judging any religion by impossible standards to indict it for not totally eradicating this tendency. What we can hope for is that it be mitigated. The question is whether a fair reading of history suggests that Christianity has aggravated this tendency at least as much as it has mitigated it. Judgments about this are very difficult to make. But I would say that, at the very least, Christianity has not produced the virtues it advocates to the degree that one could reasonably expect and, further, that it has to an extent aggravated the tendency to use coercive force against "aliens."

It has rightly been pointed out that Christian-Jewish relations cannot *simply* be categorized as one more example of the relations between "us" and "them." Christianity arose as a sect of Judaism; being a "Jew" who is not a "Christian" is in effect a denial of the central Christian claim; and the early antagonism of the "Christians" to those Jews who did not agree with them and ostracized them is reflected in the Sacred Scripture of the Christians in such a way that Judaism took on special theological significance. Due to these facts, the Christian attitude toward and treatment of Jews is a special case, although it is also an example of the more general human tendency to reduce those who are different to objects against whom the use of force is justifiable.

I have indicated three problems:

(1)   the general problem of theodicy, especially in the light of the Holocaust;

(2)   the problem of the practical value of Christianity, especially with regard to the inculcation of the virtues of "love, peace, patience, kindness, goodness, gentleness, and self-control" in relation to those who are perceived as different in some significant respect; and

(3)   the problem of the special animus that has been manifested by Christians toward Jews and Judaism.

The first problem is a purely theoretical one, which in principle can be solved by theological reformulation. The second and third problems are practical ones, involving the attitudes and behavior of Christians; but they are rooted in part in theoretical beliefs, so that theological reformulation could be relevant to overcoming them. I believe that at the root of the theoretical dimension of all three problems is one and the same issue: the understanding of God's power in relation to the world. God has been understood by traditional Jewish and Christian theology as having *coercive omnipotence*. This idea has led to an insoluble problem of evil; it has contributed to an anti-Judaistic Christology; and it has aggravated the coercive tendencies of those who have been informed by the biblical vision of the Holy Reality. My threefold thesis is that process theology's *conception* of God's omnipotence as persuasive can solve the theoretical problem of evil, that it can remove the basis for an anti-Judaistic Christology, and that, to the extent that it would become widely informative of people's *perception* of the Holy, it would mitigate their tendency to use coercion. I will discuss these three issues in order.

I. Process Theodicy

There has been considerable advocacy, for example by Irving Greenberg,[2] of the idea that the Holocaust should be perceived as a new revelation. I agree that it should, *if* it is specified that "revelation" is not being used in the strict sense here, and that the revelation is a negative one. To speak of an event as a revelation of God in the strict sense, one should mean not only that the event has been *received* by someone as revelatory of God's nature (the subjective side of revelation), but also that the event resulted from God's activity in such a way that the *event in itself*, prior to its reception at any subsequent time as a revelation of God, was a self-expression of God's nature (the objective side of revelation).[3] In endorsing the idea that the Holocaust is appropriately taken as a revelation of God, the term *revelation* is not being used in the strict sense, because the objective dimension is absent: The event was not a positive self-expression of God's nature. Insofar as it is appropriately received as a revelation, this is not because of some positive input by God, but precisely because there was *not* any special divine causal influence in a situation that seemed (to many) to call for it.

This point leads to the sense in which the revelation is negative. It has been taken by many, and it should be taken by all (at least by all who were not already consciously convinced by other data), as revealing this truth: *There is no Holy Reality with coercive omnipotence.*

This general negative truth allows for at least three variations. One would be that there is no Holy Reality at all—that is, no reality that is worthy of our total devotion. This is nihilism. A second option would be that there is a Holy Reality, but that this Holy Reality exerts no providential guidance in the processes of nature and human history. This has been Richard Rubenstein's response. A third possibility is that there is a Holy Reality that exerts providential power in the world, but this power is necessarily persuasive, not coercive. Process theology provides a version of this third view. I have developed a process theodicy at length elsewhere.[4] Here I will simply lay out four major points in very sketchy fashion.

The first point is that creativity (or energy, or power) is inherent in the world. Creativity is the twofold power of individual events (1) to determine themselves partially and (2) to influence subsequent events. This power exists in various degrees: Individual events at the electronic level have far less than do human events. But all events that are genuine individuals have at least some iota of this twofold power. (There are many entities that we ordinarily call "things" [such as rocks] and "events" [such as rock concerts] that are not genuine individuals: They have less unity than their constituents [such as the molecules in the rock and the members of the rock group and of the audience]. These mere aggregational clusters of individuals have no creative power whatsoever; all the creativity is in the individuals constituting them. In speaking of "events" and "beings," I will be referring to true individuals.)

To say that this power is *inherent* in the world is to say that the world embodies it necessarily. It is not a contingent characteristic of the world, voluntarily granted to it by God. There could be worlds other than this one; but there could, by hypothesis, be no actual world without this inherent power of creativity.

This creative power, exemplified by all creaturely individuals, is a power that cannot be overridden by God. This means that God cannot completely control any event in the world. God seeks to persuade events to actualize the best possibilities open to them. But God can only seek to persuade; God cannot dictate. God proposes; the world disposes. This feature of the God-world relation is not a feature created by God, through some form of self-limitation. This is simply, by hypothesis, the way things are, eternally and necessarily.

Accordingly, the central feature of the world, in relation to God's will, is its *ambiguity*. Each event has a divinely derived ideal aim, but this ideal aim gets embodied in an event having its own power of being. This means that the possibility of ambiguity exists in every single event in the world. Because each event is internally affected by preceding events, as well as having its own partial autonomy, there are two bases for ambiguity. First, each event gets off to an ambiguous start; the "ideal aim" proffered by God is "ideal" only in relation to those particular ambiguous circumstances. "The initial aim is the best for that *impasse*."[5] Second, should an individual perfectly actualize the possibility that is ideal for it in this sense, this eventuality would not be determined by God, but would be due to the response of the individual.

This doctrine implies that there can be no one being with a monopoly on power. Having "perfect power" simply cannot mean being the "sole power" (*contra* Emil Fackenheim). There is necessarily a multiplicity of beings with power; power is necessarily shared. This doctrine also means that God cannot coerce worldly beings, because the inherent power they have cannot be overridden. Accordingly, if there is a Holy Reality with "omnipotence," defined as *perfect power* (meaning the greatest power one being could possibly have), it cannot be coercive omnipotence. If omnipotence is attributed to God, it must be persuasive omnipotence.

The doctrine of *creatio ex nihilo*, with *nihil* understood as *absolutely* nothing, has been correlative with the doctrine of coercive omnipotence. If God created our present world out of absolutely nothing, there would be no realities that have any inherent power of their own with which to resist the divine will. Any power possessed by any of the creatures would be purely a divine gift, and could be withdrawn, or overridden (depending upon which terminology is preferred), at any time.

Process theology, by contrast, envisages God as creating our ordered world out of chaos, out of the "formless void" of Genesis 1. There are important senses in which the phrase *creatio ex nihilo* can properly be used.[6] But process theology denies that God ever was the only actuality. It also denies that worldly actualities were ever totally controllable by God. Creation is (by hypothesis) always based upon a prior state of finite actualities (although that state might be too chaotic to be properly termed a *world*), and these actualities have always had at least an iota of uncontrollable power. The divine creative action is, accordingly, always limited to encouraging the best possible advance upon the previous state of things.

In sum, the first point of a process theodicy is that creative power is inherent in the world. The corollaries of this point are the rejection of creation out of absolute nothingness, the impossibility of coercive omnipotence, and the resulting inevitability of worldly ambiguity.

The second point is that there is an order among possibilities. After A is actualized, F cannot be actualized until B, C, D, and E have been actualized. For example, human beings could not—some artificial intelligence enthusiasts notwithstanding—have been created directly out of protons and electrons. It was necessary first to have atoms, then molecules, then macromolecules, then multicelled animals. A very complex organization was necessary before a soul could emerge, especially a human soul. This point, in conjunction with the previous one, means that the creation of our world was necessarily a step-by-step process. In other words, God created our world by means of a long, slow, evolutionary process not for some mysterious reason, known only to divine omniscience; God used this process because it is the only possible way to create a world such as ours.

Having mentioned omniscience, I should pause to indicate more clearly the nature of my process theodicy, as it may well sound as if it were propounded from a viewpoint of presumed omniscience. It is proposed, rather, as a *hypothesis*, to be accepted or rejected on the same grounds as any hypothesis: in terms of its consistency, its adequacy to all the relevant facts, and its illuminating power. So, for example, the doctrine that the world necessarily consists of actualities that inherently possess power is a speculative hypothesis, as is the contrary doctrine that there could be a world devoid of power. One of the reasons for preferring the former hypothesis to the latter is that the latter creates an insoluble problem of evil. Likewise, the correlative alternatives— creation out of chaos or out of absolute nothingness, persuasive omnipotence or coercive omnipotence—are also speculative hypotheses.

Neither set of alternatives has been infallibly revealed; neither set is any more speculative than the other.

I move now to the third hypothesis of this process theodicy, which is that there exist in the nature of things positive correlations among the following variables:

(1) the capacity for enjoyment, meaning experience that is harmonious and intense;
(2) the capacity for suffering;
(3) freedom, or the power of self-determination;
(4) the power to contribute good to others; and
(5) the power to inflict suffering upon others.

(The fourth and fifth points together constitute the power of other-determination, or causal influence.)

For there to be a positive correlation among these variables means that, as any one of them rises, the other four necessarily rise proportionately. The creator's purpose throughout the evolutionary process, by hypothesis, has been to bring about creatures with more and more capacity for enjoying higher values. The increasing complexity of organisms, which is a direction observable in this process, is a pre-condition for greater variety and intensity of experience. When this greater variety plus intensity is synthesized harmoniously, the desired result is achieved. However—and this is where the second variable comes in—the same conditions that allow greater enjoyment also make greater suffering possible. The reason for this correlation is that both variables presuppose the same quality: sensitivity. At the human level, the capacity for the highest enjoyments involves sensitivity to our body's experience (as in the enjoyment of food, exercise, sex, and sights, sounds, and smells in the environment), to the welfare of others (as in the enjoyment of our children's successes), the opinion of others (as in the enjoyment of praise), and to moral, intellectual, aesthetic, and religious values. However, these same sensitivities can cause us intensely disharmonious experience, as when our bodies are starving or wracked with pain, when our children suffer or die prematurely, when others criticize us, when we feel moral or religious guilt, when our intellectual processes lead to conclusions that are horrifying, or when we find our environment ugly. Any of these experiences can induce sufficient suffering to lead to suicide. Humans enjoy positive values of which no dog dreams; but we also experience negative values that no dog dreads. The conditions that make possible the higher forms of enjoyment equally make possible the higher forms of suffering.

Suggesting that this correlation exists "in the nature of things" means that it obtains necessarily. It was not arbitrarily decided upon by God, even "before the foundations of the world." The hypothesis is that the correlation is a *metaphysical necessity*: It would obtain in any possible world God could create. Accordingly, the creative process is necessarily a risky business. The creative purpose of bringing about increasingly greater richness of experience in the creation cannot be carried out without the risk of greater suffering.

The riskiness of the creative process is intensified by the other correlations, which (by hypothesis) are equally necessary. The third variable is freedom, or the power of self-determination. According to process theology, freedom in and of itself is not the quality God is most concerned to promote. Rather, creatures with more and more freedom are evoked because increased freedom is part and parcel of the increased capacity for enjoyment. Consequently, process theodicy has a clear answer to a question that is so difficult for most other theodicies, namely: "Why did God not create beings who would have been just like us in all respects except that they would not have been genuinely free? These creatures would have been able to experience all the values we can enjoy (except those that presuppose sin), including the *belief* that they were free, but would always act rightly, never bringing unnecessary suffering to themselves or others. Why did God not create a world composed of them instead?" For process theodicy, the answer is simply: "God could not have done so, because such creatures are as impossible as round squares." It is metaphysically impossible for there be creatures with a high sensitivity to various values without a correspondingly high degree of freedom, which means freedom to violate the creator's will, or ideal aim, for them. By correlating this third variable with the second, we see that the creatures who have the greatest capacity to suffer also have the greatest capacity to reject the best possibilities for themselves and, thereby, to make themselves miserable.

Greater power for self-determination also correlates positively with greater power to influence others. The happy side of this is the fourth variable, the power to contribute good to others. The ominous side is the fifth variable, the power to inflict suffering upon others. It is when we bring this fifth variable into the picture, along with the second and third (the capacities for suffering and for self-determination), that we have the conditions for a "Holocaust Universe." On the assumption that these correlations, which *factually* obtain in our world, also *necessarily* obtain, any world God could create would necessarily be *tragic*, meaning that the greater goods would not be possible without the possibility of the greater evils. Accordingly, any universe with creatures possessing the capacity for rational self-determination, and for the enjoyment of all the values this capacity makes possible, would necessarily be a universe in which holocausts could occur. A world with creatures such as Moses, Jeremiah, Jesus, Maimonides, St. Francis, Pope John XXIII, St. Teresa, Martin Luther King, Martin Niemoeller, Abraham Heschel, and Martin Buber is simply not possible without the possibility of beings who would bring fellow human beings in chains from Africa to serve as slaves, beings who would decimate the native American population, and beings who would seek to destroy the entire Jewish population in Europe.

Would it have been better if human beings had not been created? The fourth hypothesis of this process theodicy is relevant to this question. This is the affirmation that God not only rejoices with all our joys but also suffers with all our sufferings. In fact, God is the one being who suffers all the pain in the universe, and is thereby the one being in position to judge whether the higher stages of creation have been worth the risks.

This fourth point puts a different light on the question of God's moral goodness. In the previous paragraphs, God was portrayed as urging on the universe to develop more and more complex structures in order to make possible the higher forms of value-experience. Because this divine leading also has made possible the more horrendous forms of evil, however, God could seem to be callous. But this fourth point says that the Holy Reality has never opened up the possibility of any kind or degree of suffering that It Itself was not willing to endure.

It seems that Jewish thought has emphasized this biblical insight more than Christian theology, having been less influenced by Greek notions of perfection as immutability and impassibility. One of the ironies of Christianity has been that it took the suffering death of Jesus on the cross as its central symbol and yet denied that God suffers with the world. In our century, fortunately, this contradiction of its central symbol, and of the biblical witness in general, is being overcome, as evidenced in the writings of Reinhold Niebuhr, Kazo Kitamora, Jürgen Moltmann, and various feminist theologians, as well as process theologians.

At this point, I want to draw out the contrast between the process view of God's power in relation to worldly freedom and that of the currently prevalent view. This prevalent view involves the hypothesis of a voluntary self-limitation on God's part. That is, God essentially has coercive omnipotence, but freely decides to create some beings having freedom. Deity, thereby, limits its power to control all events, because it permits the free creatures to make their own decisions, including the decision to sin. Deity voluntarily limits its power to that of persuasion.[7] I call this the *"hybrid* free-will defense," because it does not go all the way with freedom: It does not affirm it to be an ingredient inherent in the world.

From the process perspective, there are several problems with this hybrid position. First, theologians who take this position usually speak as if God gave freedom only to some of the creatures; these privileged creatures are often limited to human beings. This implies that God has coercive omnipotence in relation to the rest of creation. Accordingly, all those events usually called "natural evils," such as diseases, earthquakes, and tornadoes, receive no explanation. Of course, this problem could be solved by affirming that God has freely given some power of self-determination to every level of actuality, down to the subatomic events, but few of the theologians in question have done this. (Also, it would be a mystery as to why God would choose to give living cells the freedom to become cancerous, if this were not necessary.)

A second problem with the hybrid free-will defense is that, if God essentially has coercive omnipotence, so that the power of self-determination has been freely given to the creation, God could withdraw this power at any time. God could intervene in the "natural" course of things to prevent gross evils. The idea that God has this kind of power in reserve leads to the expectation that God should use it in particular situations. This expectation lies behind many of Elie Wiesel's most poignant passages. It lies behind Irving Greenberg's lament, "There were no thunderbolts of divine curses to check mass murder or torture." It lies behind Alexander Donat's disappointed statement, "In vain we looked at that cloudless September sky for some sign of God's wrath."[8] It lies behind thousands of other outbursts against God, and only God knows how many people have been led to atheism because of this expectation.

A third problem of the hybrid free-will position is that it makes our responsibility for the future of the world dubious. If God has the power unilaterally to bring about a perfect world, then are our efforts really essential? If God has the power to overcome the evils of the world unilaterally and yet has failed to use it for all these centuries, can the battle against evil really be very important from the ultimate point of view? These kinds of questions can undermine long-term, whole-hearted commitment to overcoming the evils of the world, including efforts to avoid the imminent destruction of the human species. Such commitment is urgently needed—at least on the assumption that there is not a good God with coercive omnipotence, which I am taking the Holocaust to have confirmed.

I turn now to the question of the kind of Christology that could be developed in harmony with this process theodicy.

II. Process Christology

I have developed a process Christology at some length elsewhere.[9] Here, I will focus on those points that are most pertinent to the present concern, which is to indicate that a process conceptuality can enable Christians to develop a Christology that, on the one hand, provides a way of intelligibly conceptualizing affirmations about Jesus that are basic to Christian faith, but does not, on the other hand, support anti-Judaistic attitudes or do violence to basic Jewish beliefs.

The last point needs explanation. By "not doing violence to basic Jewish beliefs" I do not, of course, mean that I as a Christian will not make affirmations about Jesus that some Jews cannot accept. I mean that, unlike traditional formulations, the conceptualization will neither compromise the oneness of God nor imply that God's activity in Jesus was ontologically different from God's activity in other prophets.

Of course, this negative criterion can easily be met and has been met (usually unintentionally) by much modern Christian theology, insofar as it has, through phenomenological bracketing or some other methodological device, avoided all metaphysical affirmations about deity in itself and Jesus' (special) relation to deity. Such approaches, however, although admirable in some respects, do not provide an adequate theological explication of and support for Christian faith, for reasons that I have discussed elsewhere.[10] The challenge is to meet the negative criterion of not doing violence to basic Jewish beliefs (along with the other negative criterion of not supporting anti-Judaistic attitudes), while providing a formulation of Jesus' special relation to God that is an adequate explication of what is implied by Christian faith.

There is another qualification that must be made with regard to the intention of not doing violence to basic Jewish beliefs. There is one sense in which many contemporary theistic Jews will surely think that my position does violence to basic Jewish beliefs. I have in mind particularly the things I have said and will say about what God cannot do, according to process theology. Many Jews will think that these statements undermine basic beliefs about what God has done and will do. Many Christians, however, will think the same thing, and yet I obviously do not believe that I am doing violence to basic Christian beliefs. The point is, of course, that what is "basic to" any religious tradition is a matter of judgment, and my judgment is that process theology can do justice to the basic ideas of Christian faith. By implication, therefore, it is also my judgment that process theology can do justice to the basics of Jewish faith because, with regard to the issue of how God can and cannot act in the world, there is no reason in principle for Jews to be less predisposed than Christians to accept process theology's views on this matter.

The thesis that will be made explicit in the following is already implicit in the foregoing: The presupposition that made possible an anti-Judaistic Christian theology in general, and an anti-Judaistic Christology in particular, is a presupposition shared in common by traditional Judaism and traditional Christianity. This is the presupposition that God is coercively omnipotent and can, therefore, totally determine events in the world. Recognizing its connection with anti-Judaism is not the only or even the basic reason for rejecting this presupposition. This recognition, however, may provide the psychological occasion for Jews and Christians to give serious consideration to the other good reasons for rejecting it.

It must be frankly acknowledged, of course, that this psychological element in most people's beliefs—namely, that they partly believe things because they *want* to believe them—also works the other way in this case. That is, the hope that God *will* some day unilaterally set things right, bringing about an unambiguous salvation, encourages people to hold on to the traditional belief that God *can* unilaterally determine states of affairs in the world. The question is whether the value of that hope is worth all the moral and intellectual problems entailed by holding on to the presupposition of that hope.

Given those preliminary remarks, I will now, in summary fashion, indicate how process thought can develop a Christology that does justice to basic Christian affirmations. I will then point out the ways in which such a Christology, along with the more general Christian theological position compatible with it, rules out precisely those elements that did violence to Jewish beliefs and/or gave support to anti-Judaistic attitudes.

Christians have affirmed Jesus as the supreme incarnation of God—in particular, of the divine Logos. The very idea of God's being present in worldly actualities at all has been problematic for most philosophical positions, especially in the modern period. In process philosophy, however, all actualities are centers of experience, and each experience incorporates to some extent all the other experiences in its immediate environment. Because the divine experience is all-inclusive, it is in the immediate environment of, and is thereby incorporated into, every creaturely experience. The notion that God was incarnate in Jesus, accordingly, poses no problems in itself. What needs to be explained is how God could have been incarnate in him *in a special way*, such that it is especially appropriate to relate ourselves to God through Jesus.

Process philosophy allows us to understand the presence of God in creatures to differ *in degree*: God is more present in some creatures than in others. There are two dimensions of this difference. First, for higher-level, more complex creatures, the initial aim God gives will be more complex, including more of the pure possibilities (eternal objects) contained in the primordial nature of God. Second, a creature can choose to constitute itself either by responding primarily to the complex possibility offered by God or by responding primarily to alternative possibilities offered by the past world. This is a matter of degree. Accordingly, high-level creatures, such as human beings, have the capacity to incarnate God more fully than do lower-grade ones; and those human beings who regularly determine themselves by responding with a high degree of conformity to the divinely-given aims for them incarnate God to the highest degree.

Process philosophy also allows us to understand the presence of God in us to differ *in kind*, in this sense: The divinely-given aims, which can be incorporated into creaturely experiences, differ *in content*. To explain: The primordial nature of God contains all abstract possibilities, meaning those that are possibilities in the broadest sense of the word, including possibilities that could only be instantiated in a world inconceivably different from ours a trillion years in the future. Only a small number of these abstract possibilities are *real* possibilities for a particular creature at a particular time and place. For one thing, there is an order among the possibilities: Some are incompatible with others, and particular ones can only be entertained as real possibilities after prior ones have been actualized. Accordingly, what God can proffer to a particular creature as the best possibility really open to it will depend not only upon the general kind of creature it is, but also upon the particular background out of which it arises. For example, the content of the possibilities that can be presented to a human differ drastically from those that can be presented to an electron. Also, the aims that can be presented to a human being in Israel in the fifth century B.C.E. will differ considerably from the real possibilities open to a person living at that same time in India.

The next step in the argument is that it is possible for the content of some particular aims given to creatures to reflect more directly than others God's general aim for creation as a whole. If ideal aims whose content reflected that general aim to a high degree were faithfully expressed by a human being through language and action, this language and action would be a special expression of God's purpose. Furthermore, if this symbolic expression were appropriately interpreted by some human beings, then a special revelation of God would have occurred. In these terms, process theology can interpret Jesus as a special revelation of God's purpose. Additional considerations can lead to seeing Jesus as also especially revelatory of God's character and mode of agency.

As well as showing how Jesus can intelligibly be understood as incarnating God in such a way that it is appropriate to apprehend him as a special revelation of God, process theology can also make intelligible the specialness of the incarnation of God in Jesus in such fashion as to support the conviction that Jesus is a model for human existence.

John Cobb has developed a conceptuality for understanding various ways in which the human psyche can be structured.[11] This conceptuality can account for the differences between mythical existence and axial existence in general, and also for the differences among the various structures of axial existence. Each structure of axial existence involves an authentic mode and various inauthentic modes in which it can be actualized. Given this pluralistic approach, Jesus cannot be taken as a model for humanity in general in some simple sense. Jesus can, however, be seen as a model with regard to the relation to the biblical God. People who have had their existence decisively formed in relation to this God—a Holy Reality understood as a personal God who cares about our morality—are particularly conscious of the initial aim, especially its moral dimension, and therefore of the "ought" dimension of experience. Whereas this awareness tends to produce societies that are more concerned with social justice than are other societies, it also can produce individuals who experience continual tension between duty and inclination. The ideal aim is experienced as a call to do something other than what I want to do. This tension is due to the fact that the center of my existence, my "self" or my "I," finds the initial aim from God as one of the many alien data that need to be synthesized. The "I," or organizing center, is constituted by memories and purposes from my previous experiences.

The authentic sayings of Jesus, however, suggest that he had a peculiarly undistorted view of life and a sense of immediate authority.

These characteristics can be accounted for by supposing that, at least in certain decisive moments, the divine aims were not experienced by Jesus as something alien to his selfhood, but that his selfhood was constituted as much by these ideal aims as by his own previously formed purposes (which had in turn conformed to God's aims and therefore involved the disposition to be open to God's aims in the future). In Jesus, accordingly, the tension between "desire and duty" would have been transcended, at least to a great extent and in decisive periods.

This reflection provides a way of showing how the incarnation in Jesus might have differed from the incarnation of God in most human beings not only in degree, and not only in content, but also in the role that the incarnation played in the structure of his existence, for in this portrayal the incarnation of the divine purpose is constitutive of Jesus' very self. In this sense we can take Jesus as a model for ideal human existence vis-à-vis God.

The point of the foregong Christogical sketch is that process categories for understanding God's relation to the world can explicate Christian convictions about Jesus—as special incarnation of God, as special revelation of God, and as model for ideal human existence in relation to God—in a way that does no violence to Jewish beliefs about God. Thus far, accordingly, the point has been positive. I now turn to the negative points implicit in this sketch, meaning the aspects of traditional Christian theology that are ruled out. (I believe, however, the acceptance of these negative points to be a positive move forward.)

(1)   If Jesus, thus understood, is really accepted as a special revelation of God's mode of agency in the world, then this acceptance provides no basis for attributing coercive omnipotence to God. God acted on and through Jesus by attraction or persuasion, not by coercion. This interpretation fits with the portrayal of Jesus in the synoptic gospels, once one strips away some added miraculous elements (while realizing that the *authentic* miraculous events can be understood in terms of parapsychological [as well as psychosomatic] relations)[12] and the theological rationalization of Jesus' death as planned and determined from the beginning by God. Once this later framework is removed, there is nothing in the life of Jesus— the life of a man who responded freely to God's call, sought to persuade others to respond to the present and future Reign of God, and ended up on a cross in the prime of life—if it

be taken as a special revelation of God's *modus operandi*, to suggest that God possesses coercive omnipotence.

(2) Although it is affirmed in this Christology that Jesus was a special incarnation of the divine Logos,[13] this Logos is not understood to be in any sense a subject, or a quasi-subject, with its own experience within the Godhead. Rather, the Logos is understood as an abstraction within God. There are not multiple centers, or even quasi-centers, of experience in God. The Logos is God's primordial envisagement of the eternal possibilities for finite existence with the purpose of actualizing these possibilities in such a way as to maximize the richness and joy of finite existence. This Logos is, hence, the eternal purpose of God, which came to expression in Jesus' message of the Reign of God. Accordingly, there is no basis in this Christology for a tritheistic understanding of God. Also, not thinking of the Logos as an experiencing subject removes one of the bases in traditional Christology for assuming that the "incarnation of the Logos" in Jesus somehow made Jesus less than, or more than, fully human.

(3) This incarnational Christology does not require, and in fact removes every basis for, thinking of Jesus as other than fully human in *any* sense. Jesus in no way shared in those attributes that can characterize only God, such as omniscience, omnipresence, aseity. (The telepathic and clairvoyant knowledge Jesus evidently had, for example, does not make him different in kind in this respect from several other human beings, and does not even begin to approach divine omniscience.) God was present in Jesus, but only as *experienced*, not as *experiencing subject*. The subjectivity of Jesus was not, even in part, divine subjectivity; no aspect of the normal, human type of psyche was replaced by something divine. The idea that the structure of Jesus' existence differs from that of the rest of us in being more oriented around the initial aims received from God, so that Jesus' "I" was especially constituted by the incarnation of the divine Logos, in no way contradicts this point. What is involved here is not an ingredient in Jesus that is not present in the rest of us, but a different structuring of the relations among the various ingredients. In simplest terms, Jesus was in no sense God. Accordingly, every basis for the charge of "deicide" is removed (whether the Jewish or Roman authorities be regarded as primarily responsible for Jesus' death).

(4) In whatever way Jesus may have been special with regard to his relation to God, this specialness was not unilaterally determined by God, but depended upon repeated, free, human responses. This does not mean that Jesus' specialness was not rooted in God in any sense, as implied by those Christologies that portray Jesus as simply having actualized to an optimal degree the possibilities that are presented to all humans. On the contrary, God (by hypothsis) always calls an event to realize the best possibilities open to it, given its particular past and its particular environment. Accordingly, insofar as all pasts and environments differ, especially for human beings, God's ideal aims for all human experiences differ, more or less. However—and this is the main negative point being made here—any specialness characterizing the ideal aims presented to Jesus was not a result of a unilateral decision on God's part. Rather, it depended upon the centuries of partly free responses to God in the Hebraic tradition, and upon the partly free decisions of those who were especially influential in the development of Jesus' character, and then upon the entire series of responses made by Jesus in his formative years, and finally upon those made during his active ministry. In other words, how Jesus responded to divine aims in one moment determined what aims God could present in a subsequent moment, and so on.

This view, incidentally, provides one way of explicating the Jewish saying:

> When the Israelites do God's will, they add to the power of God on high. When the Israelites do not do God's will, they, as it were, weaken the great power of God on high.[14]

God had the power to become specially incarnate in, and revealed through, Jesus only because of the long series of events in which Jesus' predecessors, and then Jesus himself, actualized God's will or ideal aims for them in their particular circumstances.

This fourth point doubly underscores Jesus' full humanity: It stresses not only that Jesus was in no way merely a puppet. It also stresses that the "special prevenient grace" that can be affirmed as part of the explanation of Jesus' life was not the result of an arbitrary, unilateral decision by God but an exemplification of God's practice always and everywhere of presenting the best aims possible for the creatures, given the particular circumstances at hand that determine what is *really* possible for those creatures. In underscoring Jesus' full humanity by stressing the role of our past in determining what God can do with us, this point also underscores Jesus' Jewishness: If Jesus was indeed a special incarnation of God, as Christians profess, this type of incarnation simply could not have occurred elsewhere than in a Jew. Accordingly, this fourth point, along with the previous ones, removes every basis for the view, expressed by "Nazi Christians" and other Marcionites, that Jesus' Jewishness was irrelevant to his specialness.[15]

(5) The question as to whether Jesus was the "Messiah who was to come" does not admit of an unambiguous answer. Because all historical events involve partially self-determining responses, God cannot know the future, and cannot unilaterally determine the present. In particular, God cannot simply decide that some pre-existent set of characteristics (what Whitehead calls a "complex eternal object") will be instantiated at such-and-such a time and place. Whether that complex abstract possibility can even be proffered as a real possibility for some individual or community will depend upon the myriad decisions that are made by the creatures in the intervening time. Also, even if that intervening history is most fortunate in respect to that complex possibility's becoming a *real* possibility (a lure for realization) for an individual or community, the issue of whether or not it then gets incarnated will be decided by the individual or community.

For these reasons, there is ambiguity at every point of the history of the expectation of a "messiah." On the one hand, there was never any unambiguous announcement from God that a messiah, however understood, would appear. There was certainly no unambiguous announcement that a particular type of messiah would appear. On the other hand, Jesus' own life was not planned and controlled by God in any detail: There were free, unforeseen responses at every point, and undoubtedly many of these were ambiguous. Jesus' life was a partially *self-creating definition* of a special agent of God, not a mere acting out of a pre-established blueprint. One can see Jesus' life and message as a particularly creative response to the tradition and the contemporary situation without saying that it was *the* response to be made, and certainly without saying that Jesus unambiguously was the expected messiah. The answer to that question, "Was Jesus the messiah?" can only be: "It depends." That is, it depends on what you mean by "messiah." It also depends on how you understand Jesus, particularly which aspects of his life you take to be primary. Christians, from this point of view, are those who have decided that Jesus' life in some sense creatively defined the nature of true messiahship. In making this confession, however, they need not conclude that those who disagree with them are wrong. There simply is no unambiguous right and wrong on this question. This issue, however, is far too complex to discuss briefly.[16]

(6)   Just as it was impossible for God totally to determine events prior to Jesus, so that none of these events can be taken as providing infallible testimony as to God's purposes, no events after Jesus' life can be taken as infallible testimony that Jesus was exactly what God had in mind (whether Jesus be considered by Christians to have perfectly fulfilled the best Jewish expectations for a messiah or to have been a surprising, unexpected fulfillment). In other words, Christians cannot take events reported in their "New Testament," or any other statements therein, as having infallibly settled the question. Even the resurrection appearances, whatever be thought to have "really happened," cannot legitimately be taken as an unambiguous statement by God that Jesus was precisely the kind of life God had planned in order to carry forward the divine purpose. As the example of the orthodox Jewish theologian Pinchas Lapide shows, one can believe in the resurrection of Jesus without drawing any messianic conclusion.[17] If some of us take Jesus as central for our relationship to God, it must be on some basis other than the assumption that we have unambiguous testimony from God on this score.

The more general point here is that we cannot take any of the events or statements in the Bible as unambiguous statements of God's will and attitudes. All the statements in the Bible are human formulations. Some of them can be thought to be based, more or less, upon ideal aims from God, as can some of the events reported in the Bible. But the events reported, the reporting itself, and the doctrinal statements all involved human self-determination and therefore the possibility (and virtual inevitability) of ignorance, wishful thinking, and ideological (self-serving) distortion. This means that the anti-Jewish polemic in the New Testament ought not to be taken as an expression of God's own attitude. The same is true of the statements of later church theologians and councils. The Holy Spirit can do many things, but She cannot guarantee that any individual or council will not fall into error and sin.

(7)   A qualification must be made, however, with regard to the previous two points, which have stressed not only that we have no infallible testimony as to whether God viewed Jesus as the "expected messiah" but also that the very notion of Messiahship or Christhood is ambiguous, allowing of multiple interpretations. The qualification is that *some* understandings of what kind of messiah could be realistically expected would be ruled out by a process perspective. A messiah who could unilaterally bring an end to the ambiguities of life cannot be realistically expected. If one were to hold this definition of messiahship to be fixed, then from a process perspective one would have to conclude that a messiah was not to be expected. To be actual is to have power, and this includes the power to resist the divine will. A multiplicity of actualities cannot be guaranteed, even by God—whether working through an earthly agent or not— to actualize themselves in conformity with the divine will and, hence, for the general good. Process theology, therefore, stands in the same negative relation to a particular formulation of the Jewish expectation of a messiah and a messianic age as it does to a particular formulation of the Christian expectation of a "second coming," according to which some agent will unilaterally bring about an unambiguous reign of peace, love, and justice. In whatever way we might retain these respective notions as symbols, we should not portray them as literal expectations. To do so implies the belief that God has coercive omnipotence held in reserve—the belief that creates the insoluble problem of evil and associated difficulties.

The denial of coercive omnipotence to God means that we have to distinguish, in a way traditional theology did not, between God's will, on the one hand, and what will actually happen, on the other. Accordingly, it is one thing to take the message of the prophets and of Jesus about a Reign of God on earth, in which there would be love, justice, and peace, as true intuitions into, or revelations of, the divine purpose. It is another step, and an unwarranted one, to assume that God's purpose will necessarily be achieved in an unambiguous form, especially in a sudden fashion.

It is at this point that many theologians of oppressed groups face their biggest dilemma. On the one hand, they want to retain the idea of God as having coercive power, so that they can retain the expectation that, some day, God will step in with coercive power and unilaterally put things right. On the other hand, if they portray God as having that kind of power, they have to wonder why God has waited so long, and has allowed so much misery already. If God has that kind of power, and yet has failed to use it on behalf of the oppressed, especially when the oppression has become horrendous, the implication is that God cares less for justice than we do, or that God is even positively evil, perhaps racist or sexist. This is the issue behind William R. Jones' query in the title of his book, *Is God a White Racist?*, and behind Richard Rubenstein's claim that *After Auschwitz* no Jew (or good Christian) should believe in a providential God of history. This issue is also reflected in the position of Eliezer Berkovits, John Roth, and Frederick Sontag, that God either is not (yet) perfectly good, or is good by some other standard than ours.[18]

The position of process theology is that, as understandable as the desire to hang onto the idea of coercive omnipotence may be, the Holocaust provides conclusive evidence, if prior history did not, that this doctrine should be given up explicitly and consistently. This should be done in the interests of realism: There is no credible evidence in favor of the hypothesis that God has this kind of power, and there is much evidence against it. This doctrine should be given up also in the interests of preserving belief in a God of perfect goodness who is worthy of our absolute worship and commitment.[19]

(8) Because God cannot control any events, and because most events can be assumed to diverge from God's will more or less significantly, we cannot assume—as Rabbi Harold Kushner has forcibly argued in *When Bad Things Happen to Good People*—that misfortune represents God's punishment. This is a key point for the problem of evil in general, and in particular for the attitudes of the powerful and fortunate in relation to those who are less powerful and fortunate. To

assume a positive correlation between fortune and divine favor is one of the most prevalent forms of ideology (in the strict sense of doctrine that distorts the truth in order to justify special benefits for oneself or one's group). The fact that Christians have time and time again reverted to this ideology is especially reprehensible in the light of the dual fact that, not only was Jesus himself killed in the prime of life. He was also portrayed as rejecting that ideological theology, saying, for example, that God makes the rain to fall on the just and the unjust alike (Matthew 5:45) and that those who suffered through catastrophes were not worse sinners than others (Luke 13:1–3).

(9) Neither Jews nor Christians can (if process theism be accepted) take convenantal statements recorded in their scriptures as accurate statements of decisions made by God. For example, Irving Greenberg points to the Holocaust as evidence that "God didn't keep his part" of the covenant with the Jews.[20] But the fact that God is depicted as making certain promises in the Hebrew scriptures—even if they should be interpreted as promising protection against such catastrophes—cannot be taken as unambiguous evidence that God actually made such promises. Likewise, particular statements in those writings that Christians refer to as the "New Testament"— even if they should be interpreted as meaning that God has made a new covenant or testament that abrogates the one with the Jews—cannot be taken as unambiguous evidence that God actually made such a decision.

In other words, one and the same presupposition—that God has coercive omnipotence and can therefore completely control historical events (including "word events")—lies behind the assumption that God made special promises to the Jews and the assumption that this special relationship was abrogated in favor of a special relationship with Christians. Once the presupposition of divine coercive omnipotence is consistently given up, the basis is gone for the belief that either Jews or Christians are especially loved, protected, or guaranteed ultimate salvation by God. This will help us overcome not only the constant disappointment that such a belief inevitably brings, but also the arrogance that Jews and Christians have found offensive in each other— and that Christians have usually been in position to be offensive about.

There will be some—both Christians and Jews—who will surely consider the prescription offered here worse than the disease. Belief in the nonexistence of a Holy Reality with coercive omnipotence is, however, advocated first of all not for its beneficial effects, although they should be legion, but because it seems to be true, given the history of what has occurred in biblical times, in the more general history of the world, and in our own individual experiences. The pragmatic value of religious beliefs is very important, and it is not illegitimate to take this value into account in determining what to affirm. But we should, insofar as possible, try to determine first of all what seems to be true, apart from the question of the probable effects of believing it. Furthermore, if we really have religious faith, in the deepest sense, we will trust that believing the truth will be, overall, more beneficial than believing falsehood, no matter how many particular benefits may have come from the acceptance of particular falsehoods.

In this essay, I have, in fact, been focusing primarily upon some of the benefits, with regard to the problem of evil in general and Jewish-Christian relations in particular, that can be derived from regarding divine omnipotence as persuasive rather than coercive. In the third section I turn to the benefits that can be expected with regard to the nature of Jewish and Christian existence, in both individual and group activities, in relation to the role of the "will to power" in our lives.

III. The *Imitatio Dei*

The argument of this section can be stated in eight theses:

(1)   Human beings have a religious drive.

(2)   This drive is to be in harmony with deity, and this means, most fundamentally, to imitate deity—that which is Holy.

(3)   It is the felt or *perceived* Holy that we primarily want to imitate, not that which is merely *conceived* (intellectually) to be Holy.

(4)   However, our *conception* of the Holy Reality, to the degree that we believe it sincerely, focus our attention on it affectively in public and private worship, have it portrayed effectively to us in stories, sermons, and the arts, and have it confirmed by others in a community of faith, can greatly mold our *perception* of the Holy.

(5)   Because creativity, or the twofold power to determine ourselves and to express ourselves so as to influence others, is

the fundamental metaphysical reality constitutive of all actualities, human beings have a metaphysical drive to exercise power on others. This dimension of the "will to power" can be actualized, however, in either primarily coercive or primarily persuasive fashion.

(6) Insofar as human beings perceive the Holy Reality as *Coercive* Omnipotence, their religious drive will reinforce the tendency to use coercion, because the exercise of coercive power will be felt to be an imitation of deity, a participation in the Holy.

(7) Insofar as the Holy Reality is perceived to be *Persuasive* Omnipotence, the religious drive of human beings will still encourage them to be effective in the world, but it will reinforce the tendency to exert influence by using persuasion whenever possible, seeking to influence others by presenting to them possibilities that *they* see as attractive. The religious drive, thus informed, will therefore mitigate the tendency to use coercion. Coercion will still have to be used in some situations, but it will be exercised with the sense of regret that persuasion has failed, not with the sense of exhilaration that comes from the sense of imitating deity.

(8) One of the ways in which theologians *qua* theologians can be most effective in improving the human exercise of power is by helping people overcome conceptions and perceptions of the Holy Reality as Coercive Omnipotence, and by presenting convincing portrayals of the Holy Reality as Persuasive Omnipotence.

The first thesis, that human beings have a religious drive, has been widely contested, especially since the eighteenth century, but I believe that the evidence of history bears it out.

The second and third theses, that this drive is most fundamentally to imitate deity as perceived (or felt, or—in Jonathan Edward's metaphor—"tasted"), can be supported by appealing to the lives and writings of those who have most deeply come to *see* and *experience* reality in terms of the conception of the Holy that they hold. For these people, the Holy Reality is less of an inference from other self-evident data than the experienced reality that determines the way in which all other things are viewed. These people, more or less consciously, strive to imitate the central characteristic of the Holy Reality as they perceive it: the Taoist to become like the Tao; the Buddhist to achieve the perfect equanimity of Nirvana and/or the perfect compassion of the Buddha; the Vedantist to become like Brahman; the Vitalist to become fully alive, especially in one's bodily and emotional being; the Rationalist (in the sense of one who sees disembodied Reason as that which creates and saves us) to be unemotionally rational; the Stoic to achieve the perfect "apathy" of the divine reality.

The fourth thesis is a Platonic point, which I also believe to be confirmed by human experience. If it were not true that our conceptions made a difference to our feelings and outer behavior, it would be hard to understand why people in every society have been passionately concerned about what is believed, especially about the Holy Reality. However, the distinction between those conceptions that do and do not become perceptions takes account of the recognition that many of our "beliefs" seem to have little effect upon our behavior. Both sides of the truth are stated by Whitehead:

> Your character is developed according to your faith. This is the primary religious truth from which no one can escape. Religion is force of belief cleansing the inward parts. For this reason the primary religious virtue is sincerity, a penetrating sincerity.
>
> A religion, on its doctrinal side, can thus be defined as a system of general truths which have the effect of transforming character when they are sincerely held and vividly apprehended.
>
> In the long run your character and your conduct of life depend upon your intimate convictions.[21]

The remaining theses seem to need no clarification, but, for some support for the overall position, I can point to Richard Rubenstein's writings. These writings show that he has most fundamentally understood deity in terms of Coercive Omnipotence. For example, he says that the world is functionally godless, because there is no punishment for violating the divine law, and that the state is in effect God, because it has the power to define what will be punished.[22] The thought that God might exercise persuasive providential influence in the world has evidently not been a live option for Rubenstein, as he poses the issue of God's reality as a dichotomy: Either the "all-powerful judge," the "omnipotent God of History," exists, or else there is no providential God at all.[23] Rubenstein's early vision of the Holy Reality as Coercive Omnipotence (which seems to have been a perception, not a mere conception) was the determining factor, according to his own account, in his choice of vocation: He confesses in retrospect that his desire to be a priest was "the quest for God-like omnipotence," an attempt to fulfill "fantasies of omnipotence."[24]

I have said in Thesis 2 that the drive to be "in harmony with" deity is most fundamentally the drive to "imitate" deity. Many might think, instead, that the drive to be in harmony with deity would give us impetus not to imitate but to obey the will of deity (that is, in those religions in which deity is conceived as a personal being who issues commands or at least has preferences). There is some truth to this. But the deeper form of the drive, I am convinced, is to imitate deity, insofar as possible. Accordingly, believers are given two messages when God is portrayed as telling them, "Do as I say, not as I do," as in Romans 12:19: "Beloved, never avenge yourselves, but leave it to the wrath of God; for it is written, 'Vengeance is mine, I will repay, says the Lord.' " At the surface level, believers are told to eschew vengeance, and the desire to be in harmony with the will of deity gives them some motivation to do this. At the deeper level, however, they receive the message that wreaking vengeance is divine activity, and their drive to imitate the nature of divinity leads them to want to participate in this activity. (My discussion of this passage from Romans concerns, to be sure, not Paul's exact intentions but only a common reading of it.)

In other biblical passages there is more evident consistency between the portrayal of God's nature and the recommendation for human existence. One of the clearest examples is in Luke 6:35–36:

> But love your enemies and do good, and lend, expecting nothing in return; and your reward will be great; and you will be sons of the Most High; for he is kind to the ungrateful and the selfish. Be merciful, even as your father is merciful.

It seems, unfortunately, that the former tendency is quite pervasive in the Bible and in both Judaism and Christianity. That is, believers are exhorted to be gentle and patient, to work through love, and to overcome evil with good; but the Holy One is too often portrayed as the ultimate coercive power, and as using this power, now or in the future, to overcome evil with evil—to take vengeance, to destroy.

I believe that this fact goes a long way (in conjunction with universal human egoism and ignorance) toward explaining that enormous difference between the "manifest values" and the "ethos" of the Judaeo-Christian tradition, to which Richard Rubenstein (and countless other critics) have called attention. The manifest values—the explicit ethical teachings—are undermined by the vision of God that has been dominant in Jewish and Christian circles, because the desire to imitate this God has led to an ethos that encourages violence, particularly against those who are "enemies" of this God and against whom this God has promised to take vengeance.

Whitehead commented on this connection between human violence and the equation of God's worshipfulness with coercive power.

> This worship of glory arising from power is not only dangerous; it arises from a barbaric conception of God. I suppose that even the world itself could not contain the bones of those slaughtered because of men intoxicated by its attraction.[25]

We underrate the importance of religion in human nature if we are not aware of the degree to which people's emotions and attitudes, and therefore their actions, are determined by their "intoxication" with their perception of the Holy. We neglect one of our most important tasks as theologians if we do not help them develop a conception and a perception of the Holy Reality that is truly worthy of worship. I would hope that this is a task upon which many Jewish and Christian theologians could agree and cooperate.[26]

Notes

1.   Richard Rubenstein says that the Holocaust raises the question of the practical value of Judaism in the modern world. He has in mind attitudes that, for the most part, distinguish Judaism from Christianity. I leave that debate to others. My discussion concerns the practical value of Judaism only insofar as Judaism and Christianity are similar.

2.   Irving Greenberg, "Cloud of Smoke, Pillar of Fire: Judaism, Christianity, and Modernity after the Holocaust," in *Auschwitz: Beginning of a New Era? Reflections on the Holocaust*, Eva Fleischner, ed. (New York: KTAV Publishing House, 1977), 7–55.

3.   I have discussed this point in *A Process Christology* (see note 9, this essay), especially ch. 9.

4.   David Ray Griffin, *God, Power, and Evil: A Process Theodicy* (Philadelphia: Westminster Press, 1977; reprint [with new preface] Lanham: University Press of America, 1991); *Evil Revisited: Responses and Reconsiderations* (Albany: State University of New York Press, 1991).

5.   Alfred North Whitehead, *Process and Reality*, Corrected Edition, David Ray Griffin and Donald W. Sherburne, eds. (New York: Free Press, 1978), 244.

6. There are at least three senses in which the expression *creatio ex nihilo* is meaningful from a process perspective.

(1) Actual entities in process thought are momentary events, termed *actual occasions* or *occasions of experience*. The individuals that endure through time, such as electrons, atoms, molecules, and psyches, are serially-ordered societies of actual occasions. In a state approaching absolute chaos, there would be no enduring individuals, but merely random actual occasions. Since by "thing" we normally mean something with stable identity through time, there would be "no-thing" in a state of chaos. Whitehead called such a state a "nothingness of confusion" ("Immortality," in Paul A. Schilpp, ed., *The Philosophy of Alfred North Whitehead* [Tudor Publishing Company, 1951], 691). Accordingly, the creation of order out of chaos would be a creation of a world out of no-thing.

(2) The occurrence of actual occasions involves the actualization of possibilities (pure possibilities are called *eternal objects*; impure ones are called *propositions*). God's creative agency in relation to an actual occasion involves the proffering of an ideal aim, which is a more-or-less complex possibility for that occasion. The reception of this ideal possibility for its existence is what gets the occasion's own self-creation started. Now, possibilities are *real*, but they are not what we usually have in mind when we speak of things that *exist*. Whitehead characterized them as having a kind of being that is a kind of not-being (*Science and the Modern World* [Macmillan, 1926], 254). Consequently, God's creation of new actual entities can be referred to, in Reinhold Niebuhr's words, as the creation of "things that are" out of "things that are not" (*Beyond Tragedy* [New York: Scribner's, 1939], 9, 149, 217–18).

(3) In a third meaning of creation out of nothing, the notion of creativity is central. Creativity is certainly not a thing, and can be compared with Buddhist "emptiness" or "nothingness" (see John B. Cobb, Jr., "Buddhist Emptiness and the Christian God," *Journal of the American Academy of Religion* XLV/1 [March 1977], 11–26, and *Beyond Dialogue: Toward a Mutual Transformation of Buddhism and Christianity* [Philadelphia: Fortress Press, 1982]). From this viewpoint, every actual occasion's self-creation, out of which its creative impact on others is derived, would originate "out of nothing." Deity's self-creative activity, out of which its creative effects on others is derived, would be the supreme example of this creation out of nothing.

These are three philosophically intelligible and existentially important ways of explicating the ancient intuition that our world is created out of nothing. (And they are compatible with the at least equally ancient intuition that our world is created out of chaos.) Process theology, accordingly, does not deny the truth or significance of that intuition; it only protests against the common error of identifying the truth of an intuition with one particular formulation of it—in this case a formulation that was based upon dubious exegesis, that allows no element of truth to the major alternative intuition, and that creates an insoluble problem of evil.

7.   In "The Concept of God after Auschwitz," reprinted in this volume, Hans Jonas presents an idea of God very similar to the one given here: a suffering, becoming, caring, non-omnipotent God. He opts, however, for the position that God created the world out of absolute nothingness, so that God's lack of omnipotence is self-limitation (even though he rightly points out that the notion of absolute power, not limited by anything, is a senseless concept, because power must be shared). He evidently accepts this view because it is preferable to the alternatives of which he is aware. He rightly rejects the idea that the Creator is eternally limited by an evil god. A second possibility, that God is eternally limited by a passive medium, is said to be inadequate to the fact of "positive evil, which implies a freedom empowered by its own authority independent of that of God." Jonas has evidently failed to see the third option, according to which the eternal source of resistance to God is not a passive medium, but active energy or creativity.

8.   Greenberg, "Cloud of Smoke," 46; Alexander Donat, *The Holocaust Kingdom* (New York: Holt, Reinhart and Winston, 1965), 100 (quoted by Greenberg, 18).

9.   David Ray Griffin, *A Process Christology* (Philadelphia: Westminster Press, 1973). In a new preface for a reprint (Lanham: University Press of America, 1991), I point out some of the objections that I now have to the position developed in that book. A Christology that I would write today, however, would be even more different than indicated in that preface. A sketch is provided in a chapter on "Incarnation Through Persuasion" in a work in progress tentatively titled *The Divine Cry of Our Time*. One important change is that, no longer considering it essential to Christian faith to think of Jesus as the "supreme incarnation" and "decisive revelation" of God, I now speak of Jesus as a "special incarnation" and "special revelation" of God.

10.   *A Process Christology*, 15–148.

11.   John B. Cobb, Jr., *The Structure of Christian Existence* (Philadelphia: Westminster Press, 1967; reprint, Lanham: University Press of America, 1990); cf. Cobb's *Christ in a Pluralistic Age* (Philadelphia: Westminster Press, 1975), ch. 8, and *Process Theology: An Introductory Exposition*, with David Ray Griffin (Philadelphia: Westminster Press, 1976), chs. 5 and 6 (which were written primarily by Cobb).

12.   See David Ray Griffin, "Parapsychology and Philosophy: A Whiteheadian Postmodern Perspective," *Journal of the American Society for*

Psychical Research 87/3 (July 1993), 217–88; the chapters on parapsycholoogy and Christology in *The Divine Cry of Our Time* (see n. 9, above); or *Parapsychology, Philosophy, and Spirituality* (forthcoming).

13. In the chapter on Christology in *The Divine Cry of Our Time*, I portray Jesus as a special incarnation of not only this dimension of God, which I there call the "Creative Love of God," but also of the other two dimensions of the immanent trinity, the "Responsive Love of God" and the "Divine Creativity." This change, however, does not affect the point at hand. Indeed, I explicitly present this account of Jesus as special incarnation of the Holy Trinity as a Christology acceptable in principle to Jews and other unitarians.

14. Quoted in H. Loewe and C. G. Montefiore, eds., *A Rabbinic Anthology* (New York: Schocken Books, 1974), 34.

15. In the "Twenty-eight Theses of the Saxon Volk Church," which was written by Walter Grundmann in 1933 and adopted as the platform of the *Reichsbewegung Deutsche Christen*, one reads: "The strife over whether Jesus was a Jew or Aryan does not reach to the essence of Jesus. Jesus was not the bearer of human ways, but rather encapsulized for us in his person the being of God" (quoted in James A. Zabel, *Nazism and the Pastors* [Chico: Scholars Press, 1976], 163).

16. I will try to provide a somewhat more adequate discussion in *The Divine Cry of Our Time* (see nn. 9 & 13, above).

17. See Pinchas Lapide, *The Resurrection of Jesus: A Jewish Perspective* (Minneapolis: Augsburg, 1983), 57, 64, 92, 143, 146, 151, 153.

18. For Berkovits, see *Faith After the Holocaust* (New York: KTAV Publishing Co., 1973). For the views of Roth and Sontag, see Stephen Davis, ed., *Encountering Evil: Live Options in Theodicy* (Atlantic: John Knox, 1981).

19. In speaking of Christianity's tendency to deny continuing revelation, Irving Greenberg says: "The desire to guarantee absolute salvation and understanding is an all too human need which both religions must resist as a snare and temptation" ("Cloud of Smoke," 25). In spite of recognizing this temptation and of seeing that classical theism as well as classical atheism needs to be transcended, however, Greenberg still holds to the idea of a God who can unilaterally fulfill the promise to bring about ultimate redemption and perfection in this world (37). Holding to this classical, unreconstructed understanding of divine power leads him to conclude that talk of a God who cares and loves is now obscene and incredible (11, 41–42). It leads him to declare: "Nothing dare evoke our absolute, unquestioning loyalty, not even our God" (38). It leads him, therefore, to defend the "revolt against God" (40). Greenberg is only one of many who show that the vision of a Holy Reality who is perfectly loving and just, and who can thereby appropriately evoke our absolute loyalty, will not be re-created as long as the conception (or image) of divine coercive omnipotence remains unreformed.

20.   Greenberg, "Cloud of Smoke," 33–34. Greenberg does stress in other passages that the Holocaust cannot be assimilated to "unreconstructed traditional categories" (25) and, in particular, that the understanding of the covenant needs to be reformulated (24, 27).

21.   Alfred North Whitehead, *Religion in the Making* (New York: Macmillan, 1926), 15.

22.   Richard L. Rubenstein, *The Cunning of History: The Holocaust and the American Future* (New York: Harper & Row, 1975).

23.   Richard L. Rubenstein, *After Auschwitz: Radical Theology and Contemporary Judaism* (Indianapolis: Bobbs-Merrill, 1966), 68–69; *Power Struggle* (New York: Scribner's, 1974), 66, 94–95. My statements about Rubenstein's views are based on the books I have cited, which were published some time ago. I have not examined his more recent writings with this question in mind.

24.   *Power Struggle*, 124, 186.

25.   Whitehead, *Religion in the Making*, 54.

26.   This is a slightly revised and updated version of an essay that was first written for a conference, "Process Theology and Evil: The Holocaust Experience," which was co-sponsored by the Center for Process Studies and the Anti-Defamation League of B'nai Brith and held at the School of Theology at Claremont in June of 1980.

Chapter 8

Theodicy in Jewish Philosophy and David Griffin's Process Theology

Norbert M. Samuelson

This essay focuses on David Griffin's claim that process theology is consistent with the "basic" teachings of Jewish philosophy. I will explore the following critical claims:

(1) Creation out of nothing can be understood to be a time-transcendent, ideal (rather than actual) origin at which God imposes order on a coextensive chaos.

(2) God's perfect knowledge excludes definite knowledge of the future.

(3) God's creatures possess freedom in both senses of the term, i.e., having options and being self-determining.

(4) Divine revelation can be both positive and negative.

(5) God has persuasive omnipotence, but not coercive omnipotence.

In dealing with these issues, I will focus my summary on the writings of a single representative of classical rabbinic philosophy, Gersonides (Levi ben Gershon, Ralbag).[1] I have chosen him as representative because his writings bear most directly on each of the above points of comparison, and they reflect Jewish philosophy at its most sophisticated, technical best in the classical period.[2]

I. Divine Attributes

Gersonides' ontology is inherited from a theological tradition of Christian, Muslim, and Jewish commentators on purportedly revealed

127

scriptures and the scientific writings of both Plato and Aristotle. The judgment that God is the most perfect being was based on the assumption that the God of Abraham, Isaac, and Jacob, who created the world, is the entity to whom philosophy referred as the first cause of the universe. Gersonides' science conceived of physics in teleological terms, where intelligibility was understood primarily in terms of reference to final causes. If God were not perfect, then there would be some end distinct from God that functions as the divine final cause, in which case the "first cause" would not really be first. A consequence of this judgment is that God in no way is subject to change. Hence, while God must perform some activity (because to act is to be alive and to be alive is superior to being dead), that activity must be invariant. In other words, what God does necessarily is timeless, eternal. There could be no time at which God did not perform this activity. Doing what God does either is or is not most perfect. If it *is* most perfect, then when God either was not or will not be performing this action, God was or will not be perfect—that is, not be God. If, on the other hand, it is *not* most perfect, then when God does perform the action, God is not perfect—that is, is not God. Furthermore, if God had two or more distinct actions, then one would be better than the other(s), and to the extent that God performed an action that was in any sense not perfect, God would not be God. Divine creation, revelation, and redemption are therefore a single action.

In general, God performs a single eternal action, which appears to be multiple actions only because of the radical limitation of human modes of conception.[3] Furthermore, that God is the first cause also entails radical oneness. There is nothing else in the universe as simple as God. Were God in any sense complex, then the simpler components that constitute God would be causally prior to God, in which case these components, and not God, would be the first cause. In the case of God, accordingly, there can be no distinction between God as the subject of action, the action itself, and the object of the action. The creator is identical with the creature, both of which are identical with the act of creation. Consequently, with respect to theology, the standard attempt to think of the universe either in terms of relations and processes, on the one hand, or in terms of subjects and substances, on the other, is transcended. The nature of God lies beyond both ways of conceptualizing reality.

In general, rabbinic tradition affirmed cosmologies in which God is something no greater than which can be conceived, something unlimited, something whose existence or nonexistence is not merely logically possible, and something that can neither come into existence nor cease to exist, but necessarily exists. Furthermore, we can stipulate logical rules that will determine *a priori* what attributions are and are not true of God.[4]

(1) No nongraded exclusion predicate can be affirmed of God.[5]

(2) If any graded predicate is less than some other graded predicate, then the lesser predicate cannot be affirmed of God.

(3) If predicating a graded predicate entails predicating a nongraded, exclusion predicate of that thing, then the graded predicate in question cannot be predicated of God.

(4) Concerning any graded predicate that does not entail a nongraded, exclusion predicate: if that predicate expresses the highest perfection possible in its class, then that predicate is affirmed of God.

(5) Concerning any class of predicates that are not exclusion predicates: if one member of that class of predicates is predicable of God, then all members of that class are predicable of God.

(6) Concerning any predicate that is not an exclusion predicate that does not entail a nongraded exclusion predicate: if it is predicable of anything, then it is predicated of God.

To these six rules, Gersonides added a seventh that expresses divine attributes in terms of *pros hen* equivocation. Given any predicate, F, that can be affirmed of God, F applies primarily to God in an absolute sense and derivatively to anything else in a less than absolute sense that admits of degrees of perfection. Furthermore, if G, whose sense differs from F, can also be affirmed of God, then G and F have the same reference, namely, God. For example, God knows himself in a single act of knowledge that is identical with God, and in knowing himself God knows everything as its cause. In contrast, we know something through multiple acts as an effect of what exists through God's causation. Furthermore, in our case the following are all distinct:

(a) each of us as the subject of the act of knowing;

(b) our acts of knowing themselves; and

(c) the objects of our knowledge.

In these ways, our knowledge is both dependent upon, and inferior to, God's knowledge.

Gersonides' formulation of divine attributes had a direct influence on how Spinoza understood the nature of God as an absolutely infinite substance. There are significant differences between

Gersonides' theory of attributes and that of his predecessor Maimonides,[6] however, and it was Maimonides' theory—commonly called his "theory of negative attributes"—that had more impact on twentieth-century Jewish philosophers, such as Hermann Cohen and his disciples. Maimonides argued that literally no univocal affirmation is possible in a sentence whose subject is God. Rather, affirmative declarative sentences are possible in a language of God-talk only when those sentences are absolutely equivocal in meaning. What it means to say that God is F, where F is any predicate whose contrary is G, is that God is not G, F is a human excellence, and G is a human vice. Maimonides' theory of negative attributes is, accordingly, really an explanation of the meaning of the principle of *imitatio dei*. In other words, statements about God do not inform us about God; rather they instruct us in human ethics—in how to behave to become more like God (but without knowing anything about God).

However, the two primary interpretations of divine attributes in classical rabbinic philosophy, those of Maimonides and Gersonides, need not be viewed as mutually exclusive. Gersonides would agree with Maimonides that every predicate attributed to God is part of an equivocal expression that affirms an absolute moral ideal for human behavior. Cohen's identification of theology and ethics is well rooted in this classical tradition of Jewish philosophy. The sole difference between Maimonides and Gersonides has to do with just how little we, in fact, know about God. According to Maimonides, we know something about ethics but absolutely nothing about God; according to Gersonides, moral and theological statements mutually entail each other, so that the very moral commandments we do know are in themselves knowledge of God. In affirming that God is F, we affirm that God is F in a primary, absolute way, which functions for human behavior as an ideal. Thus, we can differentiate between how we and God know, and can affirm that God's way of knowing is superior as an ideal that we, in fulfilling the moral obligation to gain knowledge, constantly attempt to approximate.

II. Creation

God is the sole active, positive principle of the universe. At the same time, Gersonides also discusses a related but distinct principle, which is passive and negative. It is the *nothing* out of which the world is created. All of the classical rabbinic philosophers[7] agree that divine Mosaic revelation, as recorded in the Book of Genesis, teaches that the universe was created out of nothing. What they do not agree about is what "out of nothing" means. The Greek language offered two ways to make this claim,[8] which were expressed in six different ways in Arabic,[9] four ways in Hebrew,[10] and six ways in Latin.[11] In most cases, "out of nothing" does not mean out of what is *utterly* nothing. In Gersonides' case, the nothing out of which the universe is created is what he calls both "absolute body" (*geshem meshulach*) and "final matter" (*chomer acharon*).

The three elements in Gersonides' account of the origin of the universe are

(1) first matter (*chomer rishon*),
(2) first or corporeal form (*tsurah rishonah* or *tsurah gashmiyt*),
(3) absolute body or last form.

For Gersonides, absolute body is the building block of the universe. Yet, unlike his medieval predecessors, particularly Ibn Rushd, Gersonides argues that the form of absolute body, properly speaking, is not really a form. Like God, it is something that can only be known *pros hen* equivocally. In other words, the composite universe of form and matter has two ultimate principles. The formal principle is God and the material principle is absolute body. However, this body is not a second deity, worthy of worship. In fact, it is nothing at all. God is the sole principle of what is. At the same time, it also is true that only God completely *is*.

Ours is not the world of being. It is the world of becoming, which, as such, both is and is not. Absolute body is the principle of the nonbeing. Precisely because it is by nature indefinite (it is not precisely anything at all), it is the nothing out of which God creates the world of becoming. As such, it is the indefinite stuff that God, through an act of will that is identical with his nature, informs, and, by so doing, gives definition and purpose. For those who cannot imagine what such a stuff would be, Gersonides suggests that Genesis itself provides an example. It is water. Water is a definite substance that, unlike other substances, in itself has no definite shape. Similarly, absolute body is a definite body that, like water and unlike other bodies, "does not preserve its shape."

This general cosmological schema provides the basis for Gersonides' interpretation of the Genesis account of creation. God informed an original, indefinite matter with the potential to receive from him the definitions by which the universe became differentiated into its present composition of multiple bodies in motion. It is a consequence of divine unity that in God's case no distinction can be made between the actor and the act. God's act of creation is, accordingly, indistinguishable from God. Therefore, while it is an act of will, because God desires its creation, it is also an act of necessity.[12]

Because God's one act of creation is invariable, creation itself is a unity. Because what God knows in a single act is knowable to human beings only through a conjunction of multiple acts, however, creation is knowable to everyone other than God through multiple stages. These stages can be ordered in terms of priority with respect to logical causes and natures. Each unit of logical priority is called a "day." Anything, A, created on an earlier day than a later thing, B, is prior in any one of the following respects. A exists for the sake of B, and/or A is more venerable that B, and/or A is a necessary cause of B.[13] However, this does not mean that A came into existence at some time before B. It can be said, therefore, that God created the universe in seven days. That does not mean, however, that creation involves seven divine actions or that one act occurred before another. It means, rather, that from a human perspective the creation of certain aspects of the universe is logically prior to the generation of other aspects, and that this differentiation with respect to causal order has seven levels. Scripture uses the expression "day and night" to show that the entities created within each unit are themselves hierarchically ordered, and "evening and morning" to affirm that they constitute a unity. That the causal ordering is also a moral hierarchy is indicated by calling each complete unit "good." Similarly, Scripture states that the overall ordering of all the logically distinct events is the best possible order by calling the completed universe "very good." In other words, this is the best of all possible universes.

In general, then, Jewish philosophy interprets creation out of nothing to be a time-transcendent, ideal origin at which God imposes order on a coextensive chaos. This is consistent with the process position that divine creation at a hypothetical origin of our universe is an act of imposing order on a preexistent chaos, rather than an act of willing something into existence from absolutely nothing whatsoever.

IV. Divine Providence

The extent to which the Creator can govern the creation depends on what he can know. What he cannot know necessarily lies beyond his direction. What God knows is himself in a single, invariant act, which is identical with himself. Through this single act, God knows everything that, for human beings to know, would necessarily have to be expressed in an infinitely long conjunction of simple declarative sentences. The question is: What does this "everything" in divine knowledge include? Gersonides' answer is: Everything that is knowable. This judgment in itself, however, is not an answer. It only moves the question back one step. Given that God knows everything that is knowable, what in fact is knowable? Clearly excluded is the definite truth-value of future contingents. On this point, too, Gersonides' position accords with that of process philosophers: God's perfect knowledge excludes definite knowledge of the future.

Consider any future event. Either it will necessarily occur or its occurrence is only a possibility. If it must occur, then God can know that it will occur. If, on the other hand, it need not occur, then in principle there can be no advance knowledge that it will or will not occur. At best, there can only be an informed opinion. However, opinions, no matter how reasonable or well informed, are inferior to knowledge, and for God to have opinions would contradict his perfection. Furthermore, because God cannot know that a future contingent will or will not occur, he cannot know contingent events at all. This judgment, for two different reasons, follows from the assumption of God's perfection. First, God's perfection entails that God is in no sense subject to change. Now, assume that God's knowledge could increase through time. In this case, as soon as any event becomes knowable, God knows it. However, then God would be subject to change. Second, God's perfection entails that, with respect to graded predicates, only the best member of that class is predicable of him, and that, with respect to nongraded predicates, all or none, but not some, of the members of that class are predicable of him. If to know is a graded predicate—that is, if to know some things is better than to know others things—then God can only know what is most worthy of knowledge, i.e., himself. If, on the other hand, to know anything is an ungraded predicate—that is, that knowing one member of that class does not make a knower better than knowing some other member—then either God knows everything in that class or he knows nothing. Because God cannot know every contingent event, because he cannot know those that have not yet occurred, then God cannot know any contingent events. Consequently, to the extent that any event is contingent, it lies outside of divine knowledge, and to that extent it also is excluded from the domain of divine providence.

The question now becomes, to what extent is an event contingent? Gersonides' answer is that to some extent every event exhibits a general order or structure and to some extent every actual event is unique and particular. To the extent that the event has order, it is formal: it has a form (morphe) that is knowable by God and in principle is knowable by any human being. Conversely, to the extent that the event is unique, it is material: it has matter (*hyle*), which in principle is unknowable to either God or humanity. This judgment alone, however, does not settle the issue. The question is again moved back one step.

Given that an event is knowable insofar as it is ordered and unknowable insofar as it is unique, to what extent is any temporal event in principle structured and unique? Gersonides gives no clear answer to this question. At least two different interpretations are possible. Consider the following example: There is a species of turtles that once every year deposits its fertilized eggs on the beaches of the Galapagos Islands, then returns to the sea. Every year young turtles emerge from their eggs without developed shells and dash to the safety of the sea. While they are running, birds swoop down and eat them. Approximately 90 percent of the baby turtles are eaten by the birds. The remaining 10 percent return to the sea, develop protective shells, and go on to propagate more turtles. The primary purpose of the existence of these turtles, presumably, is to feed the birds. God, presumably, knows this as its cause. God has ordered the world so that nine out of ten of these turtles will be food for the birds, and one out of ten will survive to generate more bird food in order to preserve both the bird and the turtle species. The question is: Does God only know this probability distribution, or does God also know which individual turtles will survive?

It would be consistent with what Gersonides says to answer that God only knows the exact probability curve, so that, although he knows what will happen to the turtles in general, he does not know what will happen to them individually. The birds also do not know which turtles will be eaten: they simply see a mass of turtles and they dive down to eat them. Which turtle any individual bird encounters is of no consequence either to God or to the bird.

Note, however, that in Gersonides' ontology, temporal and spatial location are functions of matter, not form. If we admit knowledge of such location, it is in principle mathematically possible to determine which individual birds will eat which individual turtles. The motions involved are all expressible as vectors, continuous movements with both direction and speed. All of the vectors involved in this case— the birds' flight, the turtles' run from their point of origin (where the eggs are hatched) to their end point (the sea), and the direction of the wind—all can be measured and the possible points of intersection between the bird and turtle vectors can be calculated. In other words, there is no reason in principle why anyone with some knowledge of mathematics cannot determine the particular situation. God's purely formal knowledge, therefore, ought to entail a knowledge of all particular events. The sole difference is that God knows them as abstract solutions to mathematical problems. This answer would be consistent with Gersonides' claim that God knows individuals insofar as they exhibit their general nature rather than as particulars. In other words, as every unique integer can be expressed as the sole integer that is both larger than a second specific integer and smaller than a third specific integer,[14] so every other individual can be uniquely mapped in terms of its spatio-temporal place in the universe in a way that is knowable to God.

The latter interpretation lies at the heart of Spinoza's determinism. Furthermore, it is consistent with the so-called classical physics of Newton (as modified by Laplace), in which the ultimate constituents of the universe occupy definite places at specific times. The former interpretation is consistent with the new physics of quantum mechanics, in which the spatio-temporal location of any fundamental particle is in principle no more than probable. The latter scientific model is a major reason why Whitehead's metaphysics embraced indeterminism, and it is Whitehead's metaphysics that is at the foundation of Griffin's process theology. Gersonides' theology, like most of Jewish philosophy, remains open to both options.

IV. Freedom

Because of the primacy of ethics in Judaism, all of Jewish philosophy is in principle committed to the judgment that there are human choices. However, it is not self-evident that determinism and human choice are incompatible theses. The term *freedom* is used in two distinct ways. It can mean either having options or being self-determined. On the one hand, it is possible to have options when your fate is completely out of your own control. For example, if you must choose between two paths in total ignorance of the consequences of either choice, your fate is undetermined and beyond your own determination. On the other hand, it is also possible to have self-determination without options. For example, when you examine all available possibilities and find that only one of them is clearly in your best interest, you determine your own fate without any viable alternative course of action. Clearly, Spinoza read Gersonides' notion of human choice as the latter (self-determination) interpretation of freedom. However, the former (having options) interpretation of freedom also is consistent with Gersonides' thought.

If the term *freedom* can be used to mean "human choice" (*bechiyrah enoshiyt*), then Jewish philosophy shares process theology's affirmation of freedom. Beyond this very general level of agreement, however, there may be differences. The emphasis in the above statement is on the word "human." While all of the individual creatures in the world are subject to contingency, Jewish philosophy seems concerned solely with *human* choice. Most Jewish philosophers are not concerned with the nature of choice of other creatures, and those who are (for example, Maimonides) extend the domain of determinism to everything that is neither human nor divine. In contrast, process theology seems to extend freedom to all actual entities. Furthermore, process theology speaks of freedom in both senses of the word: having options and being self-determined. In contrast, Jewish philosophy may be compatible with either interpretation, but it is not so necessarily. Jewish philosophy remains consistent with both positions, including the deterministic view of Spinoza, where relative freedom means relative self-determination.

V. Revelation

The overwhelming tendency in Jewish philosophy is to see divine revelation in positive and not negative terms. The matter and necessity that are the givens of creation are associated with the dark and chaos of Genesis, whereas God is associated with the light and order. Similarly, insofar as God's attributes express moral ideals that function as the end toward which history is moving, those ideals are positive and not negative. Certainly there is evil in the world, and from the evil we can learn negative lessons of what not to do. The negativity in itself, however, is not revelation. For example, at the end of *Ich und Du*[15] Martin Buber tells us that, while the course of human and natural history is a spiral between ever-increasing poles of humanity (I-Thou relations) and dehumanization (I-It relations), in which the achievement of both human good and evil in each spiral exceeds anything previously experienced, it is only the humanizing pole of the I-Thou that is the "God-side." There is an end to the spiral, furthermore, called *redemption*, in which the God-side will prevail. In this respect—both in his affirmation that God is associated only with the positive dimension of the God-human relation (revelation), and in his affirmation that in the end the good will prevail—Buber's view of process is more in accord with classical Jewish philosophy than is the process schema of Griffin. On Buber's view of history, the Holocaust could be interpreted to represent the maximum in the direction of dehumanization in the most recent spiral of human history. It is the point after which the world has most recently returned to a humanizing direction. As such, the Holocaust is a constituent part of our understanding of the interaction of God, humanity, and the world in the cosmos' movement towards redemption. If that is all Griffin means by claiming that the Holocaust is a negative revelation, then there is no inherent conflict at this point between process theology and Jewish philosophy. However, to call such evil in any sense a "revelation" is misleading. Properly speaking, Jewish philosophy never has any evil in itself as a revelation. God as God consistently is viewed to be the source only of good, and not of evil.[16] If there is room for any give-and-take on this point, it is only on the question of what these moral terms mean.

"Good" need not be human good. Similarly, "evil" need not be human evil. For example, in the not-too-distant-future (from the perspective of cosmic time), our sun will become a supernova, and everything in our solar system, including all of humankind, will be gassed. Presumably, from a divine perspective (given that the laws of nature are an expression of divine will), this destruction of an entire universe will be good. However, it remains something that is not, and cannot be, from a human perspective, a good. The lessons that classical Jewish philosophy drew from cases such as these are the following: Humanity exists for the sake of the universe, and not the universe for the sake of humanity, and the principle of *imitatio dei* is not absolute. We are not to imitate God in every respect. In fact, human imitation of God in certain respects, as in the deathcamps of the Holocaust, is itself a manifestation of absolute evil.

VI. Divine Power

Griffin assumes a sharp distinction between persuasive and coercive omnipotence that is not clear in Jewish philosophy. God is who he is, and, in being himself, he directs all of physical and human history. God is perfect. Hence, divine power is unlimited. That power is both coercive and persuasive. Insofar as the laws of nature are an expression of divine power, it is coercive. Similarly, insofar as the moral ideals that function as the end toward which all of history moves are an expression of divine goodness, and insofar as that goodness is identical with God's power, it is persuasive. In other words, what Jewish philosophy rejects is not the claim of persuasive omnipotence, but the claim that its affirmation entails a denial of coercive omnipotence.

VII. Conclusions

It should he clear from the above summary of Jewish philosophy that there is no inherent tie between the doctrine of divine perfection and creation out of absolutely nothing whatsoever. In a significant sense, according to Gersonides' understanding, divine knowledge entails divine power, which in turn entails determinism. This view, however, is independent of the extreme judgment that God creates absolutely everything, not just something. Gersonides' doctrine of creation (like that of Whitehead) has its ultimate philosophical source in Plato's *Timaeus*, where divine creation is a timeless act of imposing order on a pre-existent chaos at what is, from the perspective of time, an ideal (and not an actual) origin. To use Griffin's language, the question whether or not the universe was created from nothing or no-thing and the question whether divine omnipotence entails coercion or persuasion are independent of each other.

Griffin's assertion of general compatibility between process theology and classical Jewish philosophy is correct. God's creation is an ideal origin from which arises a seemingly unlimited number of possibilities for concrete, material instantiation, in which general principles inform concrete contingent events, all of which are to be comprehended as a general movement of human and physical history toward an ideal end, which is itself identical with God. God functions at the origin, the end, and through nature. Process theology identifies this divine activity as God's primordial and consequent natures. Jewish philosophy identifies it with divine creation, revelation, and redemption. As creator, God is the active agent from whose ordering the universe receives its ideal origin; as revealer, God is the active cause of the necessary principles that determine the course of history; as redeemer, God is the ideal end toward which all of history points.

What process theology and Jewish philosophy most significantly share in common, in opposition to all contemporary philosophy rooted in both classical and modern physical science, is the judgment that an adequate understanding of the universe must be teleological. Causes are not only mechanical. There also is an end, the comprehension of which provides the standard by which all events are properly to be judged good or bad. The most critical difference between process theology and Jewish philosophy is whether or not that end will be achieved. Griffin's process theology insists that the end is itself a future contingent that may or may not be realized. In contrast, Jewish philosophy expresses the confidence that the end, even though it may be infinitely remote from our perspective in time and space, will be realized at the end of days in the World-to-Come. Jewish philosophy has no more surety about human ability to make the correct choices between good and evil than does process theology. Nor does Jewish philosophy presuppose some form of divine intervention into the laws of nature. It does, however, have a confidence, which process philosophy lacks, that, while many paths are open, the course of interaction between God, humanity, and the world points to, and eventually will end in, the fulfillment of the messianic ideal. Although the end always remains endlessly remote, each event—the evil as well as the good—brings us closer to its realization. In short, Griffin's expression of process theology is compatible with Jewish philosophy's classical doctrines of creation and revelation, but it seems to be incompatible with Judaism's confident anticipation of redemption.

Notes

1.   Gersonides was born at Bagnols in 1288 and died April 20, 1344. Most of his life was spent in Orange and Avignon. He wrote treatises on rabbinics, mathematics, astronomy, and medicine, as well as on theology. His major philosophic work, composed in Hebrew, was *The Wars of the Lord*, which was completed in 1329 in Avignon. My discussion of what Gersonides says about God's nature and human freedom is based on books three and four of this treatise. I have written an English translation and commentary on book three (*Gersonides on God's Knowledge* [Toronto: Pontifical Institute of Mediaeval Studies, 1977]). David Bleich has written an English translation and commentary on book four (*Providence in the Philosophy of Gersonides* [New York: Yeshiva University Press, 1973]). Charles Touati has written a French translation of both books (*Les Guerres du Seigneur, Livres 3 et 4* [Paris: Mouton, 1968]). My discussion of what Gersonides says about creation is based on books five and six of this treatise. Jacob J. Staub has written an English translation and commentary on book six (*The Creation of the World According to Gersonides*, Brown Judaic Studies #24 [Chico: Scholars Press, 1982]).

2.   Note that Jewish *philosophy* is not all of Jewish *thought*. Excluded from this essay is any consideration of either the tradition of Jewish law (*Halakhah*), Jewish mysticism (*Kabbalah*), or nonphilosophic modes of Jewish thought (such as midrashim, biblical commentaries, or ethical wills), all of which are no less authentic expressions of traditional Judaism than is Jewish philosophy.

3.   This judgment is the source of Spinoza's claim that, while human beings know two divine attributes, i.e., extension and mind, God has an

absolutely infinite number of attributes, all of which are only ways of conceiving of the one divine reality.

4. The following description is a summary of what I argue in greater detail in "On Proving God's Existence," in *Judaism* 16/1 (Winter 1967), 21–36, and "That the God of the Philosophers is not the God of Abraham, Isaac, and Jacob," in *The Harvard Theological Review* 65/1 (January 1972), 1–27.

5. "Graded predicates" are classes of predicates where individuals who exemplify them are subject to comparative ratings in terms of perfection, such that if P and Q are different graded predicates, a is P and b is Q, then either a in virtue of P is greater than b in virtue of Q or b in virtue of Q is greater than a in virtue of P. An example of a class of graded predicates are bowling averages. If John has a 175 average and Mary has a 215 average, then Mary is a better bowler than John. Classes of predicates where this rule does not apply are "nongraded."

"Exclusion predicates" are classes of predicates where the members of the class are so related that it is not possible that any individual who exemplifies one member can exemplify every member of that class. For example, if something is blue all over, then it cannot be red, orange, or any other color complement of blue all over. Classes of predicates for which this rule does not apply are "nonexclusion predicates."

6. Rabbi Moses ben Maimon, also called "Rambam," was born in Cardova in 1135 and died in Egypt on December 13, 1204. He spent most of his life in Cairo, where he functioned as the leader of the Jewish community of the emirate of Egypt. His major philosophical work, composed in Judeo-Arabic between 1185 and 1190, is *The Guide of the Perplexed*. Shlomo Pines wrote an English translation (Chicago: University of Chicago Press, 1963), and Solomon Munk wrote a French translation (Paris: A. Franck, 1856–1866).

7. With the possible exception of Abraham Ibn Daud (Toledo, 1110–1180) in his *The Exalted Faith* (completed in 1160); see the critical edition, English translation and commentary by Norbert M. Samuelson and Gershon Weiss (Canbury: Associated University Presses, 1986).

8. *Ek tou me ontos* and *Ek tou me einai*

9. *Min al-ma'dum, min lays, la min shay, min la shay, min la wujud,* and *ba'd al-'adam*

10. *Me-ayin, melo davar, melo metziyut,* and *achar haheder*

11. *Ex non esse, ex nihilo, non ex aliquo, ex non existent, post non esse,* and *non fix ex aliquo*

12. In Gersonides' judgment, Maimonides' distinction between necessity and intention with respect to God's act of creation is empty. In God's

case, it has no substantive meaning, a point of criticism that will later be made explicity by Spinoza in *The Ethics.*

13. Gersonides makes a radical break from all of his predecessors, Maimonides in particular, by arguing that the more venerable entities perform their self-defining functions for the sake of the less venerable entities.

14. For example, "3" is uniquely defined as that integer which is larger that 2 and smaller than 4.

15. Martin Buber, *I and Thou,* tr. Walter Kaufmann (New York: Scribner's, 1970), 168.

16. Note that a significantly different judgment might be reached in this case if we concentrated on *kabbalah.*

Chapter 9

The Concept of God after Auschwitz: A Jewish Voice

Hans Jonas

When, with the honor of this award,[1] I also accepted the burden of delivering the oration that goes with it, and when I read in the biography of Rabbi Leopold Lucas, in whose memory the prize is named, that he died in Theresienstadt, but that his wife Dorothea, mother of the donor, was then shipped on to Auschwitz, there to suffer the fate that my mother suffered there, too, there was no resisting the force with which the theme of this lecture urged itself on my choice. I chose it with fear and trembling. But I believed I owed it to those shadows that something like an answer to their long-gone cry to a silent God be not denied to them.

What I have to offer is a piece of frankly speculative theology. Whether this behooves a philosopher is a question I leave open. Immanuel Kant has banished everything of the kind from the territory of theoretical reason and, hence, from the business of philosophy; and the logical positivism of our century, the entire dominant analytical creed, even denies to the linguistic expressions such reasonings employ for their purported subject matters this very object-significance itself, that is, any conceptual meaning at all, declaring already—prior to questions of truth and verification—the mere speech about them to be nonsensical. At this, to be sure, old Kant himself would have been utterly astounded. For he, to the contrary, held these alleged non-objects to be the highest objects of all, about which reason can never cease to be concerned, although it cannot hope ever to obtain a knowledge of them and in their pursuit is necessarily doomed to failure by the impassable limits of human cognition. But this cognitive veto, given the yet justified concern, leaves another way open besides that of complete abstention: bowing to the decree that "knowledge" eludes us here, nay, even waiving this very goal from the outset, one may yet meditate on things of this nature in terms of sense and meaning. For the contention—this fashionable contention—that not even sense and meaning pertain to them is easily disposed of as a circular, tautological inference from first having defined "sense" as that which in the end is verifiable by sense data or from generally equating "meaningful" with "knowable." To this axiomatic fiat by definition only he is bound who has first consented to it. He who has not is free, therefore, to work at the *concept* of God, even knowing that there is no *proof* of God, as a task of understanding, not of knowledge; and such working is philosophical when it keeps to the rigor of concept and its connection with the universe of concepts.

But of course, this epistemological laissez-passer is much too general and impersonal for the matter at hand. As Kant granted to the practical reason what he denied to the theoretical, so may *we* allow the force of a unique and shattering experience a voice in the question of what "is the matter" with God. And there, right away, arises the question, What did Auschwitz add to that which one could always have known about the extent of the terrible and horrendous things that humans can do to humans and from times immemorial have done? And what has it added in particular to what is familiar to us Jews from a millennial history of suffering and forms so essential a part of our collective memory? The *question of Job* has always been the main question of theodicy—of general theodicy because of the existence of evil as such in the world, and of particular theodicy in its sharpening, by the riddle of election, of the purported covenant between Israel and its God. As to this sharpening, under which our present question also falls, one could at first invoke—as the prophets did—the covenant itself for an explanation of what befell the human party to it: the "people of the covenant" had been unfaithful to it. In the long ages of faithfulness thereafter, guilt and retribution no longer furnished the explanation but the idea of "witness" did instead—this creation of the Maccabean age, which bequeathed to posterity the concept of the martyr. It is of its very meaning that precisely the innocent and the just suffer the worst. In deference to the idea of witness, whole communities in the Middle Ages met their death by sword and fire with the *Sh'ma Jisrael*, the avowal of God's Oneness, on their lips. The Hebrew name for this is *Kiddushhashem*, "sanctification of the Name," and the slaughtered were called "saints." Through their sacrifice shone the light of promise, of the final redemption by the Messiah to come.

Nothing of this is still of use in dealing with the event for which "Auschwitz" has become the symbol. Not fidelity or infidelity, belief or unbelief, not guilt and punishment, not trial, witness and messianic hope, nay, not even strength or weakness, heroism or cowardice, defiance or submission had a place there. Of all this, Auschwitz, which also devoured the infants and babes, knew nothing; to none of it (with rarest exceptions) did the factory-like working of its machine give room. Not for the *sake* of faith did the victims die (as did, after all, "Jehovah's Witnesses"), nor *because* of their faith or any self-affirmed bend of their being as persons were they murdered. Dehumanization by utter degradation and deprivation preceded their dying, no glimmer of dignity was left to the freights bound for the final solution, hardly a trace of it was found in the surviving skeleton specters of the liberated camps. And yet, paradox of paradoxes: it *was* the ancient people of the "covenant," no longer believed in by those involved, killers and victims alike, but nevertheless just this and no other people, which under the fiction of race had been chosen for this wholesale annihilation—the most monstrous inversion of election into curse, which defied all possible endowment with meaning. There does, then, in spite of all, exist a connection—of a wholly perverse kind with the god-seekers and prophets of yore, whose descendants were thus collected out of the dispersion and gathered into the unity of joint death. And God let it happen. What God could let it happen?

Here we must note that on this question the Jew is in greater theoretical difficulty than the Christian. To the Christian (of the stern variety) the world is anyway largely of the devil and always an object of suspicion—the human world in particular because of original sin. But to the Jew, who sees in "this" world the locus of divine creation, justice, and redemption, God is eminently the Lord of *History*, and in this respect "Auschwitz" calls, even for the believer, the whole traditional concept of God into question. It has, indeed, as I have just tried to show, added to the Jewish historical experience something unprecedented and of a nature no longer assimilable by the old theological categories. Accordingly, one who will not thereupon just give up the concept of God altogether—and even the philosopher has a right to such an unwillingness—must rethink it so that it still remains thinkable; and that means seeking a new answer to the old question of (and about) Job. The Lord of History, we suspect, will have to go by the board in this quest. To repeat then, What God could let it happen?

For a possible, if groping, answer, I fall back on a speculative attempt with which I once ventured to meet the different question of immortality but in which also the specter of Auschwitz already played its part. On that occasion, I resorted to a *myth* of my own invention—that vehicle of imaginative but credible conjecture that Plato allowed for the sphere beyond the knowable. Allow me to repeat it here:

In the beginning, for unknowable reasons, the ground of being, or the Divine, chose to give itself over to the chance and risk and endless variety of becoming. And wholly so: entering into the adventure of space and time, the deity held back nothing of itself: no uncommitted or unimpaired part remained to direct, correct, and ultimately guarantee the devious working-out of its destiny in creation. On this unconditional immanence the modern temper insists. It is its courage or despair, in any case its bitter honesty, to take our being-in-the-world seriously: to view the world as left to itself, its laws as brooking no interference, and the rigor of our belonging to it as not softened by extramundane providence. The same our myth postulates for God's being in the world. Not, however, in the sense of pantheistic immanence: if world and God are simply the same, the world at each moment and in each state represents his fullness, and God can neither lose nor gain. Rather, in order that the world might be, and be for itself, God renounced his being, divesting himself of his deity—to receive it back from the Odyssey of time weighted with the chance harvest of unforeseeable temporal experience: transfigured or possibly even disfigured by it. In such self-forfeiture of divine integrity for the sake of unprejudiced becoming, no other foreknowledge can be admitted than that of *possibilities* which cosmic being offers in its own terms: to these, God committed his cause in effacing himself for the world.

And for aeons his cause is safe in the slow hands of cosmic chance and probability—while all the time we may surmise a patient memory of the gyrations of matter to accumulate into an ever more expectant accompaniment of eternity to the labors of time—a hesitant emergence of transcendence from the opaqueness of immanence.

And then the first stirring of life—a new language of the world: and with it a tremendous quickening of concern in the eternal realm and a sudden leap in its growth toward recovery of its plenitude. It is the world-accident for which becoming deity had waited and with which its prodigal stake begins to show signs of being redeemed. From the infinite swell of feeling, sensing, striving, and acting, which ever more varied and intense rises above the mute eddyings of matter, eternity gains strength, filling with content after content of self-affirmation, and the awakening God can first pronounce creation to be good.

But note that with life together came death, and that mortality is the price which the new possibility of being called "life" had to pay for itself. If permanence were the point, life should not have started out in the first place, for in no possible form can it match the durability of inorganic bodies. It is essentially precarious and corruptible being, an adventure in mortality, obtaining from long-lasting matter on its terms—the short terms of metabolizing organism—the borrowed, finite careers of individual selves. Yet it is precisely through the briefly snatched self-feeling, doing, and suffering of *finite* individuals, with the pitch of awareness heightened by the very press of finitiude, that the divine landscape bursts into color and the deity comes to experience itself . . . .

Note also this that with life's innocence before the advent of knowledge God's cause cannot go wrong. Whatever variety evolution brings forth adds to the possibilities of feeling and acting, and thus enriches the self-experiencing of the ground of being. Every new dimension of world-response opened up in its course means another modality for God's trying out his hidden essence and discovering himself through the surprises of the world-adventure. And all its harvest of anxious toil, whether bright or dark, swells the transcendent treasure of temporally lived eternity. If this is true for the broadening spectrum of diversity as such, it is even truer for the heightening pitch and passion of life that go with the twin rise of perception and motility in animals. The ever more sharpened keenness of appetite and fear, pleasure and pain, triumph and anguish, love and even cruelty—their very edge is the deity's gain. Their countless, yet never blunted incidence—hence the necessity of death and new birth—supplies the tempered essence from which the godhead reconstitutes itself. All this, evolution provides in the mere lavishness of its play and the sternness of its spur. Its creatures, by merely fulfilling themselves in pursuit of their lives, vindicate the divine venture. Even their suffering deepens the fullness of the symphony. Thus, this side of good and evil, God cannot lose in the great evolutionary game.

Nor yet can he fully win in the shelter of its innocence, and a new expectancy grows in him in answer to the direction which the unconscious drift of immanence gradually takes.

And then he trembles as the thrust of evolution, carried by its own momentum, passes the threshold where innocence ceases and an entirely new criterion of success and failure takes hold of the divine stake. The advent of man means the advent of knowledge and freedom, and with this supremely double-edged gift the innocence of the mere subject of self-fulfilling life has given way to the charge of responsibility under the disjunction of good and evil. To the promise and risk of this agency the divine cause, revealed at last, henceforth finds itself committed; and its issue trembles in the balance. The image of God, haltingly begun by the universe, for so long worked upon—and left undecided—in the wide and then narrowing spirals of prehuman life, passes with this last twist, and with a dramatic quickening of the movement, into man's precarious trust, to be completed, saved, or spoiled by what he will do to himself and the world. And in this awesome impact of his deeds on God's destiny, on the very complexion of eternal being, lies the immortality of man.

With the appearance of man, transcendence awakened to itself and henceforth accompanies his doings with the bated breath of suspense, hoping and beckoning, rejoicing and grieving, approving and frowning—and, I daresay making itself felt to him even while not intervening in the dynamics of his worldly scene: for can it not be that by the reflection of its own state as it wavers with the record of man, the transcendent casts light and shadow over the human landscape?[2]

Such is the tentative myth I once proposed for consideration in a different context. It has theological implications that only later unfolded to me. Of these I shall develop here some of the more obvious ones—hoping that this translation from image into concept will somehow connect what so far must seem a strange and rather willful private fantasy with the more responsible tradition of Jewish religious thought. In this manner, I try to redeem the poetic liberties of my earlier, roving attempt.

First, and most obviously, I have been speaking of a *suffering God*—which immediately seems to clash with the biblical conception of divine majesty. There is, of course, a Christian connotation of the term "suffering God" with which my myth must not be confounded;

it does not speak, as does the former, of a special act by which the deity at one time, and for the special purpose of saving man, sends part of itself into a particular situation of suffering (the incarnation and crucifixion). If anything in what I said makes sense, then the sense is that the relation of God to the world *from the moment of creation*, and certainly from the creation of man on, involves suffering on the part of God. It involves, to be sure, suffering on the part of the creature too, but this truism has always been recognized in every theology. Not so the idea of God's suffering with creation, and of this I said that, prima facie, it clashes with the biblical conception of divine majesty. But does it really clash as extremely as it seems at first glance? Do not we also in the Bible encounter God as slighted and rejected by man and grieving over him? Do not we encounter Him as ruing that He created man, and suffering from the disappointment He experiences with him—and with His chosen people in particular? We remember the prophet Hosea, and God's love lamenting over Israel, his unfaithful wife.

Then, second, the myth suggests the picture of a *becoming God*. It is a God emerging in time instead of possessing a completed being that remains identical with itself throughout eternity. Such an idea of divine becoming is surely at variance with the Greek, Platonic-Aristotelian tradition of philosophical theology that, since its incorporation into the Jewish and Christian theological tradition, has somehow usurped for itself an authority to which it is not at all entitled by authentic Jewish (and also Christian) standards. Transtemporality, impassibility, and immutability have been taken to be necessary attributes of God. And the ontological distinction that classical thought made between "being" and "becoming," with the latter characteristic of the lower, sensible world, excluded every shadow of becoming from the pure, absolute being of the godhead. But this Hellenic concept has never accorded well with the spirit and language of the Bible, and the concept of divine becoming can actually be better reconciled with it.

For what does the becoming God mean? Even if we do not go so far as our myth suggests, that much at least we must concede of "becoming" in God as lies in the mere fact that He is affected by what happens in the world, and "affected" means altered, made different. Even apart from the fact that creation as such—the act itself and the lasting result thereof—was after all a decisive change in God's own state, insofar as He is now no longer alone, his continual *relation* to the creation, once this exists and moves in the flux of becoming, means that He experiences something with the world, that His own being is affected by what goes on in it. This holds already for the mere relation of accompanying knowledge, let alone that of caring interest. Thus, if God is in any relation to the world—which is the cardinal assumption of religion—then by that token alone the Eternal has "temporalized" Himself and progressively becomes different through the actualizations of the world process.

One incidental consequence of the idea of the becoming God is that it destroys the idea of an eternal recurrence of the same. This was Nietzsche's alternative to Christian metaphysics, which in this case is the same as Jewish metaphysics. It is indeed the extreme symbol of the turn to unconditional temporality and of the complete negation of any transcendence that could keep a memory of what happens in time, to assume that, by the mere exhaustion of the possible combinations and recombinations of material elements, it must come to pass that an "initial" configuration recurs and the whole cycle starts over again, and if once, then innumerable times—Nietzsche's "ring of rings, the ring of eternal recurrence." However, if we assume that eternity is not unaffected by what happens in time, there can never be a recurrence of the same because God will not be the same after He has gone through the experience of a world process. Any new world coming after the end of one will carry, as it were, in its own heritage the memory of what has gone before; or, in other words, there will not be an indifferent and dead eternity but an eternity that grows with the accumulating harvest of time.

Bound up with the concepts of a suffering and a becoming God is that of a *caring God*—a God not remote and detached and self-contained but involved with what He cares for. Whatever the "primordial" condition of the godhead, He ceased to be self-contained once He let himself in for the existence of a world by creating such a world or letting it come to be. God's caring about His creatures is, of course, among the most familiar tenets of Jewish faith. But my myth stresses the less familiar aspect that this caring God is not a sorcerer who in the act of caring also provides the fulfillment of His concern: He has left something for other agents to do and thereby has made His care dependent on them. He is therefore also an endangered God, a God who runs a risk. Clearly that must be so, or else the world would be in a condition of permanent perfection. The fact that it is not bespeaks one of two things: that either the One God does not exist (though more than one may), or that the One has given to an agency other than Himself, though created by Him, a power and a right to act on its own and therewith a scope for at least codetermining that which is a concern of His. This is why I said that the caring God is not a sorcerer. Somehow He has, by an act of either inscrutable wisdom or love or whatever else the divine motive may have been, forgone the guaranteeing of His self-satisfaction by His own power, after He has first, by the act of creation itself, forgone being "all in all."

And therewith we come to what is perhaps the most critical point in our speculative, theological venture: this is not an omnipotent God. We argue indeed that, for the sake of our image of God and our whole relation to the divine, for the sake of any viable theology, we cannot uphold the time-honored (medieval) doctrine of absolute, unlimited divine power. Let me argue this first, on a purely logical plane, by pointing out the paradox in the idea of absolute power. The logical situation indeed is by no means that divine omnipotence is the rationally plausible and somehow self-recommending doctrine, while that of its limitation is wayward and in need of defense. Quite the opposite. From the very concept of power, it follows that omnipotence is a self-contradictory, self-destructive, indeed, senseless concept. The situation is similar to that of freedom in the human realm: far from beginning where necessity ends, freedom consists of and lives in pitting itself against necessity. Separated from it, freedom loses its object and becomes as void as force without resistance. Absolute freedom would be empty freedom that cancels itself out. So, too, does empty power, and absolute, exclusive power would be just that. Absolute, total power means power not limited by anything, not even by the mere existence of something other than the possessor of that power; for the very existence of such another would already constitute a limitation, and the one would have to annihilate it so as to save its absoluteness. Absolute power then, in its solitude, has no object on which to act. But as objectless power it is a powerless power, canceling itself out: "all" equals "zero" here. In order for it to act, there must be something else, and as soon as there is, the one is not all-powerful anymore, even though in any comparison its power may be superior by any degree you please to imagine. The existence of another object limits the power of the most powerful agent at the same time that it allows it to be an agent. In brief, power as such is a *relational* concept and requires relation.

Again, power meeting no *resistance* in its relatum is equal to no power at all: power is exercised only in relation to something that itself has power. Power, unless otiose, consists in the capacity to overcome something; and something's existence as such is enough to provide this condition. For existence means resistance and thus opposing force. Just as, in physics, force without resistance—that is, counterforce—remains empty, so in metaphysics does power without counterpower, unequal as the latter may be. That, therefore, on which power acts must have a power of its own, even if that power derives from the first and was initially granted to it, as one with its existence, by a self-renunciation of limitless power—that is, in the act of creation.

In short, it cannot be that all power is on the side of one agent only. Power must be divided so that there be any power at all.

But besides this logical and ontological objection, there is a more theological, genuinely religious objection to the idea of absolute and unlimited divine omnipotence. We can have divine omnipotence together with divine goodness only at the price of complete divine inscrutability. Seeing the existence of evil in the world, we must sacrifice intelligibility in God to the combination of the other two attributes. Only a completely unintelligible God can be said to be absolutely good and absolutely powerful, yet tolerate the world as it is. Put more generally, the three attributes at stake—absolute goodness, absolute power, and intelligibility—stand in such a logical relation to one another that the conjunction of any two of them excludes the third. The question then is, Which are truly integral to our concept of God, and which, being of lesser force, must give way to their superior claim? Now, surely, goodness is inalienable from the concept of God and not open to qualification. Intelligibility, conditional on both God's nature and man's capacity, is on the latter count indeed subject to qualification but on no account to complete elimination. The *Deus absconditus*, the hidden God (not to speak of an absurd God), is a profoundly un-Jewish conception. Our teaching, the Torah, rests on the premise and insists that we can understand God, not completely, to be sure, but something of Him—of His will, intentions, and even nature—because He has told us. There has been revelation, we have His commandments and His law, and He has directly communicated with some—His prophets—as His mouth for all men in the language of men and their times: refracted thus in this limiting medium but not veiled in dark mystery. A completely hidden God is not an acceptable concept by Jewish norms.

But He would have to be precisely that if together with being good He were conceived as all-powerful. After Auschwitz, we can assert with greater force than ever before that an omnipotent deity would have to be either not good or (in His world rule, in which alone we can "observe" Him) totally unintelligible. But if God is to be intelligible in some manner and to some extent (and to this we must hold), then His goodness must be compatible with the existence of evil, and this it is only if He is not *all*-powerful. Only then can we uphold that He is intelligible and good, and there is yet evil in the world. And since we have found the concept of omnipotence to be dubious anyway, it is this that has to give way.

So far our argument about omnipotence has done no more than lay it down as a principle for any acceptable theology continuous with the Jewish heritage that God's power be seen as limited by something whose being in its own right and whose power to act on its own authority He Himself acknowledges.[3] Admittedly, we have the choice to interpret this as a voluntary concession on God's part, which He is free to revoke at will—that is, as the restraint of a power that He still and always possesses in full but, for the sake of creation's own autonomous right, chooses not fully to employ. To devout believers, this is probably the most palatable choice. But it will not suffice. For in view of the enormity of what, among the bearers of his image in creation, some of them time and again, and wholly unilaterally, inflict on innocent others, one would expect the good God at times to break His own, however stringent, rule of restraint and intervene with a saving miracle.[4] But no saving miracle occurred. Through the years that "Auschwitz" raged, God remained silent. The miracles that did occur came forth from man alone: the deeds of those solitary, mostly unknown "just of the nations" who did not shrink from utter sacrifice in order to help, to save, to mitigate—even, when nothing else was left, unto sharing Israel's lot. Of them I shall speak again. But God was silent. And there I say, or my myth says, Not because He chose not to, but because he He *could* not intervene did He fail to intervene. For reasons decisively prompted by contemporary experience, I entertain the idea of a God who for a time—the time of the ongoing world process—has divested Himself of any power to interfere with the physical course of things: and who responds to the impact on his being by worldly events, not "with a mighty hand and outstretched arm," as we Jews on every Passover recite in remembering the exodus from Egypt, but with the mutely insistent appeal of his unfulfilled goal.

In this, assuredly, my speculation strays far from oldest Judaic teaching. Several of Maimonides' Thirteen Articles of Faith, which we solemnly chant in our services, fall away with the "mighty hand": the assertions about God ruling the universe, His rewarding the good and punishing the wicked, even about the coming of the promised Messiah. Not, however, those about His call to the souls,[5] His inspiration of the prophets and the Torah, thus also not the idea of election: for only to the physical realm does the impotence of God refer. Most of all, the *Oneness* of God stands unabated and with it the "Hear, O Israel!" No Manichaean dualism is enlisted to explain evil; from the hearts of men alone does it arise and gain power in the world. The mere permitting, indeed, of human freedom involved a renouncing of sole divine power henceforth. And our discussion of power as such has already led us to deny divine omnipotence, anyway.

The elimination of divine omnipotence leaves the theoretical choice between the alternatives of either some preexistent—theological or ontological—*dualism*, or of God's *self*-limitation through the creation from nothing. The dualistic alternative in turn might take the Manichaean form of an active force of evil forever opposing the divine purpose in the universal scheme of things: a two-god theology; or the Platonic form of a passive medium imposing, no less universally, imperfection on the embodiment of the ideal in the world: a form-matter dualism. The first is plainly unacceptable to Judaism. The second answers at best the problem of imperfection and natural necessity but not that of positive evil, which implies a freedom empowered by its own authority independent of that of God; and it is the fact and success of deliberate evil rather than the inflictions of blind, natural causality—the use of the latter in the hands of responsible agents (Auschwitz rather than the earthquake of Lisbon)—with which Jewish theology has to contend at this hour. Only with creation from nothing do we have the oneness of the divine principle combined with that self-limitation that then permits (gives "room" to) the existence and autonomy of a world. Creation was that act of absolute sovereignty with which it consented, for the sake of self-determined finitude, to be absolute no more—an act, therefore, of divine self-restriction.

And here let us remember that Jewish tradition itself is really not quite so monolithic in the matter of divine sovereignty as official doctrine makes it appear. The mighty undercurrent of the Kabbalah, which Gershom Scholem in our days has brought to light anew, knows about a divine fate bound up with the coming-to-be of a world. There we meet highly original, very unorthodox speculations in whose company mine would not appear so wayward after all. Thus, for example, my myth at bottom only pushes further the idea of the *tzimtzum*, that cosmogonic centerconcept of the Lurianic Kabbalah.[6] *Tzimtzum* means contraction, withdrawal, self-limitation. To make room for the world, the *En-Sof* (Infinite; literally, No-End) of the beginning had to contract Himself so that, vacated by him, empty space could expand outside of Him: the "Nothing" in which and from which God could then create the world. Without this retreat into Himself, there could be no "other" outside God, and only His continued holding-Himself-in preserves the finite things from losing their separate being again into the divine "all in all."

My myth goes farther still. The contraction is total as far as power is concerned; as a whole has the Infinite ceded His power to the finite and thereby wholly delivered His cause into its hands. Does that still leave anything for a relation to God?

Let me answer this question with a last quotation from the earlier writing. By forgoing its own inviolateness, the eternal ground allowed the world to be. To this self-denial all creation owes its existence and with it has received all there is to receive from beyond. Having given Himself whole to the becoming world, God has no more to give: it is man's now to give to Him. And he may give by seeing to it in the ways of his life that it does not happen or happen too often, and not on his account, that it "repented the Lord"[7] to have made the world. This may well be the secret of the "thirty-six righteous ones" whom, according to Jewish lore, the world shall never lack[8] and of whose number in our time were possibly some of those "just of the nations" I have mentioned before: their guessed-at secret being that, with the superior valency of good over evil, which (we hope) obtains in the noncausal logic of things there, their hidden holiness can outweigh countless guilt, redress the balance of a generation, and secure the peace of the invisible realm.[9]

All this, let it be said at the end, is but stammering. Even the words of the great seers and adorers—the prophets and the psalmists—which stand beyond comparison, were stammers before the eternal mystery. Every mortal answer to Job's question, too, cannot be more than that. Mine is the opposite to the one given by the Book of Job: this, for an answer, invoked the plenitude of God's power; mine, His chosen voidance of it. And yet, strange to say, both are in praise. For the divine renunciation was made so that we, the mortals, could be. This, too, so it seems to me, is an answer to Job: that in him God Himself suffers. Which is true, if any, we can know of none of the answers ever tried. Of my poor word thereto I can only hope that it be not wholly excluded from what Goethe, in "Testament of Old-Persian Faith," thus put into Zarathustra's mouth:

All that ever stammers praising the Most High
Is in circles there assembled far and nigh.[10]

Notes

1. This is my translation of a lecture I delivered in German on the occasion of receiving the Dr. Leopold Lucas Prize for 1984 at Tübingen

University. It was published in Fritz Stern and Hans Jonas, *Reflexionen finsterer Zeit* (Tübingen: J. C. B. Mohr, 1984). The lecture expanded and recast an earlier paper with the same title ("The Concept of God after Auschwitz," in *Out of the Whirlwind*, A. H. Friedlander, ed. [New York: Union of American Hebrew Congregations, 1968], 465–76), which in turn incorporated portions of my 1961 Ingersoll Lecture, "Immortality and the Modern Temper" (see n. 2). The partly verbatim use of this previously published material is by permission.

2.   Hans Jonas, "Immortality and the Modern Temper," the 1961 Ingersoll Lecture at Harvard University, first printed in *Harvard Theological Review* 55 (1962): 1–20; also in H. Jonas, *The Phenomenon of Life* (Chicago and London: University of Chicago Press, 1982), 262–81.

3.   The same principle has been argued, with a slightly different reasoning, by Rabbi Jack Bemporad, "Toward a New Jewish Theology," *American Judaism* (Winter 1964–65), 9 ff.

4.   An occasional miracle, i.e., extramundane intervention in the closed causality of the physical realm, is not incompatible with the general validity of the laws of nature (rare exceptions do not void empirical rules) and might even, by all appearances, perfectly conform to them—on this question, see H. Jonas, *Philosophical Essays* (Chicago: University of Chicago Press, 1980), 66–67, and, more extensively, my Rudolf Bultmann Memorial address of 1976 at Marburg University, "Is Faith Still Possible? Memories of Rudolf Bultman and Reflections on the Philosophical Aspects of His Work" (*Harvard Theological Review* 75/1 [January 1982]: 1–25, esp. 9–15); see also pp. 17–18 for a statement of the religious objection against thinking of God as "Lord of History."

5.   For more about this inalienable postulate of revealed religion— the possibility of revelation itself, i.e., of God's speaking to human *minds* even if debarred from intervening in physical *things*—see Jonas, "Is Faith Still Possible?", 18–20.

6.   Originated by Isaac Luria (born 1534–died 1572).

7.   Genesis 6:6–7.

8.   Sanhedrin 97 b; Sukkah 45 b.

9.   The idea that it is we who can help God rather than God helping us I have since found movingly expressed by one of the Auschwitz victims themselves, a young Dutch Jewess, who validated it by acting on it unto death. It is found in *An Interrupted Life: The Diaries of Etty Hillesum, 1941–43* (New York: Pantheon Books, 1984). When the deportations in Holland began, in 1942, she came forward and volunteered for the Westerbork concentration camp, there to help in the hospital and to share in the fate of her people. In September, 1943, she was shipped, in one of the usual mass transports, to

Auschwitz and "died" there on November 30, 1943. Her diaries have survived but were only recently published. I quote from Neal Ascherson ("In Hell," *New York Review of Books* 31/13 [July 19, 1984]: 8–12, esp. 9): "She does not exactly 'find God,' but rather constructs one for herself. The theme of the diaries becomes increasingly religious, and many of the entries are prayers. Her God is someone to whom she makes promises, but of whom she expects and asks nothing. 'I shall try to help you, God, to stop my strength ebbing away, though I cannot vouch for it in advance. But one thing is becoming increasingly clear to me: that You cannot help us, that we must help You to help ourselves . . . . Alas, there does not seem to be much You Yourself can do about our circumstance, about our lives. Neither do I hold You responsible. You cannot help us, but we must help You and defend Your dwelling place in us to the last.' " Reading this was to me a shattering confirmation, by a true witness, of my so much later and sheltered musings—and a consoling correction of my sweeping statement that we had no martyrs there.

10. "Und was nur am Lob des Höchsten stammelt, / Ist in Kreis' um Kreise dort versammelt" (Goethe, "Vermächtnis altpersischen Glaubens").

Chapter 10

Hans Jonas as Process Theologian

John B. Cobb, Jr.

Jonas' essay is a fine piece of "process theology." I say this without regard to the question of the sources of his thought. Jonas was, of course, familiar with Whitehead's philosophy and appreciative of it. At one point in the essay he speaks of "the 'primordial' condition of the Godhead" in a way that suggests intentional evocation of Whitehead's distinction between the primordial and consequent natures of God. But I am not interested in the question of influence. Jonas thought for himself and came, through largely independent reflection, to the same conclusions as process theologians.

"The same" is strong language. Rarely is there complete agreement among any independent thinkers, even among those who explicitly appeal to a common tradition. But what is striking is that, in the clearest and most explicit formulations in this essay, Jonas' position is completely acceptable to process theologians. This is true of what Jonas says of "a suffering God," "a becoming God," and "a caring God."

Most striking of all is his agreement with process theology in the discussion of omnipotence. He rejects omnipotence for two main reasons. First, logical nonsense is involved, since power is a relational term and requires power in what is acted on in order to be actual at all. Second, it is impossible to reconcile the doctrine of divine omnipotence with that of divine goodness without a total sacrifice of intelligibility. Like process theologians, Jonas takes the doctrine of divine goodness as fundamental and regards the abandonment of the effort to attain intelligibility as a disaster.

There are, to be sure, some places where Jonas' language is not characteristic of process theologians. For example, he speaks of divine "self-limitation." Most of us avoid this language because it suggests that God remains able at all times to assert total control, refraining from doing so only for moral, not ontological, reasons. This view seems to us incompatible with divine failure to prevent events such as the Holocaust. But the view we reject is not at all what Jonas means to affirm by speaking of self-limitation. Quite the contrary, the view we oppose is explicitly opposed by him as well, and for just the same reasons. He, too, asserts that the act of creating something inherently and necessarily limits God's power. From my point of view, the language of divine self-limitation is still in danger of being misleading, but there seems to be no difference in the thought we try to express in different ways.

Probably the language of self-limitation is more appropriate from his perspective than from mine because he affirms *creatio ex nihilo*. Process theologians have sometimes used this phrase in order to show that they affirm much of its existential meaning. Process theology, like the classical doctrine of creation out of nothing, rejects the Manichean dualism of a good spirit and a bad matter. Both also reject the idea that a passive matter renders all embodiment of ideas imperfect. The reasons Jonas cites for affirming creation out of nothing are, accordingly, shared by process theology.

Nevertheless, there does seem to be a difference here. Jonas' language suggests that he takes this doctrine literally as well as existentially. It implies that there was a beginning of time and creation such that one can speculate about what God was like *before* creation in a quasi-temporal sense. Jonas writes as though it were meaningful to say that before creation God had no limitations, and that creation was an "act of absolute sovereignty." But on examination this apparent difference from process theology is less than it initially seems. Jonas' analysis of power as relational makes it clear that, apart from creation, power cannot be attributed to God at all, and that the act of creating, as an expression of relational power, must deal with the power of what is created.

Jonas seems to think that it is important to assert a literal beginning of creation and time, whereas process theologians do not. But it is hard to see what of religious or existential importance follows in Jonas' thinking from this assertion. For some Christian theologians today, the assertion of a supernatural beginning supports the anticipation of an equally supernatural end, and in their reading of Christianity such confidence in God's final victory on earth is crucial. But I find no suggestion that Jonas moves in that direction. There seems here to be between Jonas and process theologians a difference that makes no difference.

Perhaps a more significant difference lies in Jonas' language about God's leaving the creation entirely to its own devices. Process theology discerns divine grace at work throughout the creative process, although certainly not controlling it. But the difference here, too, is not as great as some of the formulations make it appear. Jonas makes plain that he does *not* exclude God's "call to the souls, His inspiration of the prophets, and the Torah." What process theologians think of as God's persuasive power is *not* excluded, at least in relation to human beings.

The question is whether Jonas limits this divine power to the relation to human beings. Or is "the mutely insistent appeal of [God's] unfulfilled goal" present elsewhere as well, as process theologians believe? The evidence here is not altogether clear. In other writings, Jonas has emphasized continuities between human beings and other living things. And in his myth in the present essay, he writes:

> every new dimension of world-response opened up in its course means another modality for God's trying out His hidden essence and discovering Himself through the world adventure.

This comes just after the introduction of life in the evolutionary process.

Nevertheless, even if God's call can be understood as effective among all living things, and not only human beings, there is here a difference between Jonas and Whitehead, one on which Jonas has commented in other writings. For Jonas, there is a dualism between living things and the inanimate world. In this essay, he contrasts God's role in calling human beings with God's impotence in the physical world. The myth, also, suggests that God is completely at the mercy of chance and probability.

But even on this point, I am not quite ready to concede a real difference. I know that Jonas does assert a duality of the inanimate and the animate and that he says that God is completely impotent with respect to the inanimate. But the myth does not make sense if these statements are taken in an unqualified way. If there were nothing at work in the inanimate world that tends to bring life into being, then would not God's total subordination of the divine to this utterly blind and directionless process have been a far greater risk than Jonas' myth suggests? Is not life, from the point of view of inanimate physical processes alone, an *extreme* improbability? Did God commit his cause to processes with so insignificant a probability of producing anything like life and humanity? In what sense was God's cause "safe in the slow hands of cosmic chance and probability?" If "all the time we may surmise a patient memory of the gyrations of matter to accumulate into an ever more expectant accompaniment of eternity to the labors of time—a hesitant emergence of transcendence from the opaqueness of immanence," does not this suggest that the total immanence of eternity was having *some* effect on time?

I know that it is wrong to impose one's views on a text that resists them. Nevertheless, I do believe that Jonas' real concerns would express themselves better if he did not differentiate so sharply the ways in which God has related to the world. The text seems to distinguish a "time" of no relation because there was no world, a drastically unique act of creation out of nothing, a long protracted period in which there was no effect of God in the world at all, and a new period when God begins to call human beings to respond to the divine lure. What would be lost in terms of Jonas' basic concerns if we argued that God has always been creating and persuading, that before the emergence of living things the range of possible responsiveness was very limited indeed, that with the emergence of life this range increased, and that with the appearance of human beings it took on whole new dimensions of significance?

In these comments I have devoted most of the time to the apparent differences between Jonas' work and process theology. That is not because I think the differences to be primary, but only because it seems better to spend one's time on what is problematic than merely summarizing the massive agreements. I do not think the remaining differences have anything to do with Jonas' Jewishness. They seem to derive from a conviction that the physical world is purely material until the emergence of life. This has certainly been a widespread view since the Enlightenment; so it is not difficult to trace its sources. Process philosophy is one of several protests against this view, a view that leads either to metaphysical dualism or to some form of reductionism. I am convinced that both of these alternatives should be avoided for both philosophical and religious reasons, reasons as relevant to Jewish as to Christian faith.

What is truly remarkable is that, despite this apparent divide, the views of God and of God's mode of relation to the world, at least the human world, are virtually identical in Jonas and in process theology. Religiously these are the most important matters. To claim Jonas as an ally is a source of great joy to this process theologian.

Chapter 11

Reversing the Reversal: Covenant and Election in Jewish and Process Thought

Clark M. Williamson

The thesis of this essay is suggested in the following quotation from Charles Hartshorne's *Omnipotence and Other Theological Mistakes*. Said Hartshorne:

> It is a conviction of mine that a test of antisemitism is in the way one answers the question: "Can I take seriously the idea that it just might be that the Jews, in their differences from Christians, have been more right all along on some issues?" If the answer is "Yes," then perhaps there is no antisemitism. If "No," then I have my suspicions.[1]

The thesis is that, on the topic of covenant and election, Jews have been more right all along than Christians. The dominant Christian position, that the price of the election of the Gentiles has been the rejection of the Jews, must itself be rejected. The reason for discarding this supersessionist understanding of covenant is not that Jews disagree with it, although they do, but the double reason that it is inappropriate to the good news of God's all-inclusive love and that it is morally and intellectually incredible. We shall return to these points later in this essay.

Hartshorne's comment is a qualified one. He does not claim that all Jews have always been completely right on all issues on which Jews and Christians have differed or that all Christians have always been wholly wrong on all such issues. Some Christians, although a minority, may have been right on the question of covenant. The constructive

163

claim of this essay will be that some few Christians were right, and that with the resources of process thought we can critically reclaim their views in a manner that befits the gospel of God's all-inclusive love and that is morally and intellectually credible.

I. Karl Barth on Judaism and the Covenant

The context in which this essay has been written is one in which we are conscious that we do our theology after the whirlwind of destruction, the *Shoah,* unleashed by the Nazis upon Jews in the heart of Christian Europe. We cannot discuss theological questions, particularly such matters as covenant and election, in an ahistorical manner. Complex though the Holocaust was, it has become increasingly clear that the pre-Holocaust praxis of Christian anti-Jewish preaching, teaching, and action was a necessary, if not sufficient, reason for its occurrence. Central to this preaching and teaching of contempt for Jews and Judaism was the issue of covenant.

The problem Christian theology faces post-Holocaust is best illustrated not by reference to such German-Christian (*Deutsche Christen*) thinkers as Gerhard Kittel, Paul Althaus, and Emanuel Hirsch, who took it upon themselves to justify the Nazi state.[2] The question whether Christian theology can survive the Holocaust is directly and best put when we look at the theology of the anti-Nazi Confessing Church theologians, chief among whom would have to be Karl Barth.

Without a doubt the most influential Protestant theologian in the twentieth century, Barth, along with Bonhoeffer and other members of the Confessing Church, resisted Hitler. In the 1930s Barth's theological work took a highly practical turn with his declaration of war against Adolf Hitler and the Nazi movement. By 1933, the German Evangelical Church had become largely a tool of the Nazi party. In April of that year, the "Evangelical Church of the German Nation" was created and published the following "guiding principles":

> We see in race, folk, and nation, orders of existence granted and entrusted to us by God. God's law for us is that we look to the preservation of these orders . . . .
>
> In the mission to the Jews we perceive a grave danger to our nationality. It is the entrance gate for alien blood into our body politic . . . . In particular, marriage between Germans and Jews is to be forbidden.

We want an evangelical Church that is rooted in our nation-hood. We repudiate the spirit of Christian world citizenship. We want the degenerating manifestations of this spirit . . . overcome by a faith in our national mission that God has committed to us.[3]

To oppose this German Christian movement, Barth, along with Martin Niemoeller, led in forming the German Confessing Church. In May of 1934, representatives of the Confessing Church met at Barmen and issued the famous Barmen confession, which was essentially the work of Barth. It asserted the sovereignty of the Word of God in Christ over all idolatrous political theologies. Declared the Barmen Confession:

In view of the errors of the "German Christians" of the present Reich Church government which are devastating the Church and are also thereby breaking up the unity of the German Evangelical Church, we confess the following evangelical truths:

Jesus Christ, as he is attested for us in Holy Scripture, is the one Word of God which we have to hear and which we have to trust and obey in life and in death.

We reject the false doctrine, as though the Church could and would have to acknowledge as a source of its proclamation, apart from and besides this one Word of God, still other events and powers, figures and truths, as God's revelation.

We reject the false doctrine, as though there were areas of our life in which we would not belong to Jesus Christ, but to other lords . . . .[4]

Along with helping to form the German Confessing Church, Barth joined with Eduard Thurneysen in giving birth to a new theological journal, *Theologische Existenz Heute*, in which the denunciation of Nazism was carried further. For Barth, personally, the upshot of all this activity was that the Nazis suspended him from his teaching post at Bonn in December of 1934, and then in the spring of the following year forced him out of Germany. He then went to and remained in Basel, the city of his birth, for the next thirty-three years.

Thirty-two years after his expulsion from Germany, Barth visited Pope Paul VI in Rome shortly after the close of the Second Vatican Council. On that occasion he said this to the members of the Secretariat for Christian Unity:

Today there are very good relations between the Roman Catholic Church and many of the Protestant churches, between the Secretariat for Christian Unity and the World Council of Churches. The number of ecumenical study—and work—groups is growing very fast. The ecumenical movement is clearly being impelled by the Spirit of the Lord. But we should not forget that there is ultimately only one truly great ecumenical question: our relation to Judaism.[5]

Barth held the view that an anti-semitic or a-semitic church loses its faith and the object of its faith.[6] He also affirmed of Israel that we Christians are "guests in their house, . . . new wood grafted onto *their* old tree."[7]

Nevertheless, his attitude toward Judaism and the Jewish people was mixed. In spite of the fact that his encounter with Nazism showed him that anti-Judaism is also anti-Christian, he continued the age-old tradition of Christian anti-Judaism. Writing while the final and systematic phase of Hitler's *Endlösung der Judenfrage* was being implemented, he saw the misfortunes of the Jewish people as a witness to Christian truth, which is precisely how the *adversus Judaeos* theological tradition, going back at least to the *Epistle of Barnabas*, had always seen them.

In 1942, Barth made a series of points to this effect, beginning with the declaration that it is God who determines that Israel will serve the elected people of God, of which Israel is a part, by reflecting the judgment from which God has rescued human beings. Israel, said Barth, "is not an obedient but an obdurate people," by whom the Messiah is delivered up and for whom he is crucified. Israel should become obedient to its election; it should "enter the Church and perform this special service in the Church."[8] Barth was not bothered by the contradiction involved in urging Israel to choose to do something that God determines that Israel shall not do.

Israel, says Barth, is disobedient to and resists its election. It forms and upholds the synagogue, seeking to "realise its true determination beside and outwith the Church," and in so doing "creates schism, a gulf, in the minds of the community of God." Outside the church, all that Israel can set forth is "the sheer, stark judgment of God," an "outmoded and superseded" revolt of fallen people against God's grace. In their unbelief, the Jews create "the spectral form of the synagogue." In the sense that Jews provide the strange witness of unbelief, a witness for which they suffer, Barth affirms that "the existence of the Jews . . . is an adequate proof of the existence of God."

The Jews of the ghetto give this demonstration involuntarily, joylessly and ingloriously, but they do give it. They have nothing to attest to the world but the shadow of the cross of Christ that falls upon them. But they, too, do actually and necessarily attest Jesus Christ Himself?

In such comments as these, we clearly see a certain view of the covenant and election of Israel. It is the church that is elect of God and in covenant with God; Israel's covenant and election are to be found within the church. By virtue of staying obdurately outside the church, Israel is disobedient to and misses its election. The suffering of the Jewish people in the ghettos of Europe in 1942 is interpreted Christologically: the shadow of the cross falls upon them. A post-Holocaust theologian might make such a remark as a piece of prophetic self-criticism from within the church. In one sense, it was the shadow of the cross that fell upon the Jews in Hitler's effort to make the earth *Judenrein*. But this was not Barth's point, and his anti-Judaism blinded him to the fact that the real shadow that fell upon the Jews of Europe in 1942 was that of the *Hakenkreuz*, the swastika.

Although Barth resisted Hitler, those who collaborated with Hitler could also agree with the negative side of Barth's dialectical stance toward Jews. Indeed, their stance was a factor in their collaboration. In 1942, an eastern European rebbe went to an archbishop to plead for Catholic intervention against the deportation of the Slovakian Jews. Tiso, the head of the Slovakian government, had previously been the archbishop's secretary and the rebbe hoped that the archbishop could persuade Tiso not to allow the deportations. Because the rebbe did not yet know of the gas chambers, he stressed the dangers of hunger and disease, expecially for women, old people, and children. The archbishop replied:

> It is not just a matter of deportation. You will not die there of hunger and disease. They will slaughter all of you there, old and young alike, women and children, at once—it is the punishment that you deserve for the death of our Lord and Redeemer, Jesus Christ—you have only one solution. Come over to our religion and I will work to annul this decree.[10]

As late as March, 1941—admittedly still before the full destruction was unleashed—Archbishop Grober of Germany, in a pastoral letter, blamed the Jews for the death of Christ and added that:

The self-imposed curse of the Jews, "His blood be upon us and upon our children," had come true terribly, until the present time, until today.[11]

In like manner, the Vatican responded to an inquiry from the Vichy government about the law of June 2, 1941, which isolated Jews and deprived them of rights:

> In principle, there is nothing in these measures which the Holy See would find to criticize.[12]

In general, throughout the Holocaust, one finds an inverse ratio between the presence of the *adversus Judaeos* ideology and the survival of Jews. Given all the variables, anti-Judaism apparently played a role in the decision not to shield Jews or to turn them over to Nazi authorities. Central to anti-Judaism is a supersessionist notion of covenant and election: that the covenant between God and the Jews has passed to the church and that the election of the Gentiles was accomplished by the rejection of the Jews.

These comments, inadequate as they are in the face of the demonic *tremendum* of evil let loose in Hitler's systematic program of *Judenvernichtung*, will have to suffice to contextualize our theological discussion of covenant and election. If credible moral practice is a norm of Christian faith (and if not, why do we bother to talk about love of the neighbor?), then Christians obviously have a lot of rethinking to do.

II. Covenant in Judaism

The purpose of this section is to state in a short synopsis the understanding of covenant within Judaism and the ways in which it has been more correct than the supersessionist deviation from it.

A covenant is a relationship between two parties in which each party voluntarily agrees to certain conditions of the relationship and both give their word to uphold the conditions. Covenant provides the central analogy in the scriptures for the bond between God and Israel. Although the origins of the idea are obscure, subsequent tradition regards the covenant as established by the revelation of God to Moses, the redemption of Israel from bondage in Egypt, the giving of the Torah, and the leading of the Israelites through the wilderness into the land. Other traditions in the scriptures carry the idea of covenant to Noah.

Christians often view the idea of covenant as easily degenerating into the notion of a mere legal relationship contracted for the mutual benefit of both parties. Although God's complaint against Israel's sin is sometimes stated in terms of a legal lawsuit ("the Lord has a controversy with the inhabitants of the land," Hosea 4:1; cf. Jeremiah 12:3), the Hebrew scriptures avoid legalism because of their emphasis on the primacy of grace in God's election of Israel. Moreover, the Torah, which is the visible seal of the covenant, is not a set of legal obligations that, once obeyed, becomes the basis for a reward claim. It, too, is a gracious revelation of the conditions necessary for a truly authentic life, particularly as that involves justice in and beyond the community. Elements of legalism can appear, particularly in popular piety, but the prophets warned against this. The covenant forms the background for the understanding of the prophets' denunciation of Israel's apostasy and for their choice of such images as marriage and adultery to illustrate the meaning of covenant. The message of the prophets is not that Israel has broken a legal contract, but that Israel has forsaken the gracious God who originally redeemed Israel, and who still remains faithful to the covenant, in spite of Israel's occasional ignoring and breaking of it.

That is the bare bones of the notion of covenant in the Hebrew scriptures. The main Hebrew term for covenant is *berit*, most probably used in the sense of binding or a bond. In both the Septuagint and the apostolic writings of the young church, *berit* is translated by the Greek term *diatheke*. The Latin term is *testamentum*, from *testare*, to bear witness.

Usually the covenant was accompanied by a sign or token to remind the parties of their obligations (e.g., Genesis 21:30; 31:44–45, 52; Joshua 24:27). The "sign of the covenant" is especially characteristic of the Priestly source. The Sabbath, the rainbow, and circumcision are the signs of the three great covenants established by God at the three critical stages of human history: the creation, the renewal of humanity after the deluge, and the beginning of the Hebrew nation. Circumcision came to be regarded as the most distinctive sign of the covenant, and is known as *berit milah*—"the covenant of circumcision."

The prophets, particularly Hosea, Jeremiah, and Ezekiel, expressed the idea of exclusive loyalty between God and Israel in the language of intimacy between wife and husband, a relationship also considered covenantal. Although the idea of marital love between God and Israel is not mentioned explicitly in the Torah, it seems to be present in a latent form. Following other gods is threatened by the statement: "For I the Lord your God am a jealous God" (Exodus 20:5; Deuteronomy 5:9; cf. Exodus 34:14; Joshua 24:19). The same root for "jealous" is used elsewhere in the technical sense of a husband who is jealous for his wife, and the verb "to whore after" is used for disloyalty. Furthermore, the formula expressing the covenantal relationship between God and Israel, "you will be my people and I will be your God" (Leviticus 26:12; Deuteronomy 29:12), is a legal formula taken from the sphere of marriage. The language of intimacy and tenderness descriptive of the relation between the people and God is Jewish language, borrowed by the church, which sometimes then claims that this language of intimacy transcends the arid and legalistic religion of Judaism.

The concept of the kingship of God in Israel also seems to have contributed to the conception of Israel as God's servant. The idea of the kingship of God was prevalent throughout the ancient Near East. In Israel, the idea was adopted before human kingship was established. Consequently, for hundreds of years the only kingship recognized and institutionalized in Israel was that of God. During the period of the judges, the Lord was the King of Israel (Judges 8:23; I Samuel 8:7; 10:19) and was not the projected image of Israel's earthly king.

The covenant between the Lord and Israel at Sinai is the original and fundamental covenant of the scriptures. But there is a tendency to read this covenant further back into history; so the J-document tells of the covenant between the Lord and Abram (Genesis 15:17–18) and in P the covenant is carried even further back to Noah (Genesis 9:8–17); the story stands as witness that God's covenant, though historically made with Israel, applies both to the whole human race and to the animal kingdom ("and with every living creature that is with you, the birds, the cattle, and every beast of the earth with you, as many as came out of the ark" (Genesis 9:10). As a further extension of the same principle, Ecclesiasticus 17:12 carries the covenant back to Adam: "He established with them an eternal covenant, and showed them his judgments."

The Lord is a God who initiates covenants, according to the Hebrew scriptures, and these covenants are God's ordinances. Indeed, "covenant making" is an attribute of the Lord expressed as *hesed*, mercy, steadfast love. So within the covenant with Israel we find further covenants. The promise to David (II Samuel 7:11–13:16) is reinterpreted as a covenant (II Samuel 23:5). The later covenants were reaffirmations in new situations of the original covenant. This is true of the new situations of the original covenant. This is true of the new covenant promised in Jeremiah 31:31–34. The content of this new covenant is the same as that of the original; only the form is different. Now the Torah is to be written on tablets of human hearts, not of stone.

Of the themes we have seen in the Hebrew Bible, two in particular are worthy of mention as they develop in Judaism. These are the grace of God in electing and establishing a covenant with Israel and the relation between particularity and universality in the covenant. Christian interpretation of Jewish life and thought has usually paid insufficient attention to both.

We begin with some rabbinic comments on grace.

"Deal with thy servant according to thy *hesed* (grace)" (Psalm 119:124). Perhaps thou hast pleasure in our good works? Merit and good works we have not: act towards us in *hesed*. The men of old whom thou didst redeem, thou didst not redeem through their works: but thou didst act towards them in *hesed* and didst redeem them. So do thou with us.

There are ten words for prayer. One of them is appeal for grace. Of all the ten, Moses used only this one, as it is said, "And I appealed for grace with the Lord at that time" (Deuteronomy 3:23). R. Johanan said: Hence you may learn that man has no claim upon God; for Moses, the greatest of the prophets, came before God only with an appeal for grace . . . . God said to Moses, "I will be gracious to whom I will be gracious. To him who has anything to his account with me, I show mercy, that is, I deal with him through the attribute of mercy; but to him who has nothing I am gracious, that is, I deal with him by gift and gratis."

"Thou didst lead them in thy mercy" (*hesed*) (Exodus 15:13). Thou hast wrought grace (*hesed*) for us, for we had no works, as it is said, "I will mention the lovingkindnesses of the Lord" (Isaiah 63:7), and again, "I will sing of the mercies of the Lord forever" (Psalm 89:1). And, from the beginning, the world was built only upon grace (*hesed*), as it is said, "I declare the world is built upon grace" (Psalm 89:2).[13]

Deuteronomy 7:7 states: "It was not because you were more in number than any other people that the Lord set his love upon you and chose you, for you were the fewest of all peoples." On this the rabbinic commentary remarks:

Not because you are greater than other nations did I choose you, not because you obey my injunctions more than the nations; for they follow my commandments, even though they were not bidden to do it, and also magnify my name more than you, as it is said, "From the rising of the sun, even unto the going down of the same, my name is great among the Gentiles" (Malachi 1:11).[14]

In this just-cited passage, we see that the implication entailed in an emphasis on the radical grace of God is increasingly realized: that God's covenanting grace is extended to all people; it is all-inclusive in scope. The prophets had already articulated this theme: "Blessed be Egypt my people, and Assyria the work of my hands, and Israel my heritage" (Isaiah 19:25). "Are you not like the Ethiopians to me, O people of Israel? says the Lord. Did I not bring up Israel from the land of Egypt, and the Philistines from Caphtor and the Syrians from Kir?" (Amos 9:7)

The logic of grace is a universalizing, inclusive logic. Being overwhelmed with the sense of being loved by God is only adequately articulated in the language of inclusion—I, too, am included, even me! Knowing oneself to be loved by God brings with it an amazement at being included. So the rabbis' claim for Israel was that, while Israel was indeed the first to be included in God's covenant, Israel was by no means to consider itself exclusively so embraced. God's original promise was understood by the community of faith to have been given to Abraham so that "all the families of the earth" shall be blessed (Genesis 12:3). The reading of the covenant back into the stories of Adam, Abraham, and Noah, increasingly universalizing and mono-theizing it, is a working out of the logic of grace. The covenant tends to become an eternal covenant. This is not to say that the faith of Israel was never parochial or nationalistic, that the covenant was never regarded as a private affair of the people of Israel, but to affirm with the Jewish thinker Manfred Vogel that such a "stance does not really represent the authentic expression of Judaism."[15]

Increasingly it was realized that God's all-inclusive love extended concretely to Gentiles, and we have seen prophetic comments to this effect. Isaiah 45:22–23, speaking for God, says:

"Turn to me and be saved, all the ends of the earth! For I am God, and there is no other. By myself I have sworn, from my mouth has gone forth in righteousness a word that shall not return: 'To me every knee shall bow, every tongue shall swear.'"

The rabbinic comment on this was: "Though his goodness, loving-kindness, and mercy are with Israel, his right hand is always stretched forward to receive *all* those who come into the world, . . . as it is said, 'Unto me every knee shall bow, every tongue shall swear.'"[16] Jeremiah calls God "the King of the Gentiles" (10:7) and Isaiah says:

"It is too light a thing that you should be my servant to raise up the tribes of Jacob and to restore the preserved of Israel; I will give you as a light to the nations [Gentiles], that my salvation may reach to the end of the earth" (49:6).

The theme of the universality of God was implemented by emphasis on the Covenant of God with Noah and on the accompanying Noachide laws, the seven laws regarded by rabbinic tradition as the minimal moral duties enjoined by the Torah on all people. Every non-Jew is a "son of the covenant of Noah," a technical term referring to all human beings except Jews. Everyone who accepts the minimal obligations of this covenant is to be regarded as a "resident stranger" and comes under the Levitical commandment toward strangers:

When a stranger sojourns with you in your land, you shall not do him wrong. The stranger who sojourns with you shall be to you as the native among you, and you shall love him as yourself; for you were strangers in the land of Egypt; I am the Lord your God (Leviticus 19:33–34).

Any *hasid* (righteous person) among the Gentiles has a share in the world to come. Such a person need not become a Jew, but need only keep the seven Noachide commandments. The six negative Noachide laws prohibit idolatry, blasphemy, bloodshed, sexual sins, theft, and eating from a living animal. The positive commandment is the injunction to establish a legal system. Muslims have been regarded as Noachides in view of their strict monotheism and Christians have been so regarded since the later Middle Ages in spite of what is regarded as *shituf* (association with idolatry) in our theological concepts (especially the trinity and the incarnation). How adequately this Noachide covenant expresses Christian self-understanding is a topic to which we will return.

The judgment that Christianity is to be regarded as a kind of monotheism and its corollary that Christians are not idolaters is found in the *Shulchan Aruch* (1542), *Yoreh Deah* 151. This development continued in the seventeenth and eighteenth centuries, particularly in the work of Rabbi Jacob Emden. Emden argued that Jesus never meant "to abrogate the Torah so far as Jews were concerned, but had wished merely to spread Jewish tenets and the Seven Noachide Commandments among non-Jews."[17]

It was left to Franz Rosenzweig to attempt, in *The Star of redemption*, to frame a statement that would manage to regard Judaism and Christianity as equally valid and mutually complementary. Judaism is the Life—the faith that was with God at the beginning—while Christianity is the way toward God of those not yet with God. Judaism is the fire, Christianity the rays. Judaism is the star of redemption turned in upon itself, Christianity the cross with its arms branched outward. This view nonetheless puts Christianity in a subordinate and dependent position. For Rosenzweig, Christianity remains second-rate and inferior in relation to Judaism. As he wrote in his famous letter to Pastor Ehrenburg: "Christianity cleaves to Jesus because it knows that the Father can be reached only through him. Precisely the good Christian forgets God Himself in the face of the Lord Jesus."[18] Although Rosenzweig tried to move things further along, it remains the case with him that Christians are Noachides dangerously flirting with idolatry.

Jewish inclusiveness and universalism with regard to the covenant have been more right, considerably, than typical Christian exclusivism and parochialism. Yet it is clear that a view of Christians as Noachides with a little *shituf* thrown in is utterly unacceptable from a Christian point of view. A Noachide does not even have to know God, but simply refrain from serving false gods. Yet if the Christian claim that having Jesus Christ as Lord is existentially the same as having the God of Israel as God,[19] an interpretation with which I agree, then the Noachide/*shituf* interpretation of Christianity is unacceptable to Christians.

What I have called the logic of grace means that as Judaism interprets and reinterprets its tradition, it tends to monotheize and universalize its understanding of itself. Had it not been for centuries of Christian belligerence toward Jews, manifest in attempts at conversion, population expulsion, mass murder, forced baptisms, child-stealing, and so on, this logic of grace would probably have worked out a more forthcoming and assertive proclamation of the radically free and universally available grace of God. The Christian tradition bears a lot of responsibility for the Jewish view of it as second-rate. Christians cannot expect both to keep Jews on the defensive and to hear from them more adequate views of the covenantal reality of Christianity.

Yet the thesis of this paper is not that all Jews have been all right all along on all issues on which they have differed from Christians, but only that most Jews have been more right than most Christians.

In addition to seeing God's covenantal grace as eternal, universal, and inclusive of Gentiles, there is also the claim, as we have seen, that the covenant is a gracious gift, founded on no works-righteousness. God gives the covenant without regard to merit, out of *hesed*—steadfast love—and God remains steadfast in faithfulness to the covenant even when the other party is not faithful. As stated in *Exodus Rabbah*, XLI.4:

> It is usual for an earthly king to bestow gifts on his subjects and furnish supplies for them, as long as they are loyal to him, being then obliged to support them; but as soon as they rebel against him, God forbid, he has no obligation whatsoever towards them, and he immediately cuts off their supplies as a penalty for denying his royal authority. With God, however, it is not so; for while they were busy provoking Him to anger on earth, He was occupied in heaven with bestowing upon them a Torah that is instinct with life.

III. Covenant in Christianity

In Judaism we have seen a strong tendency to universalize the idea of covenant; it is given to Israel on behalf of all humanity. Characteristic of Christianity is a movement in the opposite direction, to affirm the election of the Gentiles at the cost of the rejection of the Jews and to argue that the covenant has passed to a new people or, alternatively, that God made a brand new covenant (the old one being intended only provisionally) with a brand new people. One can find this interpretation in so many sources from Barnabas to Barth that here I shall only limn it. The *adversus Judaeos* mode of thinking is a double-edged model, a systematic pattern of thought for understanding both Judaism and Christianity.

On this model, Judaism was portrayed as barren, defiant, and antiquarian, clinging to what is past and resisting the novel. Judaism represents both a religious system and a people who, because they defy their own election, repudiate God and are disclaimed by God. Their repudiation of God is typified in the trail of crimes (culminating in deicide) that they committed, whereas they could have responded faithfully to the messengers whom God sent to them. This pattern of thought began some time before the gospels were finally redacted and is observable in them (see the parable of the wicked tenants in Mark 12:1–12 and its parallels in Matthew 21:33–46 and Luke 20:9–19.

The former inhabitants of the vineyard, namely Israel, will be destroyed and new tenants installed in their place).

The *adversus Judaeos* ideology also provides a model of Christianity, portraying it as a religious system and a people of innovation, universal rather than particular, spiritual rather than carnal, obedient rather than defiant. This universal new people inherits all the promises given to the prophets, while all prophetic denunciations are applied to Jews. It is also a model for how to pray, how to act, how to interpret scripture—not as the Jews do these things but in our new, spiritual, and better way.

Consonant with this are the two major themes of rejection/election and inferiority/superiority. According to the first, Gentile Christians replace Jews in the economy of salvation. On this point, Manfred Vogel is quite correct in asserting that the difference between claiming that the covenant has been abrogated and claiming that it has been fulfilled is "a distinction merely of degree, but not of kind."[20] This motif dwells heavily on the "two peoples" allegory, the elder/younger brother stories, and the reason for rejection: the trail of crimes. According to the second theme, the Jewish way (Torah) and worship are inferior, while Christian ethics and worship are superior and fulfill biblical promises. Jewish exegesis and interpretation of the Bible are "blind." Only Christians can rightly interpret the "Old" Testament, which is called "old" because it no longer applies, and its meaning turns entirely upon the "New" Testament.

The *adversus Judaeos* argument is an ideological deformation of the truth of the gospel for the sake of social interest. From very early times—sometime between Paul's writings and the writing of Mark—the church increasingly couched its message in the form of the *adversus Judaeos* ideology. When, later, the church gained influence and power, the same ideology was translated into a legal structure that excluded Jews, marginalized them socially, politically, and economically and created an image of Jews as "suited only for slaughter."[21] Hence the gospel, distorted, came to promote the oppression of the Jewish people.

IV. Reversing the Reversal

Two questions must now be addressed. First, is there an alternative to the *adversus Judaeos* tradition that has a better claim to being Christian, to being appropriate to the gospel, than does this tradition itself? Second, assuming a positive answer to the first question, can process thought help to articulate this alternative position in a way that is plausible and that shows the implausibility of anti-Judaism?

The answer to the first question is affirmative: there is an alternative that has a better claim to being Christian than does the *adversus Judaeos* ideology. This point is established as follows. To begin with, the earliest witness of faith to Jesus Christ was itself thoroughly Jewish, i.e., not Gentile. In whatever way this initial witness may be reconstructed, there is no possibility of regarding it as having anything in common with *gentilizing anti-Judaism*. The earliest church may have been at odds with other kinds of Jews, and may have said nasty things about them. The Qumran documents show that it was possible for some Jews to be disagreeable about "the Jews." At the same time, it is remarkable that there is not more evidence for hostility between the earliest Jerusalem church and the surrounding community. Had Rome and the local power structure wished to, they could have wiped out this church rather easily. As late as Paul's time "the apostles in Jerusalem were not being persecuted. Both his letters and Acts depict him as visiting them with no difficulty."[22] Gentilizing anti-Judaism is a later development. Therefore, if we take the earliest Christian witness as the norm of appropriateness for Christian theology, a methodological point that has, to my satisfaction, been established,[23] then supersessionist (displacement) understandings of the covenant have no place in it. This earliest witness, when demythologized (as the prophetic nature of biblical thought requires), testifies to the all-inclusive love of God and, therefore, to the command of God for justice to all. Such a promise and command are incompatible with the ideology of displacement.

The next response to the first question is to point out that the displacement myth has no warrant in the theology of Paul. Two dilemmas confront any interpreter of Paul. If we assume that Paul wrote to Jews about Judaism and its problems, then we have to conclude with H. J. Schoeps that Paul did not know what he was talking about, that he was fundamentally confused.[24] If he was so confused, there is little point in reading him. If he is to be taken seriously, we must conclude that he was not complaining about Judaism but about Gentiles playing at being Jewish by having themselves circumcised. The second dilemma has to do with Paul's commitment that he would go to the Gentiles and that the other apostles would go to the Jews (Galatians 2:1–10). We can take Paul at his word on this, that he went only to Gentiles, or we can decide that he was a liar. If the latter, again, there is no reason to take him seriously. If we should take him seriously, we have to conclude that he went only to Gentiles and discussed with them *their* problems.

Interpreting Paul from his own writings (not from Acts, the pastoral epistles, or the letters of dubious authorship, such as II Thessalonians), we see that he interprets his dramatic experience with Christ on the model of the call to a prophet to go to the Gentiles (Galatians 1:15–17; cf. Isaiah 49:1, 6, Jeremiah 1:5). As Krister Stendahl has amply demonstrated, it is inappropriate to speak of this as a conversion from one religion to another.[25] Also we see that his letters are addressed to Gentiles: for example, "you turned to God from idols" (I Thessalonians 1:9); "when you were Gentiles you were led astray to dumb idols" (I Corinthians 12:2); "when you did not know God, you were in bondage to gods who essentially are not" (Galatians 4:8).

On the relation of Gentile Jesus-followers to Jews and the role of Christ, Paul speaks as follows: "For I tell you that Christ became a servant to the circumcised to show God's truthfulness, in order to *confirm* the promises given to the patriarchs, and in order that the Gentiles might glorify God for his mercy. As it is written, 'Therefore I will praise thee among the Gentiles' " (Romans 15:8–9; emphasis added). Paul's language here is typical of him; he never says that Jesus Christ fulfills the promises. Jesus is the one who re-presents God's act of including Gentiles, an act that is a renewal of God's prior acts and promises in this regard. There is much more to Paul's thought than this, but enough has been said to indicate that the displacement ideology finds no warrant in him.[26]

There is, then, an alternative and more appropriately Christian position than the supersessionist ideology. We find it in the earliest Christian witness and in Paul. Even in the rest of the New Testament, deeply affected as much of it is with this ideology, we find no mention of the church as the "new Israel" nor any claim that salvation is made possible only through Christ. This alternative position would say something like this: in the providence of God, Jesus of Nazareth became the one by whom, through the preaching of the church, Gentile Christians came to understand themselves in relation to the God of Israel as the gracious and creative ground and end of their being. We who sat in darkness have seen a great light in Jesus Christ, "a light for revelation to the Gentiles and for glory to . . . [the] people of Israel" (Luke 2:32). Further, this spreading of the covenantal relation with the gracious God testifies not to the falsity but to the verity of that which had previously been known only by Jews: the "conversion of the Gentiles is both the effect of truth and the test of truth."[27]

We turn now to the second question, whether process thought can articulate this alternative position so as to show its credibility? Central to process thought is a well worked-out theory of internal and external relations. Jewish thinkers point out that covenant is a relational category delineating "not individual entities in themselves but the relation between them."[28] Furthermore, this kind of relationality between God and people requires God to be thought of as a Thou, One who is free and conscious.[29] The question whether process thought can adequately articulate the covenantal reality seems to be stood on its head: Can any other position articulate the covenant adequately? No other theology speaks coherently of the all-encompassing divine mystery as "the" person in the strict sense of the term,[30] nor works out a comprehensive theory of internal and external relations of which God is the eminent or perfect case. That is, God is externally related to all other individuals as their creator, the one by knowing whom all the others are enabled to come into being, graciously empowered to become and, at the same time, commanded to attain and contribute, the highest relevant possibility available to them. God is the one person known by all others, to which knowledge their very being attests (although it is quite clear that they/we do not all or always know God *as* God).

Also, as internally related, bonded, to all others, God is the only one who knows all others and who takes all others into account, the one to whom all others matter, who bestows upon their fleeting days abiding worth. God is the chief exemplification of the metaphysical principles and therefore supremely free, primordially self-determining and *causa sui*.[31] God is the reason for the decisions that God makes. Thus, the metaphors of process thought (appealing for the imaginative leap that they require) articulate a view of the divine mystery that gives voice to God's covenanting grace on the very points that are important: a covenanting God must be personal, social, and free, not an "it."

Sometimes we process thinkers, trying to express ourselves economically, shortchange the radicality of our perspective and thereby leave room for misapprehension. Let me stress, then, that this is in no way a "substance" point of view. God in process thought does not offer an initial aim to an actual entity that is already there. The actual entity is a unit of becoming that begins as a many; the one novel occasion is enabled to arise and become only because of the initial aim offered by God. God is the creator of the world, without whom there would be nothing (which is not the same thing as saying that there ever was a nothing), and is the gracious ground of the becoming and being of each of us. As such, God offers us the past with our perspective on it, our freedom and agency, the possibility of efficacy upon the future, and the promise that we count with God who everlastingly presides over the world with a tender care that nothing be lost. This God is the same one with whom all others also count and is the God of a quite singular promise and demand: the promise is that our life is grounded in God's free and gracious action toward us and that its final meaning is found in and only in God's consequent love of us; the demand is that, because God also loves all others, so must we exercise love and justice (justice being the social form of love) toward them.

This metaphysical model, which process thinkers say sheds *some* light on the circumambient mystery, makes sense of a certain view of the Christian covenant with God: the particularity, the Jewishness of Jesus, is required by the very universality of the gospel. That is, Jesus' Jewishness was a necessary condition whereby the peoples of the world, the Gentiles, could have access to God's gracious gift and irrevocable calling. This new access is not a matter of an ontological change, but of an epistemological one. *Coram deo* all people were, are, and will be responsible for knowing God and for understanding themselves in relation to the one who is the gracious and creative alpha and omega of their being. Ontologically, the covenant is universal. Epistemologically, it only includes those who have been given to understand themselves in relation to the God who continually recreates them transformatively out of their narrow and sinful pasts, and who decide to appropriate that understanding in the most passionate and personal way. The new covenant, then, is a re-presentation, a re-newal of the same covenant, not somehow fulfilled and transcended but, as Paul put it, ratified, confirmed (Romans 15:8). The Gentiles are now to understand themselves as children of Abraham and by grace are freed to keep all the laws summarized in the dual commandment of love of God and the neighbor.

I now turn to the argument that process thought can *in one respect* intelligibly articulate this alterntive view of the covenant. It can express a view of covenant that does not entail the abrogation of the covenant with Jews. However, the emphasis on what Paul calls God's "irrevocable" call (Romans 11:29) is usually made by theologians who base their argument on the consideration that God, by God's very own constitution, cannot change in any respect, for example cannot change the divine mind or act differently in one situation from another, because such change would be incompatible with the divine perfection. Process theologians obviously do not hold these views, and might

be led to disagree with Paul on this point. Furthermore, I have demonstrated that process theologians (with some exceptions) have fallen
into the supersessionist trap as quickly if not as deeply as any other
group of Christian theologians.[32] In that demonstration, I tried to
show that the fall into supersessionism on the part of process theologians was only possible on the pain of incoherence, trying thereby
to indicate that process thought itself was not the reason for supersessionism in process thinkers. The reason, rather, is that, on Christology,
process thinkers, as a rule, have been less willing to revolutionize the
Christian tradition than they have been with regard to the doctrine
of God. Thus, the problem is that process theologians are too traditional, not too process-oriented, in their Christologies. The last task
of this essay will be, briefly, to warrant this claim or to indicate how
it can be warranted.

By rights, a process thinker has to agree with the *Exodus Rabbah*
that God, because God is not like an earthly king, cannot be unfaithful
to God's fundamentally gracious relation to the world. The covenant,
in any form, re-presents God's relational bond to the creatures and
God's intent that they be bonded in love and justice to one another.
No more than Jewish theology can process theology literalize the
action of God in covenanting with a people. Literalized myth images
God as an earthly ruler who, in wrath, might empty the vineyard. The
prophetic insight, which rejects as idolatry the identification of God
with an earthly ruler or envisaging God in such terms, pointedly
asserts that God is not such an in-the-world-being, one among others,
but the one who transcends and includes all. Process theology must
agree that what it calls God's categorical uniqueness requires a deliter-
alizing and indeed a rejection of the notion that God covenants with
human beings conditionally and abrogates covenants conditionally.
Covenant is a sign of God's *hesed*, or steadfast love, and as such not
something or a sign of something that God can break.

Exodus 32:9–14, 31–32 depicts God as willing to consume the
people with wrath because of their sin and Moses as so identifying
with the people that, in his intercession with God, he would prefer
to be blotted out of God's book than that the people go unforgiven.
Paul reminds us of Moses in Romans 8:3, when he says ". . . . I could
wish that I were myself accursed and cut off from Christ for the sake
of my brethren, . . ." Moses was offered a deal—that God would destroy
the people and with Moses make a new one—and refused it. The
people were saved and God learned a lesson of faithfulness. Supersessionist theology makes precisely the assumption about Jesus Christ
that Exodus 32 denies about Moses: it seems ready to believe that

Jesus assented to precisely the offer that Moses declined. Moses is obviously the more efficacious mediator, Jesus the shadowy, imperfect approximation, to reverse the usual run of typology.

Process theology has to affirm two things: first, the mode of God's action upon the world is always the same. The way God acts in Christ is disclosive of how God acts everywhere and anywhere. This follows from the strictly universal character of God's agency. Second, God's particular grace for special occasions, the initial aims around which each actual entity arises, is always in higher-grade occasions at the kind of possibility that will enhance both the occasion's ability to be sensitive to its environment, to be more adequately related to, and aware of, those around, and to overcome exclusivism and dichotomies in its experience. "Now process," says Whitehead, "is the way by which the universe escapes the exclusions of inconsistency."[33] The *adversus Judaeos* ideology is nothing but the inconsistent exclusion of a people from the grace of an utterly gratuitous God.

V. Epilogue

The work of John B. Cobb, Jr., in collaboration with Joseph C. Hough, Jr., on a proposed curriculum for theological education in America articulates a view of Christian identity *vis-à-vis* Judaism that is radical in its implications for that curriculum. Cobb faces fully the consequences of the history of Christian anti-Judaism, rejects the exclusivism of it, and defines Christianity as "that movement . . . in which the efficacy of Israel's witness to God's creative and redemptive work has been mediated through Jesus and the apostolic witness to God's activity in him."[34] On that kind of basis, he and Hough propose a new theological curriculum focused on this new understanding of Christian identity.

This is the first thorough-going reconception of ministerial education based on the kinds of considerations discussed in this essay. If picked up, it will have widespread, beneficial effect. I mention it here because what Rabbi Yeshua of Nazareth taught us long ago remains true: By their fruits you shall know them.

Notes

1.   Charles Hartshorne, *Omnipotence and Other Theological Mistakes* (Albany: State University of New York Press, 1984), 98.

2.   Robert P. Ericksen, *Theologians Under Hitler: Gerhard Kittel, Paul Althaus, and Emanuel Hirsch* (New Haven: Yale University Press, 1985).

3.   Arthur C. Cochrane, *The Church's Confession Under Hitler* (Philadelphia: Westminster, 1962), 222–23.

4.   Ibid., 239–40.

5.   Pinchas E. Lapide, "Christians and Jews—A New Protestant Beginning," *Journal of Ecumenical Studies*, 12/4 (Fall 1975), 36.

6.   Karl Barth, *Church Dogmatics*, Vol. 2, Part 2, trans. G.W. Bromiley (Edinburgh: T. & T. Clark, 1957), 236.

7.   Karl Barth, "The Jewish Problem and the Christian Answer," in *Against the Stream* (London: SCM Press, 1954), 200.

8.   Karl Barth, *Church Dogmatics*, Vol. 2, Part 2, 206–07.

9.   Ibid., 208–09.

10.   Michael Dov Weissmandl, *Min Hametzar* (Jerusalem, reprint edition, n.d.). Cited in *Auschwitz: Beginning of a New Era*, Eva Fleischner, ed. (New York: KTAV Publishing House, 1977), 24.

11.   Gunther Lewy, *The Catholic Church and Nazi Germany* (New York: McGraw-Hill, 1974), 294.

12.   Saul Friedlander, *Pius XII and the Third Reich* (New York: Knopf, 1966), 91–92.

13.   H. Loewe and C.G. Montefiore, eds., *A Rabbinic Anthology* (New York: Schocken Books, 1974), 91, 89.

14.   Jacob Neusner, ed., *Understanding Jewish Theology* (New York: KTAV Publishing House, 1973), 70.

15.   Manfred Vogel, "Covenant and the Interreligious Encounter," in *Issues in the Jewish-Christian Dialogue*, Helga Croner and Leon Klenicki, eds. (New York: Paulist Press, 1979), 75.

16.   Jacob Neusner, *Understanding Jewish Theology*, 72.

17.   Rabbi Jacob Emden cited in David Ellenson, "Jewish Covenant and Christian Trinitarianism," in *Jewish Civilization: Essays and Studies*, Ronald A. Brauner, ed. (Philadelphia: Reconstructionist Rabbinical College, 1985), 88.

18.   Franz Rosenzweig cited in F. E. Talmage, ed., *Disputation and Dialogue: Readings in the Jewish-Christian Encounter* (New York: KTAV Publishing House, 1975), 245.

19.   Schubert M. Ogden, *The Reality of God and Other Essays* (New York: Harper & Row, 1966), 201.

20.   Manfred Vogel, "Covenant and the Interreligious Encounter," 70.

21.   John Chrysostom cited in Clark M. Williamson, *Has God Rejected His People?* (Nashville: Abingdon Press, 1982), 90.

22.   E. P. Sanders, *Jesus and Judaism* (Philadelphia: Fortress Press, 1985), 282.

23.   Schubert M. Ogden, *The Point of Christology* (San Francisco: Harper & Row, 1982), 97–105.

24.   H. J. Schoeps, *Paul: The Theology of the Apostle in the Light of Jewish Religious History,* trans. H. Knight (Philadelphia: Westminster Press, 1961).

25.   Krister Stendahl, *Paul Among Jews and Gentiles* (Philadelphia: Fortress Press, 1976), 7–12.

26.   Lloyd Gaston, "Paul and the Torah," in *Antisemitism and the Foundations of Christianity,* Alan Davies, ed. (New York: Paulist Press, 1979), 48–71.

27.   Alfred North Whitehead, *Religion in the Making* (New York: Meridian Books, 1960), 133.

28.   Manfred Vogel, "Covenant and the Interreligious Encounter," 63.

29.   Ibid.

30.   Charles Hartshorne, *The Divine Relativity: A Social Conception of God* (New Haven: Yale University Press, 1948), 142–47.

31.   Alfred North Whitehead, *Process and Reality: An Essay in Cosmology,* Corrected Edition, David Ray Griffin and Donald W. Sherburne, eds. (New York: The Free Press, 1978), 343, 88.

32.   Clark M. Williamson, "Anti-Judaism in Process Christologies?" *Process Studies,* 10/3–4 (Fall-Winter 1980), 73–92.

33.   Alfred North Whitehead, *Modes of Thought* (New York: The Free Press, 1938), 54.

34.   John B. Cobb, Jr., and Joseph C. Hough, Jr., *Christian Identity and Theological Education* (Chico, Calif.: Scholars Press, 1985), 21–24.

Chapter 12

In the Presence of Mystery: Process Theology and Interfaith Relations

Anson Laytner

To read an essay arguing that Christian supersessionism must be rejected as immoral and unChristian is both distressing and encouraging. It is distressing to realize that, fifty years after the Holocaust, the subject remains one of discussion in some Christian circles. But it is simultaneously encouraging to know that the issue nonetheless is—better late than never—finally being addressed constructively by some Christians.

Clark Williamson's essay marks another positive step in the reformation of Christian attitudes toward Judaism. His clear understanding of the relationship between the Holocaust and the Christian *adversus Judaeos* ideology, his appreciation of both the particular and universal aspects of the Jewish concept of the covenant, and his willingness to address the need for changes in Christian attitudes toward Judaism represent real progress toward a reconciliation between the two faiths.

But, as Williamson writes, "We cannot discuss theological questions, particularly such matters as covenant and election, in an ahistorical manner." The impetus on the Christian side for building this new relationship may, unfortunately, be the Holocaust, but the context for this new relationship rests in understanding how relations between Judaism and Christianity were strained from the outset. To do so, one must return to the origins of the conflict nearly two thousand years ago. What is learned from the historic separation of Christianity from Judaism may prove helpful to those of us interested in forging a new relationship based on mutual respect, understanding, and acceptance of both our similarities and our differences.

I. Jewish-Christian Relations

What many people fail to realize about the two faiths is that Judaism is both mother and sister to Christianity (and to Islam also, for that matter). Christianity has always loved Judaism the mother, the Judaism of its "Old Testament," but it has always loathed Judaism the sister, the Judaism of the Pharisaic sages and the Rabbis, which was developing at the very time that Christianity was. As a result of the Jewish revolts against Rome, and through the success of its Gentile mission, Christianity left the Judaic soil from which it had grown, to develop along a new route. As it grew to become the religion of the Roman Empire, its mother-sister completed its transformation from a Temple-based Judaism to Rabbinic Judaism, remaining an extremely vital religion in its own right and exerting a powerful influence upon Christianity throughout the early centuries of the Common Era. Because Christianity "froze" Judaism as the "Old Testament" mother-faith, and hated its Rabbinic-Jewish sister-faith, the relationship between the two during this period was primarily one of conflict and competition between a growing and mission-oriented Church and an equally vital and proselytizing Judaism.[1]

Only when Christianity became the imperial religion did this relationship begin to change, with Christianity using its newly acquired political power to begin restraining first Jewish proselytism and eventually Jewish life itself. With some few bright exceptions, so relations remained in the European world up until the modern era (French Revolution), when they finally appear to have begun to change slowly—and not without tragic steps backwards—for the better. This is the broad historical context in which Williamson places his essay on covenant and election; it is against this backdrop that process theology will have to act if it is to help heal this centuries-long breach.

If Jews and Christians today are to begin building a new relationship, then an excellent place to start would seem to be in their mutual recognition that, along with Islam, they shared a common purpose, as Williamson rightly observes. In traditional terms—indeed the very terms that may have appealed to the pagan population of the Greco-Roman world—that mission was "that all the peoples of the earth may know that YHVH is God and there is none else" (I Kings 8:60) and, knowing this, would "walk in His paths" (Isaiah 2:2f). Each of the three great monotheist faiths contributed to the spread of this message, even though, in most times and places, members of all three faiths were oblivious to this fact and detested one another bitterly.[2]

A cardinal principle of process theology is that reality is in constant flux. As generations grow up and pass away, so do their perceptions of reality. The processive reality that led to the evolution of Christianity and Rabbinic Judaism is long past, as are the realities that led to centuries of conflict. Recognizing this fact can serve as a major step toward effecting a Christian-Jewish reconciliation. Because all religions evolve in time and space, Christians ought to free themselves from viewing Judaism in only its Old Testament or even New Testament Pharisaic modes, and Jews need to stop seeing Christianity as a Jewish heresy and as an oppressor. Both traditions live in the present, not the past—even though the past continues to exert powerful influences on us, the living. We need to give one another the spiritual space in which to grow together.

Much work is already being undertaken by scholars of both faiths in this regard, and Williamson's work is part of this noble endeavor.[3] He cites the impact of the Holocaust on contemporary Christian thinking with regard to Judaism, but I think three other factors are at least equally important in promoting a Christian change of heart toward Judaism. First and foremost, I think that the "wall of separation" between church and state in this country, which has thus far prevented the marriage of any particular faith with the power of government, has had an impact on American religion far greater than many have realized. Second, the revolutionary American model of church-state relations continues to exert a great impact around the globe, even where it is condemned. With the state officially neutral, our various religions have had to eschew direct political power, which has meant more tolerance on the whole. (Not that some groups in this country haven't tried to take direct political power both in the past and the present.)[4] A corollary of this official disinterest is that many consider religion to be of lesser importance than it is elsewhere, much as one's ethnicity, even in this age of multiculturalism, is still less polarizing here than it is in other parts of the world. Third, the rise of the cult of science—and the triumph of science over traditional religion—as the ideology of the modern world has also diminished religion's power (and, hence, its ability to do harm as well as good) in much of the world. Consequently, with fewer vested interests and less prestige, our religions can afford to coexist peacefully and even to cooperate with one another.

All this, in my opinion, has been for the better. In the past hundred years—from the first World Parliament of Religions at the

Chicago World's Fair until the Centennial in Chicago in 1993—we have witnessed the birth of a worldwide interfaith movement and the efforts of many people of many different faiths to overcome past misconceptions and hatreds in their common endeavor to find shared spiritual ground.

One possible route to a full reconciliation between Judaism and Christianity today would be to follow along the path already taken by those whom both faiths have rejected for backsliding, namely the Judeo-Christians, past and present. Jews still shun them for embracing Jesus as the Messiah, and many Christians find their observance of circumcision, Shabbat, and other Jewish holy days, their keeping kosher, and their praying with the Hebrew liturgy to be as perplexing and unpalatable today as in days of old.

But, by living with a foot in two different faiths, these doubly fringe groups point to a truth that normative Christianity and Judaism have both sought to ignore: that Jesus was a Jew and that his way was a Jewish path. It is not necessary for Jews to accept Jesus as the Messiah, nor is it important that Christians live a Jewish lifestyle, but the more that Jews and Christians can regard Jesus as a great charismatic Jewish teacher and look upon the early church as one of the Jewish movements of the turbulent first century C.E., the more progress on the road to reconciliation will have been made.[5]

II. Process Theology and Interfaith Dialogue

It seems to me that the real question Jews and Christians ought to be asking themselves today is what meaning terms like *election* can have in a world in which all faiths can equally lay claim to the divine. This, ironically, is more a problem for Christianity than Judaism, even though the concept of "chosenness" lies at the heart of traditional Judaism. However, as Williamson shows, in Judaism this concept is more than balanced by other concepts: the Noahide covenant, the *hasidei oomot ha-olam* (righteous ones of the world's nations), and the emphasis on righteous living as God's primary measure for humanity.

The questions that Williamson asks of contemporary Christianity regarding Judaism, and the solutions he looks to process theology to provide, pale beside the questions that must be asked, and the answers that must be provided, regarding those religions that are much more distant theologically than Judaism is from Christianity. If some Christians are only now learning to accept the idea that God's grace extends to the Jewish people, what of those peoples and faiths beyond the covenanting tradition? Is Christianity ready to accept the concept that all religions may be equally valid (or even partially valid) paths to that which it calls God and Christ? And if it is ready to do so, is it really prepared to give up its nearly two thousand-year-old "mission to the Gentiles," all of whom, whether in Africa or Asia (or, for some Protestant groups, in Catholic South America), have perfectly wonderful and equally legitimate religious traditions of their own? To misquote Hartshorne:

> Can I take seriously the idea that it just might be that *any religion*, in its differences from Christians, has been *equally* right all along on some issues? If the answer is "Yes," then perhaps there is no *Christian supremacism*. If "No," then I have my suspicions.

For Christianity to seek a reconciliation with Judaism is well and good (and long overdue); the real task for the twenty-first century will be for Christianity, in particular, to extend this reconciliation and loving acceptance to the other religions of humanity as well.

Clark Williamson looks to process theology to assist in this reconciliation and, like him, I believe that process theology is uniquely able to play this important role.[6] First, process theology is a product of our times and thus takes for granted certain things that we all acknowledge: the relative positions of science and religion in our society, for example, and the growth in interfaith contacts over the past century. It recognizes that advances in technology, particularly industrial and military technology, have made us more aware than ever of our interdependency on one another and on the natural world, just as advances in travel and communication have made greater human interaction possible. Ironically, as our world has gotten smaller and more interdependent, God, as traditionally conceived, has grown more remote. As we have learned more about ourselves and our world, we are less certain about what we know about God.

Because process theology bases itself on this understanding of things, it is less inclined than more traditional theologies to say what or whom God is; it is less certain of what we really can know about the divine (as opposed to what we say we know or what we believe). Process theology recognizes that all depictions of the divine are human expressions, and thus are limited by personal, historical, and cultural constraints. God, however, is ultimately unknowable—or if knowable, the experience is ineffable; therefore our descriptions of the divine are all flawed. Not only does this stance make process theology very compatible with certain Jewish perspectives, it also makes process theology uniquely able to address the subject of interfaith reconciliation. I would suggest that the unknowability of reality allows room for genuine dialogue and growth among people of diverse faith traditions.

Judaism has traditionally accepted the premise that God is essentially unknowable and unnameable, as the Divine Reality Itself purportedly told Moses on several occasions (Exodus 3:13–14 and Exodus 33:18–20). "The Lord," YHVH, is literally (and grammatically) pure potential being, indefinable, and ineffable. The Name (as traditional Jews call God) means "I am who/what I am" or "I will be who/what I will be." Thus "God" represents the infusion of constant creativity—pure positive potentiality—into the world, which in turn gives us the power and autonomy to live and grow, both individually and collectively. Supremely pragmatic for a religion, Judaism basically says: "We can't really say anything concrete about God, but we know how we are supposed to act." (See Deuteronomy 29:28 and 30:11–14, for example.) Among classic Jewish theologies, Maimonides' *via negativa* stands out as the most respectful of all we don't know about God.

Process theology's point of departure is very similar to this Jewish way of perceiving "God." On the one hand, "I am" represents the primordial God, the God prior to the world (that is, prior to any particular moment of the world's existence), God the whole. On the other hand, "I will be" represents the consequent nature of God, the God who is affected by our deeds and who chooses how to be in the future in response to our deeds. Because "God" is seen as ultimately unknowable and ineffable, all our theologies are flawed. But they are identically flawed in that they are all limited by our human capabilities. Nonetheless, they also all point to a shared truth: That humanity perceives that there is "Being" somehow greater than us. Each religion has a unique perspective of this "Being" and has built distinctive systems of belief and practice upon that perspective.

Like a gem, "God" may be thought of as being multifaceted, offering many different perspectives to be observed. Each faith is capable of describing only one or two divine facets—and then arguing with other faiths about which facet is more true—but never the whole "gem." Our efforts at theology are like the parable of the blind men and the elephant, or, as the Hindus more charitably say, they are different paths up the same mountain. Our theologies—including process theology—are *our* metaphysical constructs, not eternal verities; they represent conceptions based upon our perceptions of "God," but not "God" the ineffable.

Process theology also can draw upon other theological concepts in Jewish and Christian traditions to build a common foundation of understanding and purpose. Process theology holds that religions clothe the universal in particular dress and that we ought to recognize that, being siblings, Judaism and Christianity are more similar than different.

Both traditions image a suffering God. Various *midrashim* portray an anthropopathetic God who simultaneously could be just and merciful, wrathful and grief-stricken, omnipotent and self-limiting, who causes Israel to suffer yet suffers alongside Israel in Exile, a God who judges but with whom one can argue based on a universal principle of justice by which even God is bound to abide.[7]

In Christianity, Jesus *is* the suffering God incarnate, who suffers eternally with humanity as it suffers. Thus, in both traditions, we have the power to increase or decrease God's suffering (as it were).

Both have traditions of an immanent God: In Judaism, there is the concept of the *Shekhinah*, God's indwelling, feminine presence; while in Christianity, God actually becomes a human being who dwells on earth for a time and thereafter remains forever humanly accessible.

Both at times have viewed God as self-limiting cosmologically. In the Jewish mystical tradition, God creates the universe by self-contracting (*tsimtsum*); in Christianity, for God to become human is, by definition, self-limiting.

Both also see the world as incomplete, imperfect (the Jewish mystical concept of the "breaking of the divine vessels and the scattering of the divine sparks"; the primarily Christian amplification of the story of the Fall and Original Sin), and both believe humanity stands in need of God's intervention in the future (the Coming of the Messiah/the Second Coming). Paradoxically, both also view this divine intervention as being dependent on human behavior.

Lastly, both cherish a personal God, one who is guided by principles of justice and mercy, who hears prayer (praise, petition, and protest) and responds, who somehow exists beyond this world as creator and sustainer of all yet gives humankind the space and the opportunity to choose how to live.

By drawing on these and other similarities, process theology can begin to build a common ground between Judaism and Christianity and with other faiths as well. By recognizing our human limitations regarding knowledge of God, by acknowledging our multiple perspectives on "God," and by placing responsibility for the well-being of the world squarely on our collective shoulders, process theology sets the stage for interfaith reconciliation and new spiritual growth.

Over the centuries, our religious differences have obscured our religious similarities, leading to discrimination, persecution, wars, much death, and needless suffering. Casting blame for these tragedies is pointless—it is easy to do but so harmful for future relations. The past does have power in the present, but because "God is active"—because God constantly infuses potentiality into the present—we are not doomed to repeat the past. Each occasion inherits history but also a moment of divine potentiality, or novelty, which can enable us to transcend our pasts.

Conflict-resolution begins by letting go of the past. Perhaps, as with children and parents, religions must separate one from another and grow apart as they develop their own unique messages and accomplishments. Process theology suggests that humanity, the world and God are whole and interrelated. If we recognize our internal relatedness, then, through our efforts to understand one another better, we come to understand more about ourselves, our world, and our diverse views of God. The past is past; the future lies ahead—*ehyeh asher ehyeh* ("I am who/what I am; I will be who/what I will be."). Now is the time for people of faith to come together, not to seek proselytes among those already spiritual, but to deepen our own faith perspectives, to share and learn from one another, and to begin to repair the world.

Notes

1. For background on this subject, see George F. Moore, *Judaism in the First Centuries of the Christian Era* (New York: Schocken Books, 1971; reprint of the Harvard University Press edition of 1928, 1930); Joseph R. Rosenbloom, *Conversion to Judaism: From the Biblical Period to the Present* (Cincinnati: Hebrew Union College Press, 1978); William G. Braude, *Jewish Proselyting* (Providence: Brown University Press, 1940); Bernard J. Bamberger, *Proselytism in the Talmudic Period* (Cincinnati: Hebrew Union College Press, 1939); Rosemary R. Ruether, *Faith and Fratricide* (New York: Seabury Press, 1974); Marvin Wilson, *Our Father Abraham: Jewish Roots of the Christian Faith* (Grand Rapids: Eerdmans Publishing, 1989).

2. For an introduction to the Jewish-Christian-Muslim trilogue, see Francis E. Peters, *Children of Abraham: Judaism, Christianity and Islam* (Princeton: Princeton University Press, 1982).

3. For a bibliographic summary of some of the recent major contributions in this field, see Eugene J. Fisher, "Jewish-Christian Relations 1989–1993: A Bibliographic Update," *CCAR Journal: A Reform Jewish Quarterly*, Winter 1994: 7–35. On the Jewish side, see in particular Leon Klenicki, ed., *Toward a Theological Encounter: Jewish Understanding of Christianity* (New York: Paulist Press, 1991), which includes essays by a number of leading contemporary American Jewish scholars.

4. For more on the efforts of these groups to "Christianize" our country's government and culture, see David Cantor, *The Religious Right: The Assault on Tolerance and Pluralism in America* (New York: Anti-Defamation League, 1994).

5. For some thinking on this subject, see Irving Zeitlin, *Jesus and the Judaism of His Time* (Cambridge, U.K.: Polity Press, 1988); Geza Vermes, *Jesus and the World of Judaism* (Philadelphia: Fortress Press, 1984), and Samuel Cohon, "The Place of Jesus in the Religious Life of His Day," reprinted in Jacob B. Agus, *Judaism and Christianity: Selected Accounts 1892–1962* (New York: Arno Press, 1973).

6. Process theology has in fact already been at work in this field. See, for example, John B. Cobb, Jr., *Beyond Dialogue: Toward a Mutual Transformation of Christianity and Buddhism* (Philadelphia: Fortress Press, 1982), and Sandra B. Lubarsky, *Tolerance and Transformation: Jewish Approaches to Religious Pluralism* (Cincinnati: Hebrew Union College Press, 1990).

7. See Anson Laytner, *Arguing with God: A Jewish Tradition* (Livingston: Jason Aronson, 1990), for a full treatment of this concept and references cited in notes 41–49 (268) for specifics on the midrashic suffering God. The tradition of protesting to God is so ancient and long-lived in Judaism that it ought to be viewed as a fundamental (and perhaps uniquely) Jewish perception of the divine-human relationship, one in which God the ruler and judge of the universe nonetheless allows humankind the freedom and the power to challenge God's governance when confronted by perceived injustice and unwarranted suffering.

For some Christian theological perspectives on "arguing with God," see John K. Roth, "A Theodicy of Protest," critiques by Stephen T. Davis, Frederick Sontag, David R. Griffin, and John H. Hick, and Roth's response to them, in Stephen T. Davis, ed., *Encountering Evil: Live Options in Theodicy* (Atlanta: John Knox Press, 1981), 7–37.

Two recent books have taken the concept of "a theology of protest" and applied it to daily life. For a Jewish perspective, see David R. Blumenthal, *Facing the Abusing God: A Theology of Protest* (Louisville: Westminster/John Knox Press, 1993); for an evangelical Christian perrpective, see Dan B. Allender and Tremper Longman, III, *The Cry of the Soul: How Our Emotions Reveal Our Deepest Questions About God* (Colorado Springs: Navpress, 1994).

Chapter 13

Rabbinic Text Process Theology

Peter W. Ochs

I. Preface

If it adopted the *a priori* principles of A. N. Whitehead and of Christian process theology, a Jewish process theology would be a Jewish variety of natural theology. Mordecai Kaplan's reconstructionism came close to this. It might even be termed a Jewish natural process theology, with a strong sense of the natural role of tradition and, thus, in this case, an openness to the cultural milieu of rabbinic tradition, as well as a commitment to the pragmatisms of William James and John Dewey. Kaplan cited Whitehead favorably; his reconstructionism is at the very least compatible with process theology and thus illustrates one version of what a Jewish process theology would look like in practice.

What would a Jewish process theology look like, however, if it also adopted, rather than borrowed selectively from, the *a priori* principles of rabbinic Judaism—among them, the authority of Torah given on Sinai, a historically particular revelation of divine instruction for a particular people, and the authority of the Oral Torah, a historically evolving hermeneutic, according to which that revelation becomes normative practice for communities of observant Jews? I trust this would not be a naturalism, since it would be a theology that found its grammar or regulative logic in a textual hermeneutic rather than in an account of the orders of perception and imagination. It would not, for the same token, be an anti-naturalism, but rather a theology for which the distinction between natural and super- or non-natural was not definitional. For such a theology, for example, the world out there would belong to the order of creation (*maaseh bereshit*), rather than to "nature." This would mean that, since God creates through words, language (at least some sort of language) and world would be intimately connected rather than extrinsic phenomena. It would mean, furthermore, that for language to "know" the world would not be surprising and that something like a form of realism would not be out of the question. While it would presuppose the authority of divine speech and even of some human interpretations of it, this other-than natural theology would not, as naturalists might suppose, present a heteronomous conception of divine law. If the distinction of nature/not nature would not be definitive for this theology, neither would those of autonomy/heteronomy, body/spirit, this world/other world. This theology would present its own variety of neutral monism; in this case, however, the undifferentiated plenum would be termed a plenum of undifferentiated signification (or pure semiosis), of which undifferentiated feeling (or pure experience) was an instance; "prehension" would be another term for interpretation.

Max Kadushin was the first and, as far as I know, the only Jewish thinker to articulate a process theology in the service of what he considered the behavioral or *halakhic* authority of classical rabbinic literature. In this paper, I examine Kadushin's work as the foundation of a rabbinic text process theology. I assume, from the outset, that such a theology may complement a Jewish natural process theology and that a Jewish process theology, in general, would appear as a process of dialogue between textual and natural process theologies.

II. Max Kadushin's Organismic Study of Rabbinic Judaism

From the time of his doctoral studies at The Jewish Theological Seminary of America (New York) in the 1930s, Kadushin sought to identify the rationality of classical rabbinic discourse, or of what he later called "the rabbinic mind."[1] Typical of the class of post- or "aftermodern" Jewish thinkers that includes Martin Buber,[2] he was educated in the traditions of both rabbinic Judaism and the Western university and emerged from the latter dissatisfied with traditional Judaism's contemporary self-understanding. Searching within modern social science and philosophy for the intellectual tools that would enable him to identify Jewish norms for life in the modern world, he allied himself with Mordecai Kaplan and was one of the early exponents of Kaplan's Reconstructionism. With Kaplan, he was attentive to the powers of change and process within rabbinic Judaism and argued for radical reformation within the context of the Conservative variety of observant Judaism.

Like other aftermodern thinkers, however, Kadushin was also suspicious of essentialist or apriorist tendencies in modern social science and philosophy, which tendencies he considered symptoms of the dogmatism and individualism he rejected in any system of thought and practice. From the start, he believed that rabbinic Judaism was in its indigenous patterns anti-dogmatic, social, and particularly attentive to the integration of ethics into the details of everyday life and experience. Kadushin was thus attracted to some of his contemporaries' pragmatic and organicist criticisms of the dogmatism and individualism that accompanied what many now call "modernist thinking."[3] At the same time, he observed that pragmatists and organicists also displayed these modernist tendencies, at times presenting their alternatives to modernity in dogmatic and individualistic ways. He judged that, at a certain point, Kaplan went this way, betraying his organicist commitments in favor of a dogmatic and idiosyncratic philosophy of organism. Eventually, Kadushin parted company with Kaplan's Reconstructionist movement and sought to construct a place for himself within Conservative Judaism, with its dual allegiances to rabbinic Judaism and to modern, but non-modernist, modes of reform.[4]

Kadushin's scholarly project was to identify the rationality in rabbinic discourse. In part, his project was an index of his reformatory critique of traditionalist tendencies in observant Judaism: in this respect, "rationality" signified reasoned grounds for responsible change. In part, his project was an index of his apologetic defense of Jewish religiosity in the face of what he took to be Western philosophy's slanderous criticisms of rabbinic Judaism's "irrationality." Kadushin believed[5] that the dogmatism and individualism he rejected in modern thinking accompanied the university's promoting both sides of a modernist antimony: between reductive, scientistic rationality, on the one hand, and reductive, emotivist irrationality, on the other. He believed that criticisms of rabbinic Judaism came from thinkers burdened by either side of this antimony: rationalists criticized rabbinic literature for its irrationality and emotivists criticized it for its heteronomy.[6] Kadushin grew critical of Reconstructionism when he began to see in its claims symptoms of the modernist antimony. He was unprepared to part company with Kaplan, however, until he was convinced that he could find a clear alternative to modernism—a non-reductive reasonableness—within rabbinic Judaism.

For his doctoral thesis, Kadushin sought to identify the rationality that was displayed, indigenously, within one literary document of rabbinic Judaism, the homiletic or midrashic text *Seder Eliahu*.[7] His method was to reduce the text to its rhetorically fundamental units of meaning and then to attempt to identify the rational principle on the basis of which the units were organized into a coherent whole. He described his discovering such a principle as a "eureka" experience, culminating months of detailed textual work. He discovered that, in his estimation, previous scholars had misunderstood the way in which rabbinic *midrash* displays its principles of rationality. Expecting individual statements of *midrash* (the text's fundamental units of meaning) to display these principles, they judged the literature "non-rational" when they found that individual statements, even those attributed to the same author, are often contradictory. The problem was that they were looking,

> apparently, for an organizational principle which would systematize the many and varied rabbinic *statements*, and they soon found that these statements would not fit into any logical scheme.[8]

Kadushin's method was, instead, to go "behind the statements to the *concepts* which the statement embodied" and which belonged to a coherent or rational system of values. What became his life's work was to examine the inner logic, or grammar, of this system, including its actualizations in this and, as he would claim, in all documents and practices of rabbinic Judaism.

Kadushin labeled the rationality of the rabbinic system of concepts "organic," later reporting that he described it this way before a friend, Horace Kallen, introduced him to what would become his storehouse of literature on the principle of organism or organicism.[9] In the storehouse were works by Whitehead, Dorothy Emmet (on Whitehead), Henri Bergson, John Dewey, Raymond Wheeler, and, perhaps most influential, William Ritter and R. Bailey.[10] Kadushin claimed it was not first this organismic theory but his empirical studies of the actual character of rabbinic thinking that convinced him precisely what was missing in modernist models of rationality and in modern as well as classical philosophic characterizations of rabbinic thought. Whatever impressed him first, Kadushin delivered his mature description of what he called "organic thinking" and "the rabbinic mind" by integrating organismic theory with literary data and with his own responsiveness to contemporary theological needs.

In the historical-critical mode of his peers, Kadushin claimed to offer his theological constructions as reconstructions of what was really going on in the literary documents he examined. As recent critics have noted, he tended, in fact, to generalize beyond and at times independently of these documents.[11] If this means that Kadushin's work displayed more of the imaginative than he would have liked, it also means that this work may be more pertinent to the constructive work of process theology than he would have thought. The following section offers a summary of the process theology Kadushin developed throughout his career.

III. Kadushin's Process Theology of Rabbinic Judaism

Kadushin's process theology was what he considered a descriptive study of the form of organismic or process thinking that was displayed in the scriptural hermeneutics of rabbinic Judaism. The fundamental elements in this theology were *organic concepts*, or, more specifically, what he later called *value-concepts*; their modes of interrelation in an *organic complex*, illustrated in the case of what he later called *the rabbinic mind*; and their modes of actualization in fundamental units of literature (which units he called individual statements) or of religious behavior (acts of worship, charity, and so on).

He offered this general definition of organic concepts:

> Organic concepts are concepts in a whole complex of concepts none of which can be inferred from the others but all of which are so mutually interrelated that every individual concept, though possessing its own distinctive features, nevertheless depends for its character on the character of the complex as a whole which, in turn, depends on the character of the individual concepts. Each organic concept, therefore, implicates the whole complex without being completely descriptive of the complex, retaining, at the same time, its own distinctive features.[12]

The organic concepts of particular interest to Kadushin were the value-concepts of rabbinic Judaism, as displayed or actualized in the literature and conduct of rabbinic Jews. The following are among the most prominent features Kadushin attributed to these rabbinic value-concepts.[13]

The concepts are all named by value-terms displayed in the indigenous language of rabbinic literature. While the grammatical roots of these terms may all be found in the Hebrew Bible, many of the terms acquire levels of meaning that do not appear in the Bible. They are therefore biblically inspired, but not biblical. For example, "in rabbinic usage, the term *tsedakah* almost always connotes 'charity' or 'love', while in biblical usage it connotes 'righteousness'."[14] Other examples of rabbinic value-terms are *torah, Israel,* humanity (*adam*), loving-kindness (*gemilut hasadim*), God's mercy (*middat harachamim*), God's justice (*middat hadin*).

The value-concepts are actualized or concretized in interpretive events whose records are individual literary statements or individual acts of observable conduct. Kadushin believed that the rabbis displayed their religious values most clearly in their collections of scriptural homilies, or *midrash aggadah.* He claimed that, in the absence of an independent practice of philosophic reflection, the rabbis adopted homiletic reflection as their means of conceptualizing these values.[15] Within this literature, he identified individual "haggadic statements" as authoritative records of the value concepts' actualizations. For example, in the midrashic collection on Genesis, *Genesis Rabbah,* we find this interpretation of the scriptural passage, "And God saw everything that [God] had made: and behold, it was very good" (Genesis 1:31).[16]

> (a) In the copy of R. [Rabbi] Meir's Torah [Pentateuch] was found written: "And behold, it was very [*me'od*] good": and behold, death [*maweth*] was good . . . .
> (c) A. Johanan said: "Why was death decreed against the wicked? Because as long as the wicked live they anger the Lord, as it is written, 'Ye have wearied the Lord with your words' [Mal. 2:17]; but when they die they cease to anger Him as it is written, 'There the wicked cease from raging' [Job 3:17], which means, there the wicked cease from enraging the Holy One blessed be he. . . ."

According to Kadushin, these are two *haggadic statements,* each of which actualizes different elements of the rabbinic value-concept on the occasion of its interpreting the text of Genesis. Examining the first text philologically, the text's modern editor observes, "This may mean either that Rabbi Meir's manuscript read *maweth* ('death') instead of *me'od* ('very') or that this was inserted as a marginal comment."[17] Kadushin might have said that, in either case, Rabbi Meir interpreted a textual idiosyncrasy in a way that poses the question, "How can death be good?" As suggested by the second statement, his rabbinic readers inferred the answer, "Death is a potent force for repentance."[18] In other words, Rabbi Meir's observing a textual idiosyncrasy became an occasion for the rabbis' actualizing such value-concepts as Repentance (the wicked repent through their death), "The Wicked" Creation (God's creation includes death), God's Justice (the wicked are punished through death), and God's Mercy (that punishment removes God's wrath).

Value-concepts have both cognitive and valuational components. They refer to objects in the world as occasions for displaying rabbinic values. In the haggadic statements from *Genesis Rabbah*, for example, reference to death occasions interpretations about repentance, mercy, and so on. In Kadushin's terms, value-concepts "express approval or disapproval of a phenomenon [or mode of behavior] and thus endow it with whatever significance it has for us. And they imply the reason for the judgment they express."[19] The value-concepts are to be distinguished from "cognitive concepts," which "describe whatever we perceive through the senses . . . such as table, chair, tall, round";[20] and from poetic or "connotative concepts," which "are not tied to any particular manifestation."[21]

Connotative value-terms also refer to identifiable, though not definable, notions. These notions, such as "loving-kindness" and "God's mercy," are defined only *in situ*, which means that every definition is an actualization, or concretization, of the value-concept, of which there are innumerable such actualizations. *The value-concepts display a drive toward concretization:* put differently they are performative or pragmatic concepts and cannot therefore be reduced to any particular set of semantic definitions. "A value-concept is not an idea which is inferred and can never be the result of speculation or observation."[22] Hence, value-concepts are not deducible one from the other and cannot be arranged in a hierarchical order.[23]

"Since value-concepts are 'defined' by the situations that concretize them, the value-concepts of a society are embedded in the pattern of life of that society and are included in its vernacular. Since the valuational concepts of a group and their embodiment in its pattern of life distinguish it from all other historic groups, the maintenance of the special character of the group is thus to a large extent a matter of the transmission of the valuation terms."[24]

The value-concepts therefore participate in a complex of value concepts with respect to which they display their meanings. Within this complex, each value-concept "interweaves" with every other, which means that it may be actualized in relation to any other value-concept. The individual concept is itself a complex of sub-concepts, each of which, while an aspect of the more general concept, also preserves its own individuality. For example, the concept *torah* includes the sub-concepts of *the study of torah, the efficacy of torah, commandments,* and so on. "The more concepts [that are] concretized in any given situation, the more meaningful . . . [the] situation will be."[25] In fact, the concepts "possess the characteristic of potential simultaneity," which "means that the whole complex is brought into play upon every situation"; the potential is limited only by circumstances and mood.[26]

   The potential simultaneity of concepts introduces an element of paradox. Since concepts with apparently contrary connotations may be actualized in a single situation, the meaning of the situation may appear paradoxical. "The rabbis studied the Torah with both love and fear or awe in their hearts, emotions having conceptual parallels, respectively, in God's love and in [God's] justice; and these contradictory feelings are perfectly natural."[27] The value-complex is therefore *fluid*, as well. A given situation may be interpreted by different concepts, and interpretive tendencies may vary over time, or evolve.

IV. Kadushin as both Disciple and Critic of Whitehead

   Evaluating Whitehead's *Science and the Modern World, Process and Reality*, and *Religion in the Making*, Kadushin noted that the following "metaphysical concepts can be taken as generalizations of the characteristics of rabbinic theology":

> In his notion of "prehension" we see the generalization of *the potential simultaneity of concepts*; in his idea of "appetition" [the urge to actualization] that of the *concretization of concepts*; in his idea of "a cosmic epoch" that of *organic levels*; in his idea of a "society" that of the relation between the *organic complex* and the *individual configurations of it*; in his idea of "rhythms" [the idea that every great rhythm contains lesser rhythms without which it could not be] that of the relation of the *concept* to its *sub-concepts*.[28]

He noted other parallels as well, but these are the most conspicuous. Kadushin's comment suggests that, in Whiteheadian terms, he conceived of rabbinic Judaism as a conceptual organism, or society of interpretive events, which collectively prehends an antecedent organism, biblical Judaism, at the same time that its members prehend other members.

   Kadushin's empirical evidence for this conception was that no other model provided a better explanation of the indigenous organization of rabbinic literature. He considered each document of rabbinic homiletics, or *midrash*, a document of rabbinic theology and conceived of it as a society of individual midrashic statements, which he identified, in turn, with theological judgments or prehensions. For example, the second haggadic statement cited earlier from *Genesis Rabbah*—"why was death decreed against the wicked?"—prehended the statement from Genesis, "and God saw everything . . . ." Each such prehension entails a synthesis of what Kadushin first called "organismic concepts" and later called "value-concepts," such as Repentance, Creation, and so on. These correspond in Kadushin's system to Whitehead's "eternal objects."[29]

Kadushin noted that the value-concepts had both a cognitive component and an affective one, the concepts' "warmth," as he called it. Like Whitehead, he associated the affective with the valuational, thus providing a psychodynamic place for value-judgments:

> every rabbinic value-concept had a drive toward actualization or concretization; and many of them, such as charity, . . . repentance, the study of Torah, and numerous others, directly impelled the individual to appropriate overt actions. But impulse alone would have made such drives only sporadic at best; it could hardly have ensured steady concretization. Being mental factors, however, the concepts were subject to conscious direction. They could not only be embodied in Haggadah but also in Halakah, in commonly observed laws or rules for concretization. These laws, fashioned by the rabbis, . . . ensured steady concretization. The concretization of the concept of charity, to give several examples, was made certain by the various agricultural regulations, including the tithes for the poor, *pe'ah* ([leaving ungleaned the] "corner of the field") . . . , and by the institutions of *tamchuy* (community plate) [and so on] . . . .
>
> These and all the other concretizations of the value-concepts in law . . . are not "legalism." They did not crowd out the possibilities for spontaneous concretizations; for proof, we need only point to such a rabbinic concept as deeds of loving-kindness which has reference also to deeds of love done beyond what is required by law. Moreover, Halakah is itself a product of the value-concepts' drive towards concretization, and without doubt the most important product. Lacking Halakah, the value-concepts, with their need for steady concretization in actual life, might not have functioned at all.[30]

Kadushin considered the individual midrashic statement a product
(for Whitehead, a concrescence) of the value-concepts' drive to actualization: an individual event of interpretation (prehension) guided by
some limited configuration, or set of relations, among value-concepts.
Each such statement is authored by some individual person, such as
Rabbi Meir: for the integrative process of the rabbinic value system
as a whole is inseparable from the integrative processes of the individual persons who constitute rabbinic society. "The maintenance of
the special character of the group is . . . , to an extent, a matter of the
transmission of the valuational terms,"[31] but the valuational terms
are [themselves] only symbols of the concepts, which "are, in fact, often
drives to action" within a society of individual persons. Each such
person, finally, "is less an entity than a continuous process making
for an entity. Every individual is a more or less successful integrative
process in constant function. In this process of integration, the value-
concepts seem to play an enormous, perhaps a decisive role."[32]

To be guided by these value-concepts is to live a life of holiness,
in *imitatio dei*. A process theologian might want to spell out the
theological implication that these concepts would, in their simultaneity, constitute what Whitehead called the Primordial Nature of
God.[33] Their valuational character would represent the "appetitive"
aspect of the Primordial Nature, and God's Consequent Nature would
be known by the fruits of this appetition: what the rabbis call halakhic
practice as *imitatio dei*. In these terms, we might expect Kadushin
to have conceived of the homiletic *midrash aggadah* as a literary
concrescence of God's Primordial Nature[34] within the context of
rabbinic practice, the legal *midrash halakhah* as a literary concrescence of God's Consequent Nature within this context and his analysis
of the value-concepts, abstracted from their literary context, as the
rabbinic equivalent of Whitehead's philosophical theology.

However, respecting a strong tendency in rabbinic thought,
Kadushin was reluctant to refer to God other than through God's
actions, and he was strongly critical of metaphysical speculation,
including that of the medieval Jewish philosophers, such as Saadya,
Maimonides, and so on. His reluctance appears to have reflected his
sense of the redundancy of attempts to conceptualize God's immanence: God, he might have said, is already present as partner in all
rabbinic discourse and as communicant in all words used about this
world; actions taken on behalf of the rabbinic system of *halakhah* are
actions in which God's presence is concretely, or even tactily, embodied.[35] Rabbinic discourse is profoundly anthropomorphic, but it
does not make anthropomorphism itself a conceptual issue. Kadushin

argued that the *aggadah's* anthropomorphisms, as well as its references to God's otherness, were expressions of the rabbis' varying *experiences* of God as near and as distant and that neither experience should be foreclosed by philosophic argument.[36] He believed that the rabbis were wary of essentialism because the construction of verbal forms of essence might have distanced them from the One with whom they were already in such intimate relationship, reducing a subtly detailed process of relationship to the less subtle terms of conceptual definition.

For such reasons, Kadushin found aspects of Whitehead's system both inapplicable to the rabbinic model and out of keeping with an organicist program. He wrote that Whitehead's

> idea of the "mutual relatedness" of "eternal objects" cannot be taken as a generalization of the *integration of organic concepts* because "eternal objects" are not organic concepts. Organic concepts are altogether inseparable from the organic process whereas "eternal objects" must, in some sense, be fixed, and are, to that extent, independent of the process . . . .
>
> Exactly the same inconsistency is to be found in Whitehead's view of religion. Whitehead declares that "the topic of religion is individuality in community" and that the "individual is formative of the society, the society is formative of the individual." These and similar statements depict religion as organismic . . . . [Yet, Whitehead also says that] "theoretically rational religion could have arisen in complete independence of the antecedent social religions of ritual and mythical belief," adding that, of course, this was not the case historically. The organismic Process which means that "the topic of religion is individuality in community" is, then, according to Whitehead, theoretically superfluous since rational ideas, those which are eternal, whether rising from religious or other fields can, theoretically, be arrived at by the individual *sans* community . . . . "[I]nstitutions . . . bibles . . . codes of behaviour," he remarks, "are the trappings of religion, its passing forms." If religion consists primarily of eternal ideas, this is correct; but if religion is an organismic Process, its materials, its social institutions, cannot be separated from the Process itself.[37]

Kadushin argued, in sum, that Whitehead's "description of religion as an organismic process must necessarily conflict with his description of it as a rational system of metaphysical concepts."[38] He objected to the formality of these concepts: their specificity, definiteness, and eternality, and the process through which he believed philosophic theologians would abstract them from particular organic systems and then over-generalize their domain of reference to all possible systems. He argued that since, for Whitehead, " 'eternal objects' are envisioned in 'the primordial mind of God,' " they could therefore not be described definitively by human interpreters. This was not to say that they could not be described at all, only that the descriptions would be vaguer than Whitehead allowed. In other words, Kadushin's alternative to metaphysics was neither a strictly negative theology nor the sort of agnosticism process theologians might identify with a relativistic postmodernism. It was, instead, a text, as opposed to a natural, process theology.

We have come to the turning point in our discussion. Kadushin was both disciple and critic of Whitehead, because Whitehead provided him a vocabulary to fill only half of his needs: a process vocabulary, but not a text process one. Kadushin concluded that he had to complete the job himself, inventing his ingenious but also idiosyncratic and imprecise theory of value-concepts. His conclusion was an unfortunate one, because it kept him from making more complete and critical use of the logic that I suspect already influenced his theory: the logic of symbols, or semiotics, of the American philosopher Charles Peirce (d. 1914). We have evidence that Kadushin studied Peirce's work,[39] and I have found that Kadushin's theory of value-concepts resembles Peirce's logic of symbols more closely than it does the theory of "eternal objects" and "prehensions" after which Kadushin claimed to base his presentation. On the following pages, I will therefore describe Kadushin's differences with Whitehead from the perspective of Peirce's semiotics.

If the value-concepts of Kadushin's text process theology function in many ways like the eternal objects of Whitehead's natural process thought, they differ, specifically, in both their logical modality[40] and their etiology.[41] Modally, the value-concepts represent what Charles Peirce called "would-be's," or real possibilities. Like the eternal objects, they are non-individual, but their generality is of the sort Peirce labeled indefiniteness or vagueness: the generality of an indefinite description of some existent thing, as opposed to the generality of an indeterminacy, or abstract possibility, definitely described. To distinguish the two, Peirce suggested that the principle of contradiction did not apply to what was vague, while the law of excluded middle did not apply to what was general.[42] He drew another distinction, which readers may find more helpful:

A sign . . . is objectively *general* in so far as it extends to the interpreter the privilege of carrying its determination further. *Example*: "Human beings[43] are mortal." To the question, Which human beings? the reply is that the proposition explicitly leaves it to you to apply its assertion to what human beings you will . . . . A sign . . . is objectively vague in so far as it reserves further determination to be made in some other conceivable sign, or at least does not appoint the interpreter as its deputy in this office. *Example*: "A man I could mention seems to be a little conceited." The *suggestion* here is that the man in view is the person addressed; but the utterer does not authorize such an interpretation or *any* other application of what she says. She can still say, if she likes, that she does *not* mean the person addressed. Every utterance naturally leaves the right of further exposition in the utterer.[44]

In addition to their vagueness, value-concepts are also to be distinguished by their performative character. Their meaning is made fully definite, within context-specific occasions of action or judgment, *to those engaged in the actions or judgments entailed in their meaning.*[45] In these terms, the rabbinic value-concepts function as divine utterances *to* members of the rabbinic society, guiding those members of rabbinic society who receive them to act or judge in certain ways on certain occasions. Each value-concept displays a range of context-dependent definitions, which, if viewed simultaneously, may appear contradictory, and which admit of no summary, context-independent definition. Yet, the organic system coheres as a whole.

According to Kadushin, the text process theologian lacks discrete and definite concepts which would iconize that coherence: there is no knowledge of God's mind *totum simul*. In place of such a totalizing knowledge, the theologian possesses what we might call a symbolizing knowledge of God. Classifying the ways in which signs may refer to their objects, Peirce distinguished among three different kinds of signs. He said *an icon* (such as a sculpture depicting some person) refers to its object by virtue of characters of its own and does so whether or not the object actually exists; *an index* (such as a weather vane pointing to the wind's direction) refers to its object by virtue of being actually affected by the object and thus by virtue of qualities that it shares with the object; a *symbol* (such as a word) refers to its object by virtue of a law that causes the symbol to be interpreted as referring to the object.[46] In these terms, we may say that the value-concept terms are icons of the theologian's knowledge of God. The indices of that knowledge are the peaceful heart (*lev shalom*) of faith and of relational knowing (*yidia*). The complete symbols of that knowledge are the interpretive activities by way of which societies of individual persons live in God's image (*b'tselem elokim*). Kadushin claimed that, by way of contrast, the metaphysician's concepts—such as Whitehead's "eternal objects"—display the generality of abstract possibility and are, therefore, non-organismic. Such concepts come to us fully defined but indifferent to context.[47] We are each, consequently, free to apply them as we see fit, but we remain, for the same reason, powerless to influence their essential definition.

The etiological differences between value-concepts and eternal objects are equally significant. For Kadushin, the value-concepts receive their characterizations from indigenous practitioners of the organic system of rabbinic Judaism, rather than from scholarly or cross-cultural analyses of them.[48] As Peirce said of the word "God," value-concepts belong to the vernacular and thus to a societal organism whose individuality and conceptual integrity is the starting point of organicist studies. The concepts are to be characterized intrasystematically or, in the language of another recent hermeneutic, intratextually.[49] Kadushin argued, on the other hand, that Whitehead's eternal objects did not belong to any organic systems of lived practice and were, therefore, only "analytic tools." He applied to them the same disclaimers he applied to his own analytic vocabulary *about* value-concepts:

> We have seen . . . that generalizations epitomizing aspects of the organismic process in general are only *analytic tools*, not organismic concepts. In other words, the logical method here remains the same as in all other types of scientific research. It must, of course, remain the same if it is to be valid. The organismic approach differs from other types of scientific study only in its hypothesis: We are *utilizing* the organismic approach when we attempt to prove by logical means that the subject under analysis is organismic.[50]

Kadushin did not object to Whitehead's—or his own—engagement in scientific analysis. He objected only to Whitehead's mistaking the categories of scientific analysis for concepts of religion. It would be consistent with Kadushin's argument to say both that analytic, including metaphysical, concepts belonged to vocabularies independent of organic systems and that they reified characters selectively abstracted from such systems. From this perspective, Kadushin believed that, in finding his analytic concepts religiously interesting, White-head committed what he himself termed the fallacy of misplaced concreteness: in this case treating as organic, and thus concrete, concepts that were abstractly general.

Kadushin argued, further, that organicist thinkers tended to underdevelop as well as misplace their analyses.

> The basic fallacy of many philosophies of organism consists in the failure to take account of the fact that each organismic form has its own individuality, the organismic character of which must be demonstrated with respect to the constituents peculiar to itself. Generalizations or concepts epitomizing aspects of the organismic process *in general* are only *descriptive or analytic*, not organic concepts . . . .
>
> Social philosophies of organism are especially apt to suffer from what we have termed "the basic fallacy." The organismic approach in the social sciences demands, first of all, minute and painstaking analysis in order to discover the particular organismic forms, each with its own individual characteristics, in which social life abounds. Until these organismic social forms are identified in detail, all generalizations, even if couched in terms of the organismic approach, are bound to prove sterile.[51]

To respect the individuality of organic systems, Kadushin sought to keep his organicist theology within the limits of an empirical study of rabbinic Judaism in its literary self-expression. Recent scholarly criticisms of Kadushin's inadequate empiricism have reinforced his principle, if not his practice. Jacob Neusner writes, for example, that Kadushin

> addressed the issue of a descriptive theology of the Dual Torah that seems to me urgent . . . . I believe Kadushin was the only scholar before this writer who took seriously the documentary boundaries of texts . . . . [But] his error lay in interpreting too soon, describing too little, analyzing altogether too much out of context. He missed the specificities, but, alas, that is where God lives: only in the details . . . . Despite his own good method he ignored the bounds of the documents, treating the canon as essentially uniform and limited only by its outer frontiers. So he leapt directly into words and their definitions. That accounts for the unnuanced character of his results.[52]

Neusner's words suggest that, beyond modal and etiological differences between value-concepts and eternal objects, and beyond differences between the organismic studies of texts and of perceptual experience, text and natural process theologies may differ in their relative tolerances for generalization. The text process theologian may be more willing to sacrifice generality for the sake of attentiveness to concrete detail.

V. Text and Natural Process Theologies: Summing up the Differences

Partly supportive, partly critical of Whitehead, Kadushin's rabbinic theology is best described as a process theology unlike other process theologies: a text process theology in dialogue with, but not identical to, Whitehead's natural process theology. Reinforcing Whitehead's nonrelativistic postmodernism, Kadushin criticized modernist notions of rationality without abandoning the reasoned study of religious knowledge. He offered a non-sensationalist, non-mechanistic epistemology, which allowed for the direct perception of values and, by way of those values, the direct experience of God's presence. He portrayed knowable, individual entities (such as judgments, homilies, texts, persons, or communities) as both societies of member entities and as members of societies of comparable entities. He portrayed each such entity, furthermore, as a concretizing interpretation, or prehension, of other entities. The interpretation is guided by eternal objects, here labeled value-concepts. These value-concepts manifest God's creativity, but they are not God's alone, since human interpreters contribute to the process through which the value-concepts emerge as earthly guides. Kadushin's rabbinic theology thus supported a personalist conception of creativity and was compatible with an anthropomorphic conception of divinity. It recommended forms of inquiry that integrate realms of theory and practice.

Kadushin denied the indeterminate generality and definiteness that Whitehead attributed to eternal objects, describing them instead as irremediably vague and, thus, subject to development or redefinition (even if this development belongs to a different temporal order than that of the development of individual entities). He denied philosophers a privileged role in the process of concretizing eternal objects: the value-concepts display their meaning within the lived practice of the community of religious practitioners. Denying his own inquiry a privileged—or even normalized—place within that community, Kadushin therefore denied a special place to "ontology" as a privileged science managed by a privileged class of thinkers. His theology thus represented a variety of what Peirce called "critical common-sensism,"[53] characterized by a common-sense realism.

As a common-sense realist, Kadushin argued that activities of linguistic description are themselves realia: what, in a Peircean mode, we might label *pragmata* ("deeds"), or event-activities in which value-concepts are concretized in context-specific actions. These pragmata may interpret (prehend) other event-activities, linguistic or extralinguistic. From this perspective, neither linguistic nor extra-linguistic realia are reduced to the other, since both represent modes of prehension. Natural process theologians object to distinctions between "supernatural" and "natural." Kadushin judged arguments for or against such distinctions to be expressions of the reductive preoccupations of modernity. For him, references to "nature" are references to "the order of creation" (*maaseh bereshit*): since all such references are interpretive acts, guided by the value-concepts, distinctions between "nature" and "non-nature" are simply indices of ways in which the value-concepts interrelate in certain contexts of interpretation. Linguistic and non-linguistic events are both realia, each interpretive of the other. Rabbinic Jews, for example, may respond to reading rabbinic *midrash* as they would respond to observing everyday social events of normative significance. This is a sign of what Kadushin would call the integration of critical thinking and everyday moral practice in rabbinic Judaism. He considered the value-concepts' acquiring linguistic labels in the *midrash* to be a sign of the rabbis' critical thinking.

Kadushin did not fully explicate his theory of critical thinking, but I would imagine it went somewhat as follows. Biblical religion represented one organic level of Judaism (in Whitehead's terms, one "cosmic epoch"), rabbinic Judaism represented another level.[54] Biblical religion actualized a complex of value-concepts that are actualized, in new ways, in rabbinic Judaism: as an individual value-complex (organism), the one religion interpreted the other. The literary products of rabbinic Judaism—Mishnah, the Talmuds, the collections of *midrash*—represent stages in the later religion's process of development. Not only individual religions, but also their *value-concepts as well* represent societies of their individual actualizations. The development from biblical to rabbinic Judaism was marked by gradual modifications in the societies of entities that characterized each of the value-concepts and the value-complex as a whole. The midrashic literature is an index of the rabbis having made these modifications a subject of explicit inquiry. Puzzled—at once troubled and excited—by what appeared to be differences between the Bible's and their own value-concepts, they sought both to demonstrate their fidelity to the explicit biblical text and at the same time to perfect methods of creatively transforming the values implicit in it. Kadushin believed that the rabbis' definitive move was to invent noun-forms to label these values.[55] This invention marked the emergence of an explicit, rabbinic science of normative change. Having iconized or diagrammed the value-concepts, the rabbis gained the power not only to teach rabbinic, as opposed to biblical, values explicitly, but also—and more modestly—to manipulate or experimentally modify the values. Since the values represented societies of actualizations, the rabbis could not alter them by definition, that is, in strictly *a priori* fashion. Instead, they altered them by adding significant quantities of new actualizations, each one a *midrash*, or literary concretization of the value-concept in its altered state. For the philosophic or *a priori* thinker, rabbinic literature appears hampered by self-contradiction. For Kadushin, these apparent contradictions display only the ironic character of a process of conservatory reform or stability-in-change, in which the value-concepts were transformed from the ground up and the old forms were displayed alongside the new. Since the rabbis' presented their *midrashim* within the idiom of everyday communal discourse, there was, ideally, no separation between the literary expression of the rabbis' critical thinking and popular practice.[56] As teachers, the rabbis' burden was no longer to translate or apply their reforms to everyday reality, but only to multiply instances, providing their constituencies more opportunities for observing the value-concepts at work and, thus, for acquiring reformed habits of practice and belief. Kadushin shared with Whitehead, as well as with Peirce, Aristotle, and Maimonides, a habit-theory of moral law or virtue.[57]

What, then, guided the rabbis' reforms? Here we see Kadushin's differences with Whitehead displayed in their divergent theories of moral change. Whitehead's notion of the definiteness of the eternal objects corresponds to the concern of contemporary process theologians to define the principles of responsible moral change. Kadushin believed that a value-concept may be defined only vaguely, through a series of interpretive narratives, or *midrashim*, each of which represents an event-activity guided by the value-concept in association with some configuration of other value-concepts. To attempt to define the value-concept more discretely would be to abstract, hypostatize and over-generalize selective features of such event-activities and, thus, to commit what Whitehead called the error of misplaced concreteness. Kadushin argued that, without explicit principles, the rabbis were guided in their reforms by the evolving complex itself. They made judgments, *a posteriori*, about concrete cases, with sensitivities heightened by emergent tendencies of thought which they need not have hypostatized. Not above offering some provisional hypostases of his own, Kadushin called these tendencies *emphatic trends*, noting that, without crystallizing into value-concepts, they influenced how the value-concepts developed from out of the biblical complex. Among the emphatic trends, Kadushin identified what he called the rabbis' concerns for universalism and for personal individuality. Beyond that, Kadushin had no more general, normative claims to make. His ethics was an empirical account of how the value-concepts displayed themselves in classical rabbinic Judaism. As for contemporary ethics, Kadushin offered observations only about his own community of Conservative Judaism. He was a reformist within that community, but refused to adopt any general principle of ethics as a principle of reform. He assumed, instead, that reformists would offer their judgments *ad hoc*, guided by their sense of how the complex of value-concepts as a whole had evolved in response to changing conditions of judgment.

In sum, Kadushin believed that ethical language was meaningful only intrasystematically, and he suspected ethical universalists of what we might call ethical imperialism. With Peirce, he believed that ethics, along with religion, belongs to the vernacular. At the same time, again along with Peirce, Kadushin offered a universalizable, meta-ethical theory of how value complexes may behave in general. Philosophic and social scientific accounts of organism contributed to this theory, but by contributing to an explanatory model that he believed would adequately account for the facts of human value-conceptual life. He was therefore searching for an empirical model with the broadest possible domain of reference, but not for an *a priori* model. In this search, he found that Whitehead and other organicists offered him the most viable analytic paradigms, while the rabbis offered him a prototypical case of organismic or value-conceptual thought and practice.

Within Kadushin's writings, the difference between what I have labeled natural and text process theologies appears starkly as the difference between an ontologizing and a non-ontologizing form of theological inquiry. The differences may not foreclose dialogue, however, since each form of inquiry may expose weaknesses in the other. Natural process theologies appear weakest in their limited attention to the linguistic and semiotic presuppositions of ontology and to the vagueness inherent in performatives—including all metaphysical concepts with performative or normative significance. Kadushin's text process theology appears weakest in its rigid dichotomization of the theoretical and practical dimensions of inquiry. I will conclude this section with comments about the latter.

As noted earlier, Kadushin argued that "generalizations epitomizing aspects of the organismic process in general are only *analytic tools*, not organismic concepts."[58] He criticized Whitehead for overlooking this distinction and treating his metaphysical generalizations as pregnant with religious and thus organismic meaning. We might reply, on the other hand, that Kadushin's dichotomy may reflect a romanticized distinction of "unsullied" folk practice and "objectivistic" science. Does critical thinking introduce an unwanted discontinuity into the organic process of vernacular discourse? If so, how does Kadushin distinguish the rabbis' critical thinking about their value-concepts from his own? Perhaps he might have argued more strongly that analytic languages are languages of cultural borrowers, who translate the discourse of one organism into the terminology of another. If he replied that this other is simply "science," we might answer, again, that various postmodern epistemologists, from Peirce to Ludwig Wittgenstein to the more radical Paul Feyerabend, have urged us to consider the organismic contexts of scientific inquiry itself. Kadushin's language of analysis may represent the terms one community of inquiry employs to inspect the way another community conducts its inquiry. Kadushin's final reply might be more anguished: "You don't seem to realize that I belong to two different and unmediated communities: a community of science and a community of religious practice. Respecting the integrity of each, I apply the analytic language of one to the practical language of the other." I am not convinced that Kadushin identified his two communities carefully. He tended to assimilate his actual religious community to the community of practice he attributed to the authors of the rabbinic literature. As a result, he tended, on the one hand, to misrepresent his own analysis as an activity of "science in general," rather than as one of the normative activities of his distinctly contemporary rabbinic community. On the other hand, he tended to misrepresent his description of rabbinic values as a reconstruction of extra-scientific traditional claims, rather than as part of a contemporary practice of rabbinic interpretation, informed by the sciences of interest to contemporary practitioners. In the process, he attempted to isolate rabbinic values from the critical intelligence that informed his own analytic work and that would inform the practice of those values in his contemporary rabbinic community.

Responding to these objections, I conclude this paper by presenting an emended version of Kadushin's text process theology. This is an abstract of a "Rabbinic Process Textualism," prepared for the sake of introducing Kadushin's theology into a transforming dialogue with naturalistic process theologies, Jewish and Christian and other.

VI. Conclusion: A Rabbinic Process Textualism

A text process theology that adopts rabbinic modes of scriptural interpretation as normative cannot also adopt a process ontology as normative, because it cannot assign general or universal validity to any single ontology. If we define ontology as a description of the most general characters of an entity, specifically of an entity of very expansive domain, then a rabbinic theology is meta-ontological, since it refers to God's creativity as that with respect to which any entity—including any organismic system of law—may become other than it is. For rabbinic theology, all actual entities—organisms or finite systems of being—are creatures of God. This means that they cannot be described adequately if God's creativity is excluded from their description. That creativity contributes a surd element to all such descriptions, which must then be probabilistic, since no set of characters will exhaustively describe any class of two or more such entities. We may therefore construct ontologies with as much certainty as is permitted in any probabilistic science, but the ontologies are necessarily descriptive and specific to the domain of description. This does not preclude a transcendental ontology[59]—which remains a sophisticated way of inspecting innate ideas—but it does mean that any such inspection describes the characters of a thinking entity in its particular domain of activity. This thinking entity may have a very expansive domain, indeed, but any such expanse remains finite, or not simply general. Thus, to any ontology, no matter how expansive, another may be added, and we must speak of ontologies, rather than ontology.

In this approach, ontology is defined as an empirical or descriptive science, whose practitioners identify the most general features of a given entity, usually of the most expansive entity with which they are acquainted.[60] The language of ontology is necessarily iconic or image-making. This means that the ontologist's reader or listener is supposed to receive the ontologist's descriptions as predicates of a process of thinking that would correspond, in the reader's imagination, to the entity's process of being what it is. If the ontology is a good one, this correspondence should enable the reader to make accurate predictions about what may be observed of the entity on a given occasion. Expansive ontologies describe entities in which ontologist and reader are participants. In this case, a good ontology would enable ontologist and reader to make accurate predictions about their own behavior, which means that the ontology would have normative value. Because every entity contains a surd element and could thus be other than it is, ontologies are necessarily selective: iconic representations are representations with respect to a particular, interpreting entity— what the semiotician would call the ontologist's *interpretant* (or interpreting prehension). "The ontologist's reader or listener" represents such an interpretant. This is not to suggest that the ontologist's interpretant *need* be so narrowly conceived: no matter how expansive it is, it must simply remain finite. Ontological descriptions are therefore not nominal, but they are partial; the relation of entity (as what the semiotician calls *object*) to interpreting entity (interpretant) is a real, but finite, relation.

A rabbinic text process theology is meta-ontological, because it refers to God's creativity, which is that with respect to which ontologies display their finitude. With respect to particular ontologies, such references appear as limitations or as sources of learned ignorance, and rabbinic theology appears as negative theology. There are no iconic representations of God's creativity and, thus, we have no intuitive knowledge of revelation. Nevertheless, there are non-iconic forms of representation, and we may have nonintuitive knowledge of revelation. Rabbinic text process theology understands the revelation of Torah on Mount Sinai to mean that we have knowledge of the meta-ontological: we can say something about how entities display their finitude and become other than they are. This means there are rules to God's creativity, even if the rules are themselves probabilistic ones, or incompletely determined.

For rabbinic text process theology, revelation signifies an interruption in a finite entity's processual life, as well as in any ontology that serves it. The interruption is manifested with respect to a particular moment in such a life, and the intuitive or iconizing knowledge we have of the revelatory moment is *of that life*, rather than of the interruption *per se*. To study the revelation itself, however, is to study verbal, and usually textual, testimony about the life of that entity *before and after or in response* to revelation, which is the life of that entity as it has become *other* than it is (was). The mark of revelation is our interpretive judgment about how life has changed or become other that it was in response to revelation. This mark is both an indexical and a symbolizing sign (two different forms of prehension). In Peirce's semiotic, an index marks the thatness of an interruptive event; it points without describing. Radical difference in the life of an entity points to the revelatory event, without describing it. For the semiotician, a symbol refers to its event-object by leading its interpreter to re-enact, in its relation to the symbol, the symbol's own relation to the event-object. The re-enactment is a form of imitation, marked by its own uniqueness, which will have symbolic significance to yet another interpreter, and so on. Revelation thus displays its meaning to a potentially indefinite series of symbolizing interpretants: in rabbinic theology, these constitute the revelation's text process.

In a recent study, Steven Fraade examines this text process as displayed in the third-century rabbinic commentary on Deuteronomy, the Sifre Deuteronomy, or *Sifre*. He writes that "rabbinic literature is a medium dedicated *both* to transmission and transformation: its texts not only transmit received traditions from an earlier time, but simultaneously and often subtly transform—for purposes of their own place and program in time—what they seek to transmit."[61] To illustrate the point, he examines a well-known passage from "Chapters of the Fathers."

> *"Moses received [qibbel]* Torah from Sinai and transmitted [*māsar*] it to Joshua, and Joshua to the elders. and the elders to the prophets, and the prophets transmitted it to the men of the Great Assembly. They said three things: Be thorough in judgment, raise up many disciples, and make a fence around the Torah. Simon the Just [ca. 200 b.c.e.] was among the last of the Great Assembly. He used to say: . . . Antigonus of Soko received [Torah] from Simeon the Just. He used to say: . . . " (*Abot* 1:1–3)

Fraade explains:

> This "chain of tradition" continues with fives pairs of teachers, each of whom adds one or more teachings to what he has received before transmitting the newly transformed Torah to the next link in the chain. The last pair is that of Hillel and Shammai [ca. 30 b.c.e.–10 c.e.], who in turn [despite some kinks in the chain] transmit what they have received and taught to Rabban Jochanan ben Zakkai [2:8], who together with his five students establishes, at the time of the destruction of the Second Temple in 70 c.e., the first specifically rabbinic center for learning at Yavneh [Jamnia].
>
> In this geneological chain each "link" [explicitly beginning with the men of the Great Assembly, but implicitly for their predecessors] transforms as it transmits Torah. That which is

newly added at each successive link in the chain is no less Torah than that which precedes it as it takes its place within the cumulative tradition, which is said to originate in the divine revelation at Sinai.[62]

As an example of the way the chain works, Fraade examines *Sifre's* reinterpretation of Deuteronomy 32:7, from Moses' parting song to Israel: "Remember the days of old, consider the years of each and every generation: ask your father, and he will inform you, your elders, and they will tell you." *Sifre* interprets,

> . . . [C] "Ask your father and he will inform you": These are the prophets as it says, "When Elisha beheld it he cried out [to Elijah], 'Father, father' " (2 Kings 2:12).
> [D] "Ask your elders and they will tell you": These are the elders, as it is said, "Gather for Me seventy men of the elders of Israel" (Numbers 11:16).
> Another interpretation: . . .
> [C'] "Ask your father and he will inform you": In the future Israel will be able to see and hear as if hearing from the Holy One . . . , as it is said, "Your ears shall hear a word behind you" (Isa. 30:21), and it says, "Your teacher [= God] shall not hide himself any more, and your eyes shall see your teacher" (Isa. 30:20).
> [D'] "Your elders and they will tell you": What I [= God] revealed to the elders on the mountain, as it is said, "And to Moses He said, 'Ascend to God [you and Aaron, Abihu, and the seventy elders of Israel]' " (Exod. 24:1).

Fraade explains:

> The terms *father* and *elders*, appearing in parallel construction in the biblical text, are understood as signifying not one's own biological father and the elderly of one's family or community as sources of wisdom, . . . but *inspired biblical leadership classes.* The word *father* is deicrically interpreted . . . to signify "prophets." The word *elders* is similarly interpreted as signifying "elders," . . . those nonpriests who were divinely authorized to share in Moses' leadership and judiciary functions. . . .
> [The] second set of interpretations . . . shifts our attention to the distant, messianic future. . . . The verse's *father* . . . is now interpreted less directly as signifying God, who in the messianic

future will be the teacher of *all* of Israel, obviating the need for
mediating prophets.
. . . [T]he elders alone remain constant . . . between the two
sets of interpretations. [The exegetical significations of all the
other terms have changed.] But *elders* are always the elders—
the inspired class of elders that is—whose biblically assigned
roles inrevelation and its societal adjudication remains operative
(unlike those of the prophets) . . . until such time as Israel's direct
hearing and seeing of God . . . will make their mediating
functions unnecessary.[63]

A text process theologian might interpret Fraade's illustration
in the following way. For the community that receives the Torah as
revelatory, "Honor your father and mother" (Exodus 20) are words that
interrupt its customary ways of understanding "honor," "father" and
"mother." A member of the community might think "this is what
'father' means," or "this is who he is." But, as a consequence of receiving those words as revelatory, this person might be led to think
somewhat differently: "yet, if honored, 'father' would mean more this,
and this person must then be that . . . ." The scriptural word "father"
would therefore no longer refer to this entity of which the person had
a particular image, but would, instead, come to refer to a way of
transforming his or her understanding of this entity and, then, of any
entity called "father." The word—to use Austin's terminology[64]—might
have any number of constative meanings, or images of "father," but
its ultimate meaning would be a perlocutionary one: this "way of
transforming understanding." From this perspective, the goals of *Sifre*
were both to declare that Scripture displayed its meanings in this
performative fashion and to identify the performative meaning of
certain words within the rabbinic community. Who is "father?" *Sifre*
did not claim that what was once called biological father actually
referred to prophets or to God, or that it changed its meaning from
father to prophet: the scriptural term remains "father," not "prophet"
or "God." It claimed, rather, that "father" in Deuteronomy 32 is a
symbol which refers not to being—which must appear as some particular being, such as "biological father"—but the potential interruption of being, which appears, then, for that community, as "biological
father who now acquires the role of witness to Moses' words," and
now, for this community, as "prophet," and then for the community
to come, as "God." Each interruption introduces a new performative
command: "no longer understand your father to be mere father; he

is now witness to Torah," then "no longer as mere witness, now prophet," and so on. From this perspective, *Sifre* is not re-assigning scripture's ontological meaning, but revealing scripture's meta-ontological depth. The text interpretation is, therefore, non-iconic. "Father" is not an icon of "biological father" or of "prophet." It remains a symbol of the process through which each potential icon is made to refer beyond itself: the passage from father(f) to prophet(p) to Gods(*) refers to some processual symbol (fp . . . n*). For any given interpreter, the ultimate meaning, or interpretant, of this symbol is the transformed habit of under-standing and action which will enable the interpreter, at a given time, to assign a given value (n) to "father" or some other value to "elder." Fraade notes that, for the rabbinic authors of *Sifre*, "fathers" are pro-phets and "elders" are the rabbis themselves, who interpret these words and their performative meanings. We have yet to hear how these values might be transformed as Fraade receives *Sifre's* words into his own community of practice.

For the text process theologian, in sum, *to know a revelation is not to depict it, but to walk in its way: to participate in an interpretive process which displays, in the habit-changes which accompany inter-pretation, the meaning of God's creativity.* The developmental aspect of the rabbinic text process is thus *halakhah* (from the root *halakh*, "to walk"): the rabbinic "way," or law, in which the meaning of revela-tion is displayed in behavioral guidelines particular to each generation in its time and place. This law is a mediating symbol of revelation, whose ultimate interpretant is habit-change. The habit-change, rather than the law itself, is the mark of revelation, *imitatio dei*, and must itself, therefore, manifest divine creativity.[65]

For rabbinic text process theology, habit-change is the ultimate subject matter of ethics as a nonontological science. From this perspec-tive, there are three forms of ethical inquiry. The only strictly onto-logical ethics is the empirical study of the most general, normative features of the societal entities—including the most expansive ones—in which the inquirer is a participant or participant-observer. Here, "normative" features are those that could influence participants' decisions about how to act. From this perspective, ontological ethics would tend to be a form of ethnography, call it ethno-ethics. What is usually called "rabbinic ethics" would refer to a species of meta-ontological ethics, which may be identified in the biblical traditions with theological ethics. This is the descriptive—and, in that sense, empirical—study of the most general, normative features of a revela-tion's text process, in which process the inquirer is a participant or participant-observer. In his study of rabbinic ethics, for example,

Kadushin labeled the normative features of rabbinic Judaism "value-concepts." The value-concepts behave in some ways like the normative features of an ontological ethics, since they are general and may guide conduct. The difference is that the conduct represents a revelatory way, or *halakhah*, and therefore has habit-change, rather than the continuation of some way of being, as its ultimate interpretant. This means that "loving-kindness" (*gemilut hasadim*) and "God's attribute of mercy" (*middat harachamim*) are attributes of not-being and, in that sense, of becoming, rather than of being. These are attributes of the ways in which entities become other than they are in relation to other entities: not just any way other, but other in the particular ways displayed in this particular revelatory text process. One feature of the rabbinic text process as a whole is the eschatological hope that these attributes of non-being may become as-if attributes of being. The "as if" is a reminder, however, that, in this world, or this mode of temporality, being and not-being are not identical. Interpreting *Sifre*, for example, we cannot assign any final value to "father." Technically, this means that we cannot represent the value-concepts iconically or eidetically, but only indexically and symbolically through narratives and exempla, rather than through definitions.

Rabbinic ethics, and theological ethics in general, are context specific, but in a less limiting way than are ontological ethics. In a particular revelatory text process, God's creativity is displayed as the occasion of habit-change in a particular societal entity: *gemilut hasadim*, for example, is a value-concept for rabbinic Jews of the Talmudic period. Since it refers to a form of change, however, rather than to any particular form of being, the value-concept refers to a form of relation that will characterize at least two classes of entity (a Jewish habit changed and not-yet changed) and may conceivably characterize an indefinite number of societal entities, rabbinic and other. Within a particular theological ethics, there is, however, only one linguistic category for referring to a value-concept in its maximal generality. This is the category of names for God: the one whose creativity is otherwise displayed only in the particular way particular habits are changed. Even then, such names tend to appear as value-concepts, stark indices of the one, but informative icons only of its appearances among the many.[66] The rabbinic ethicist supposes that *gemilut hasadim*, for example, displays the divine concern that will also appear within some other revelatory traditions, but not necessarily in the same way it appears in the rabbinic one.[67] Within the domain of ethics itself, the only medium that links the one and the many is relationship, which is itself the one in its concrete and context-specific manifestation.

Otherwise put, two systems of ethics are linked only through con-versations and other forms of interaction between them, rather than through any form of inquiry undertaken by members of either system independently of such interaction.

The sort of analysis I have offered in the preceding two paragraphs illustrates the third form of ethical inquiry, meta-ethics. It is the only form of ethics which supplies a vocabulary for making generalizations about two or more systems of ontology or two or more text processes. In exchange for this privilege, meta-ethics is deprived of the kind of ontological meaning and ethical force that are associated with the first two forms of ethics. As meta-ethicist, Kadushin coined such terms as "value-concept" and "organic thinking" and analyzed rabbinic ethics in terms meaningful to academics interested in ethical phenomena in general. By insisting that these terms referred, themselves, to "analytic" rather than "organic" concepts, he sought to protect the integrity of ethical systems from the intrusions of science. He feared the misplaced concretenesses of scientists who mistake the categories of analysis for those of the analysand. As I suggested earlier, however, Kadushin may have been overly protective. Separating analytic and organic concepts too sharply, he failed to identify the particular entity with respect to which scientific inquiry—including his inquiry—has its own variety of meta-ontological meaning.

Meta-ethics has its place in Western academia,[68] understood as a hybrid and highly contested collection of text processes, interpreting testimonies of both biblical and non-biblical revelations of divine creativity (so-named and not so-named!). What are called "analytic" or "scientific" vocabularies function within academia the way "value-conceptual" or "organic" vocabularies function within particular rev-elatory text processes. That is to say, scientific vocabularies are not particular to this or that vernacular (in our terms, they are not onto-logical), but they are particular to some text process, for which they name rules of habit-change and thus have ethical force (that is, they are meta-ontological). They are different from revelatory text processes in the specific virtues they inculcate and in their claim to general rather than indefinite indeterminacy: that is, in their presumption of context-independence. The organicist science that attracted Kadushin belonged to one of a set of academia's contested text processes. Its proponents promoted it as the correct member of this set, arguing on behalf of its usefulness not only as a means of describing phenomena particular to any of the ontologies of interest to academics, but also as a norm for evaluating the various systems of ontological ethics and for encouraging certain kinds of habit-change within them. When he objected to certain aspects of Bergson's or Whitehead's thinking, Kadushin was objecting to what he considered the limits not only of their explanatory schemes, but also of their meta-ontological ethics. He argued, on philosophic grounds, that Bergson and Whitehead were incompletely loyal to their organicist principles, since they treated some of the analytic concepts of their science as if they were the value-concepts of some system of ethics.[69] He might have sought, instead, to identify the academic text process to which those "analytic" concepts belonged and on behalf of which Bergson and Whitehead promoted value-concepts, of which at least one appears to have been incompatible with those of his rabbinic ethics. This is the concept of God as being.

From a text process perspective, the error of attempting to describe the presence of God as being is the error of attempting to iconize God's creativity. As we have seen, the alternative is to describe the presence of God in its non-being and to symbolize God's creativity in an indefinite process of transformatory interpretations. Kadushin argued that such a process is an organism whose individuality and context-specificity Whitehead failed to appreciate. Does this mean that text process theology is simply incompatible with a natural process theology? To introduce the answer that I hope we might be able to find on another occasion, I close with an illustrative scenario of how apparent differences between the two forms of process theology might be resolved.

In this scenario, what natural process theologians call ontological claims would be simply relabeled and divided (in text process terms) into a set of meta-ontological and a set of meta-ethical claims.[70] Each set of claims would be attached to a different level of ethical inquiry within academe, undertaken by potentially different communities of inquirers. On the level of meta-ontological inquiry, text process and natural meta-ontologies would represent mutually-irreducible but complementary forms of inquiry. These forms would be undertaken by several different sub-groups of inquirers, such as rabbinic text process theologians, Jewish natural-process theologians, Christian natural-process theologians, and so on. Text- and natural-process theologies would employ contrasting vocabularies (referring, for example, to nature vs. creation, supernatural vs. textual, or being vs. non-being) to communicate to their different sub-groups of inquirers ways of promoting the virtues of habit-change in different societal entities. On the level of meta-ethical inquiry, a single community of process meta-ethicists would develop a single vocabulary for describing the different forms of process meta-ontology. This community would share the virtues which promote the forms of habit-change that are appropriate to this level of academic inquiry. According to this scenario, one person might function both as rabbinic meta-ontologist and process meta-ethicist, and another both as natural process meta-ontologist and process meta-ethicist. Their differences would be constructive and instructive.[71]

VII. Glossary

Here is a glossary of technical terms used in this essay. The ultimate sources of the terms are indicated as follows: K, Kadushin; W, Whitehead; P, Peirce. If I have varied an author's term to suit my purposes, I add a +. [For Whiteheadian definitions, I have consulted Kadushin's favorite interpreter of Whitehead: Dorothy Emmet, *Whitehead's Philosophy of Organism* (London: MacMillan and Co., 1932).]

Appetition: an urge to realize some relevant possibility, combined with a valuation in support of that urge (W). In Kadushin's terminology, this corresponds to a value's *"drive for concretization"* (K).

Concrescence: the process by which the elements (for example, prehensions) of an actual entity grow together into a unity. The entity is this concrescence (W).

Consequent Nature of God: God's everlasting prehension of the actual occasions in the temporal world. This is the source of all objectification (W).

Eternal object: a "pure potential for the specific determination of matters of fact," that is, a real possibility to be actualized; or a form of definiteness in the process of becoming (W).

Events: the ultimate facts of nature, which include every conceivable occurrence; an event is a nexus of interrelated occasions. Actual *occasions* or *entities* are what in everyday language we call "things," understood as processes of concrescence. Thus, events interconnect things (W).

Interpretation: the activity in the context of which a sign or symbol refers to its meaning or object (P).

Interpretive events: occurrences of interpretation (K+).

Modernist thinking: the "Cartesian" or Cartesian-like tendency to generalize doubts about aspects of a tradition of thought-and-practice into doubts about inherited knowledge as such, and the "Cartesian" attempt to substitute the authority of certain individual perceptions and judgments for the authority of inherited traditions of knowledge (P+).

Organism: nexus, or the fact of togetherness among actual entities; every
entity is also a nexus of its prehensions of other entities (W). Thus,
conceptual organism refers to a nexus of concepts (W+, K).

Prehension: a "grasping," the way one actual entity appropriates aspects
of other actual entities in its own development. The actual entity
is thus composed of its prehensions of other entities (W). I identify
both feelings and interpretations as prehensions.

Primordial Nature of God: God's eternal ordering of the universe of
all possibilities; or God's conception of the order of all eternal
objects. This is the primordial source of both novelty and limitation in the universe (W).

Notes

1. For biographical details, see Theodore Steinberg, "Max Kadushin:
An Intellectual Biography," in *Understanding the Rabbinic Mind: Essays on
The Hermeneutic of Max Kadushin* (henceforth *URM*), P. Ochs, ed. (Atlanta:
Scholar's Press for South Florida Studies in the History of Judaism, 1990), 1–18.
See also, Theodore Steinberg, *Max Kadushin, Scholar of Rabbinic Judaism:
A Study of His Life, Work, and Theory of Valuational Thought,* Ph.D.
Dissertation, New York University, 1979.

2. See P. Ochs, "Max Kadushin as Rabbinic Pragmatist," in *URM,*
165–96. I argue there that Kadushin is most appropriately classified among
the group of "aftermoderns," including Buber, Franz Rosenzweig, Hermann
Cohen, and Emil Fackenheim. I note that this group displays a characteristic
pattern of inquiry, among the major stages of which are:

(a) university training (from which they emerge as critics of traditional
forms of Jewish self-understanding, turning to modern philosophy
as a tool for improving this self-understanding);

(b) subsequent disillusionment with the modernist thinking they
acquired in the university (which breeds an attempt to locate
indigenous forms of self-understanding within traditional Jewish
practices and literatures)

(c) an attempt to nurture reformational communities of Jewish
inquirers, informed by both traditional Jewish norms of practice
and Western-academic norms of inquiry.

3. See the glossary at the end of this essay.

4. Steinberg suggests that Kaplan and Kadushin had a "father-son
relationship" and that their parting may also have stemmed "from personality
conflict, perhaps exacerbated by the emotional conflicts that often erupt in

father-son relationships, whether surrogate or natural" (Steinberg, *Max Kadushin*, 7).

5. I am personifying Kadushin's position a bit here, attributing claims to him that I believe are implicit in many of his explicit arguments.

6. Guided by the dogmatist's law of excluded middle, either side saw in rabbinic Judaism its contrary. Consider, for example, the critics addressed by Moses Mendelssohn: neo-orthodox emotivists like Johann Lavater and those enlightened rationalists who considered the Talmud "a work composed only of insipid foolery" [from Mendelssohn's *Litteraturbriefe*, cited in Michael Meyer, *The Origins of the Modern Jew* (Detroit: Wayne State, 1967), 21]. While Kadushin did not offer such examples in print, Simon Greenberg suggests Mendelssohn's responses to such critics prefigured Kadushin's responses (Greenberg, "Coherence and Change in the Rabbinic Universe of Discourse: Kadushin's Theory of the Value Concept," in *URM*, 19–43). Simon Greenberg suggests that Kadushin continued Moses Mendelssohn's response to his contemporaries' rationalist criticisms of the Talmud's "inanities and eccentricities."

7. Most likely a ninth-century midrashic compilation from the Land of Israel. Kadushin published his study of *Seder Eliahu* as *The Theology of Seder Eliahu: A Study in Rabbinic Judaism* (New York: Bloch Publishing, 1932). For a discussion of Kadushin's use of *Seder Eliahu*, see Richard Sarason, "Kadushin's Study of Midrash: Value Concepts and Their Literary Embodiment," in *URM*, 45–77.

8. Max Kadushin, *The Rabbinic Mind*, 3rd edition (New York: Bloch Publishing, 1972), 31.

9. Concerning Kadushin's use of the terms "organic" and "organismic," Steinberg writes that "both words have the same connotation in Kadushin's writings. 'Organic' is the term he used in his earlier writings. He changed to 'organismic' . . . [when] he noted that 'organic' is commonly used in fascist philosophies to glamorize pseudo-science and racial prejudice" ("Max Kadushin: An Intellectual Biography," in *URM*, 4 n.8.) See Max Kadushin, *Organic Thinking: A Study in Rabbinic Thought* (New York: Bloch Publishing, 1938), 252.

10. Kadushin refers to Whitehead, *Process and Reality* (New York: Macmillan, 1929), *Religion in the Making* (New York: Macmillan, 1926), and *Science in the Modern World* (New York: Macmillan, 1925); to Emmet, *Whitehead's Philosophy of Organism* (New York: Macmillan, 1932); to Dewey, *Experience and Nature* (Chicago: Open court, 1925); to Bergson, *Creative Evolution* (New York, 1911) and *The Two Sources of Morality and Religion* (New York: Henry Holt and Co., 1935); to Wheeler, "Organismic Logic in the History of Science," *Philosophy of Science* 5/1 (January 1936), 26–61; to Ritter, *The Unity of the Organism* (Boston: Richard G. Badger, The Gorham Press,

1919); and to Ritter and Bailey, *The Organismic Conception: Its Place in Science and Its Bearing on Philosophy* (Berkeley: University of California, 1928).

11.   In *URM*, see Jacob Neusner, "Foreword," ix–xvi; Richard Sarason, "Kadushin's Study of Midrash," 45–73; and Alan Avery-Peck, "Max Kadusin as Exegete: The Conceptual Commentary to Leviticus Rabbah," 73–95.

12.   Kadushin, *Organic Thinking*, 184. He cites with favor Ritter and Bailey's definition of the "organismal conception" as "the conclusion that . . . wholes are so related to their parts that not only does the existence of the whole depend on the orderly cooperation and interdependence of its parts, but the whole exercises a measure of determinative control over its parts" (from *The Organismic Conception*, cited in *Organic Thinking*, 185).

13.   This list, which paraphrases Kadushin's claims, is suggested by Simon Greenberg's summary of these features in Greenberg, "Coherence and Change," 19–44.

14.   Ibid., 26.

15.   From P. Ochs, "Max Kadushin as Rabbinic Pragmatist," in *URM*, 179.

16.   From *Midrash Rabbah* I–X, Freedman and Simon, ed. (London: Soncino Press, 1939, 1961).

17.   Ibid., I: 66–67.

18.   Ibid.

19.   Kadushin, *The Rabbinic Mind*, 294.

20.   Ibid., 50–51. This and the following definitions are drawn from P. Ochs. "Max Kadushin as Rabbinic Pragmatist," in *URM*, 182.

21.   Kadushin apparently drew a distinction between reference, or the way a concept referred to objects in the world, and sense, or the way it was associated with certain meanings. It appears that "cognitive" and "connotative" concepts refer to ideal types: the one tending to have reference without sense; the other, sense without reference.

22.   Kadushin, *The Rabbinic Mind*, 22.

23.   Greenberg, "Coherence and Change," 26.

24.   Kadushin, *The Rabbinic Mind*, 78, cited in Greenberg, "Coherence and Change," 27.

25.   Kadushin, *Organic Thinking*, 193.

26.   Ibid., 194–95.

27.   Ibid., 196.

28. Ibid., 247–48.

29. To be sure, Kadushin says explicitly that " 'eternal objects' are not organic concepts" (ibid., 248), but the two notions function comparably in the two thinkers' systems. In the following paragraphs, I discuss similarities and differences between the two notions.

30. *The Rabbinic Mind*, 79–80. Kadushin read with favor Emmet's study of Whitehead. She wrote, "Whitehead defines [the 'eternal objects'] broadly as 'forms of definiteness,' or 'pure potentials for the specific determination of matters of fact.' The metaphysical status of an eternal object is, therefore, to be a possibility for actualization" (*Whitehead's Philosophy of Organism*, 113). Of possible interpretations of the status of eternal objects, she favored this one: that Whitehead "might define universals as recurrent types of uniformity exhibited in the process, but without any status outside it" (107). God and world are thus interdependent, as are concept and concrescence, the Primordial and the Consequent or, for Kadushin, the value-concept and the *halakhah*.

31. Kadushin, *The Rabbinic Mind*, p. 78.

32. Ibid., 81.

33. See glossary at the end of this essay for definitions of technical terms to follow.

34. Perhaps the "mental pole" of this nature (cf. Emmet, 258–60) or its "conceptual phase" (cf. Kenneth Thompson, *Whitehead's Philosophy of Religion* (The Hague, Paris: Mouton, 1971), 66–68.

35. As illustrated, *in extremis*, in the teaching that, when one reaches into his or her pocket for charity-money, the hand that reaches is literally God's hand (from the *Tanya* of Rabbi Schneur Zalman of Liadi).

36. Kadushin, *The Rabbinic Mind*, 273–75.

37. Kadushin, *Organic Thinking*, 248–49.

38. Ibid., 251.

39. According to the biblical scholar and philosopher Yohanan Muffs, Kadushin rarely referred to Peirce in writing, but "I think you might like to know that Kadushin was a careful reader of Peirce's writings and talked of them at great length. We used to walk down Riverside Drive together [in the 1960s], coming home from the [Jewish Theological] Seminary. One of us would hold a volume of Peirce's *Collected Papers*, and we would discuss his philosophy in detail" (from a conversation I had with Muffs in 1988).

40. Or in the way they contribute to the modalities (necessity, possibility, impossibility, etc.) of the propositions in which they appear.

41. Or in that from which they are derived.

42. With regard to the general, he added, "Thus, although it is true that 'Any proposition you please, *once you have determined its identity*, is either true or false'; yet *so long as it remains indeterminate and so without identity*, it need neither be true that any proposition you please is true, nor that any proposition you please is false." With regard to the vague, he added, "So likewise, while it is false that 'A proposition *whose identity I have determined* [a vague reference] is both true and false,' yet until it is determinate, it may be true that a proposition is true and that a proposition is false" (Charles Peirce, *Collected Papers*, 6 vols., Charles Hartshorne and Paul Weiss, eds. [Cambridge: Harvard University, 1931, 1935], vol. 5, par. 448. Future reference to these volumes will be to volume and paragraph number: e.g., 5.448).

43. I have rendered Peirce's example gender neutral.

44. Peirce, *Collected Papers*, 5.447.

45. The rabbis' value-conceptual language is thus performative. Adopting the terminology of J.L. Austin (*How To Do Things with Words* [Cambridge: Harvard University, 1978]), Edith Wyschogrod has recently described "classical Judaism" as "a perlocutionary language" ("Works that 'Faith': The Grammar of Ethics in Judaism," *Cross Currents: Religion and Intellectual Life* 40/2 (Summer, 1990), 176–93, 178). This means that the use of the value-concepts in rabbinic writing or speech is intended to have consequences. In Austin's terms, perlocutionary speech acts are those in which "saying something will often, or even normally, produce certain consequential effects upon the feelings, thoughts or actions of the audience, or of the speaker or of other persons" (88; cited in Wyschogrod).

46. Paraphrased from Peirce, *Collected Papers*, 2.247–49 (1903).

47. In Austin's terms, they are merely "constative," or representational, but non-performative.

48. In the language of ethnoscience, the characterizations are "emic," rather than "etic," although the ethnoscientist—here, Kadushin—does sort them out and refine them for scholarly inspection.

49. See George Lindbeck, *The Nature of Doctrine: Religion and Theology in a Postliberal Age* (Philadelphia: Westminster, 1984), *passim*.

50. Kadushin, *Organic Thinking*, 251.

51. Ibid., 250–51.

52. "Foreword," to *URM*, xi, xii, xiii, xiv. Richard Sarason adds, "It is ironic . . . that despite his vigorous objections to the model of systematic philosophical theology and his insistence on the experiential character and origin of the rabbinic value concepts, [Kadushin's] own analysis owed more to philosophy than to history" ("Kadushin's Study of Midrash," *URM*, 51).

53.   See Peirce, "Issues of Pragmaticism," *The Monist* 15 (1905), 481–99, in *Collected Papers*, 5.438ff., and his manuscript "Consequences of Critical Common-Sensism," in *Collected Papers*, 5.505ff.

54.   "The Bible and rabbinic theology are, then, successive organic levels, with the second emerging from the first . . . . Because the rabbinic complex has a wider range of concretization and hence enriches with significance a wider sphere of situations, it is . . . richer than the biblical" (Kadushin, *Organic Thinking*, 227; cf. 219ff., also *The Rabbinic Mind*, 273ff, 303ff.).

55.   See Kadushin, *The Rabbinic Mind*, 35ff.

56.   Kadushin idealized the degree to which "there [was] no gap between the authors or teachers and the folk" (*The Rabbinic Mind*, 85).

57.   I am identifying Whitehead's general theory of concretion and of individual entities with a habit-theory of conduct. See his *Religion in the Making*, ch. I and *passim*. For a general discussion of recent applications of Aristotle's theory, see Alasdair MacIntyre, *After Virtue: A Study in Moral Theory* (Notre Dame: University of Notre Dame Press, 1984), 181ff. For Maimonides, see, for example, his *Guide of the Perplexed*, I.34, III.53 and, in general, his *Eight Chapters*. For Peirce, see, for example, his 1903 comments on "Ideals of Conduct," in *Collected Papers*, 1.591ff.

58.   *Organic Thinking*, 251.

59.   That is, an ontology constructed by identifying the conditions according to which existence as we know it is (appears) possible. I am claiming that such an ontology—Kantian, Husserlian, or other—must be presented, in nondogmatic fashion, as a fallibilistic, or probabilistic, science.

60.   The idea is to replace dogmatic claims about "universality" with far-reaching yet fallibilistic claims about "expansiveness."

61.   From Chapter 3, "The Early Rabbinic Sage and His Torah in the Text of the *Sifre*," of Steven D. Fraade, *From Tradition to Commentary* (Albany: State University of New York Press, 1991), 69–121, at 69.

62.   Ibid., 70.

63.   Ibid., 76–79.

64.   See n. 41 above.

65.   Thus, a moment of God's creativity can be interpreted only by another moment of God's creativity. This claim corresponds to traditional Jewish and Christian claims that scriptural interpretations can be authentic or non-authentic, and that the authentic ones are informed by God's spirit (however named). Such claims may be evaluated quantitatively as well as qualitatively: God's spirit may be listened to more or less attentively and,

thus, interpretations may be more or less reflective of God's creativity. To discuss who is to judge this would be to replay, from a text-process perspective, familiar arguments about the relative authority of communal and specialized decision-making procedures. Rabbinic theology regards the Torah as authentic testimony about a revelation of God's creativity and the rabbinic tradition of scriptural interpretation as an authentic process of interpreting the meaning of that revelation. The tradition displays, intrasystemically, critera for evaluating the authority of supportive testimony about God's creativity and of the interpretations which serve such testimony. As an evolving process of interpretation, the tradition constitutes an individual entity—as long as it is not identified with any single, context–specific description of it. In its finitude, this tradition cannot include all possible testimonies about God's creativity, nor all text-processes that may possibly interpret the Sinaitic testimony. In its finitude, furthermore, the tradition pressupposes the existence of other text-processes and other testimonies and the possibility of interaction or dialogue with them.

66. See Kadushin's study of the conceptual terms for God: *The Rabbinic Mind*, 194–201. Also, P. Ochs, "There's No God-Talk Unless God Talks: A Study of Max Kadushin as Rabbinic Pragmatist," in *Proceedings of the Academy for Jewish Philosophy* (Atlanta: Scholar's Press, 1990).

67. The way a value-concept appears within a tradition may be judged by the set of concretizations that illustrate it. Two value-concepts would appear similar if their respective sets of concretizations appeared to be isomorphic.

68. "Western" is used here as a term of origination and not of exclusion. The following analysis draws on research that was made possible by a grant from the Spencer Foundation.

69. If Kadushin differed so sharply on certain points from Whitehead, it may be because Kadushin tended to assimilate his philosophic to his vernacular activity, while Whitehead may have tended to assimilate his vernacular to his philosophic activity. A process naturalist may or may not object to the latter form of assimilation; a non-relativistic process textualist must object to either form.

70. In a letter to me, Norbert Samuelson notes that such a text process theology "sounds like Hermann Cohen's particular brand of idealism, and Kadushin's rabbinic Judaism sounds like Cohen's *Religion of Reason out of the Sources of Judaism*." He adds that "the concept of God, functioning as a value term which stands outside of any perceived reality, is most compatible with Cohen's Kantian notion of a world that 'ought to be' standing outside of the world that 'is'. "

71. I am indebted to Sandra Lubarsky and David Griffin for stimulating this essay, and to Norbert Samuelson for offering extensive suggestions for its revision.

Chapter 14

The Organic Relation Between Natural and Text Process Theologies

John B. Cobb, Jr.

As a Christian process theologian I have long been interested in working through the implications of process thought for the interpretation of history and specifically of religious traditions such as Christianity. In Peter Ochs' terms I am a natural process theologian in that I take my cue from Whitehead's analysis of the actual entity. This may mean that from his point of view my approach to historical events and texts is *a priori*, although I do not accept that characterization. I am aided also by Whitehead's own not inconsiderable discussion of history and values, especially in *Adventures of Ideas*.

My conclusions have been that religious traditions, such as Christianity, should be thought of as social-historical processes or movements. I find myself in agreement here with leaders of the socio-historical school at the University of Chicago in the early decades of this century. This is not a surprising conclusion for a process theologian to reach, but it leads to results that are far from being widely accepted.

It means, of course, that Christianity has no essence. There is no doctrine, no set of values, no way of life, no ecclesiastical practice, no mode of being in the world, that defines what Christianity always and at all places must be. Christianity is a living community that has its identity from remembering a shared history. But which features of that history are emphasized, how they are interpreted, what implications are drawn from them—all that changes.

It is possible to distinguish healthy changes from decadence. Healthy changes involve a creative transformation of the received tradition. Decadence involves the decay of memory, the loss of serious-ness, the ossification of tradition into something to be objectively affirmed without subjective involvement, or defensive closure against truth and criticism from within or without the community.

That there has been and continues to be change in Christianity is not disputed. Also, most agree that some of the changes are desirable and even necessary. But there is great resistance to viewing Christianity entirely in process terms. There is widespread effort to establish some final authority, some court of appeal that is not itself in process. For Catholics this may be the living tradition as interpreted by the curia. This seems to come close to a process view, but it fails in two respects. First, it usually understands the tradition as unfolding truths that have been implicit from the beginning. Second, it attributes to certain papal pronouncements a finality, even an inerrancy, that, from the process point of view, cannot belong to anything human.

Protestants have been more likely to attribute final authority to Scripture as the Word of God. It has taken two centuries of historical-critical scholarship to show the process character of what is congealed in the canonized text. Only now is it becoming possible to think more of the ongoing process of canonization than of a once-and-for-all fixed canon. Even those who have opposed biblicism have typically appealed to something fixed—an essence of Christianity, the spirit of Jesus, or the kerygma. The vast changes that have actually occurred are taken to be changing interpretations of some defined and given core. The unequivocal denial that there is any such core, called for by a genuinely processive approach, is rare.

Viewed from the distance of Christianity, rabbinic Judaism has appeared to be less resistant to a processive interpretation. It seems to be constantly in the process of determining what Judaism con-cretely and normatively is. Of course, in this process it appeals to its texts, indeed to a vast array of texts, but the determination is made now as a creative act rather than as a deduction from a supposed unchanging principle.

Imagine my delight to learn that even without any prior in-fluence of process philosophers, a profound Jewish thinker, Max Kadushin, developed an account of "the rationality of classical rabbinic discourse" along these lines.[1] The account is rich in detail beyond my imagination. Indeed, I am not sure that I am able to follow every nuance. But I *am* sure that it shows that a vital, long-sustained move-ment can flourish without the illusion that it is something other than a process. It provides a model from which Christians have much to learn.

I. The Need for Organic Relations between
Communities of Discourse

As long as I attend only to what is affirmed positively about "text process theology," I feel no need for reconciliation with "natural process theology." I experience instead a harmonious fit. But since that is not the perception of either Kadushin or Ochs, it may be important to explore the tensions they identify.

Ochs himself points out how one may overcome one of the tensions with which Kadushin struggles. Kadushin thought of scientific analysis as standing outside the effort of a community to clarify its thought in relation to its practice. Ochs rightly shows that this is not the case, that it is a matter of different communities. There are scientific and philosophical communities as well as religious ones, and their work has the same kind of organic character as that of religious communities.

But Ochs leaves us with these several communities as quite discrete, each dealing with its separate questions. Ochs allows that one person might operate in more than one community, but the intellectual activities engaged in would, I gather, not influence one another. In this way Ochs is less exclusivist than Kadushin, but the result, from my point of view as a Christian process theologian, is not satisfactory. It is to reaffirm the fragmentation of thinking that Whitehead worked so hard to overcome and that, from my Christian perspective, is profoundly unhealthy. It affirms several organic systems of thought, but it does not allow for organic relations among them. I do not believe that Judaism has any stake in maintaining this fragmentation, but of course I cannot speak with any authority on that issue.

Ochs provides us with a clear indication of the problem as he sees it. For Jewish text process theology, "God's creativity is displayed as the occasion of habit-change in a particular societal entity."[2] Elsewhere, Kadushin calls this *creative transformation*. But he and Ochs contrast their view with what they assert to be Whitehead's understanding of "God as being."[3] Kadushin presumably wants to exclude the latter altogether, whereas Ochs wants to allow it to be discussed in a distinct community, but only in such a way as not to be brought to bear on text theology.

It is certainly the case that the style of thinking typical of the rabbis and that typical of philosophy are very different. There *is* a problem. However, the problem of positively connecting Whitehead's theistic speculations with rabbinic text theology is exaggerated in the formulations I have quoted. Whitehead, of course, does not, strictly speaking, understand God as being. What is rightly meant, I think, is that he does understand God as an "actual entity," and that such an understanding provides a basis for further speculation.

On the side of the rabbinic texts themselves, it is not clear to me that there is anything like the consistent opposition to conceiving God as an actual entity that Ochs' essay suggests. Certainly, there is much textual imagery that positively suggests this interpretation. That the dominant focus of attention is on changing habits and not on answering questions about a divine actual entity is surely true. But I believe it would be possible to construe this as a matter of emphasis rather than of strict exclusion. Indeed, I find it hard to read the texts without thinking that most of the rabbis thought of God as an actual entity.

I believe also that the texts often discern God's creativity in the natural world, as well as in the human one. I have thought that one advantage of Judaism over modern Christianity is that it did not separate the human from the natural so radically. Perhaps I am wrong, but if so, then I hope that Jewish text process theology will be creatively transformed so as to work against this dualism. Hence, I hope that any distinction between natural and text process theology, based on the strict restriction of interest in the latter to the human sphere, will be overcome through their interaction rather than rigidly maintained by separating the communities of discourse.

My point is not at all that there is no distinction between philosophical theology and process text theology. There certainly is. The former, in its process form, sometimes takes off from the conviction that God is an actual entity and speculates about the implications of that fact. The latter focuses on God's work in human life. The data and the style of work are profoundly different. Ochs is correct that the communities within which the work goes on are also different, even though some people participate in both. Perhaps as matters now stand, his solution is the best available.

However, I want to keep as a goal an organic relation between these communities of discourse. From my perspective as a Christian natural process theologian, natural process theology needs to be deeply informed by text process theology. And I also believe that textual hermeneutics can be informed by what is understood of God in the community of natural process theologians.

I will not pursue further this questioning of Jewish text process theology. It seems to have found inexhaustible internal resources for its own continuous creative transformation. Perhaps it has no need to learn from natural process theology or from Christianity. But if so, I would not judge that in this respect it is a good model for Christian text process theology. It *is* important that Christianity learn from living Judaism. The creative transformation that is God's creativity at work in Christianity includes this reception from Judaism of elements of its wisdom that are still not appreciated or internalized.

Even if I am wrong, and it be true that rabbinic texts refuse to consider God as an actual entity, this is not the case with Christian texts. Many scholars today want to exclude God's own reality, transcending its effects in human life, from Christian consideration. But this is the effect of particular features of modernity rather than of the major Christian texts themselves. Of course, the texts vary as to their openness to speculation, and, from the point of view of many, Whitehead goes too far. But this is a debate within the texts and the community of their interpreters rather than a matter to be decided *a priori* because of the textual focus. The Christian cannot so easily distribute the several topics Ochs considers at the end among separate communities of discourse.

II. The Shared Conviction of Divine Creativity

In conclusion, I would like to respond to some of the comments made by Ochs about ontology. He says:

> a text process theology which adopts rabbinic modes of Scriptural interpretation as normative cannot also adopt a process ontology as normative, because it cannot assign general universal validity to any single ontology. If we define ontology as a description of the most general characters of an entity, specifically of an entity of very expansive domain, then a rabbinic theology is meta-ontological, since it refers to God's creativity as that with respect to which any entity—including any organismic system of law—may become other than it is. For rabbinic theology, all actual entities—organisms or finite systems of being—are creatures of God. This means that they cannot be described adequately if God's creativity is excluded from their description. That creativity contributes a surd element to all such descriptions, which must then be probabilistic, since no set of characters will exhaustively describe any class of two or more such entities.[4]

The theory of multiple ontologies is an interesting one. I understand it in the sense of the regional ontologies proposed by Husserl.

However, I follow Whitehead's different approach. He does not talk about various ontologies. He talks instead of the various "fields" in which the airplane of speculative philosophy is landed. In each field one probes for the most illuminating generalizations one can find. But one believes that in fact there are connections between the several fields. So one tries out the hypothesis that something that is applicable in one field *may* be applicable in another as well.

Ochs' main point in the passage quoted above is that none of the regional ontologies works adequately because they all omit the divine element. God's creativity acts in all the things with which these ontologies deal, and it is the nature of this creativity to make them other than they have been. For Whitehead also, this is one of the findings of speculative philosophy. Any generalizations about particular fields that omits this creative and transformative working of God are finally inadequate and misleading for just the reason that Ochs states.

There may be good reasons that text process theology cannot adopt Whitehead's speculative scheme as normative. Indeed, the idea of adopting it as *normative* is somewhat un-Whiteheadian. The scheme is a complex *hypothesis* to be continuously tried out and modified in that process. It is normative only in the way that scientific hypotheses are normative, that is, their considerable success warrants taking them quite seriously and continuing to employ and test them until their limits are discovered. In this sense, I do not understand why text process theology cannot make provisional use of a speculative system that shares its "meta-ontological" convictions so exactly. In doing so it may help to establish both the extent and the limits of its applicability, while finding it illuminating in at least some instances.

My comments are not in opposition to what is said in Ochs' essay. They are not in any way a criticism of what is said about text process theology as such. They are a response to what seem to me to be misunderstandings about natural process theology that lead to building too much of a wall between the two aspects of process theology. I hope that in the process of distinguishing my sense of what is now needed, at least among Christians, from the views of Kadushin and Ochs, I am not building another wall between us.

Notes

1. Peter Ochs, "Rabbinic Text Process Theology," in this volume, 206.

2. Ibid., 231.

3. Ibid., 233.
4. Ibid., 225.

Chapter 15

Biblical Hermeneutics and Process Thought

William A. Beardslee

In his book on *The Poetics of Biblical Narrative*, Meir Sternberg faults Robert Alter's *The Art of Biblical Narrative* for taking fiction as the model for biblical prose. Alter had found modern fiction a useful point of comparison because studies of fiction have helped us to understand how the narrator communicates an imagined world and its values. Sternberg holds that the biblical narratives are not intended as fiction but as history. However, in making this point he indicates that the historian is just as much concerned with imaginative construction, portrayal of character (which does not appear immediately in the events, but has to be presented by the historian in the narrative), and moral values as is the writer of fiction. Further, Sternberg clearly sees that his generic identification of the biblical narratives as history does not directly deal with their truth–value; he is dealing with truth-claims implied by the rhetorical choices made by the writers, and from his literary point of view he does not have to judge the truth-value of what he calls ideological, or what we might call faith, claims.[1]

I. Scripture-and-Interpretation

We do not have to arbitrate the debate between Alter and Sternberg. In my view we can learn a great deal from each of them. But though the discussion as framed does not necessarily raise the question of the happenedness of the events narrated in a tradition, almost inevitably we move to this question. Hermeneutics is so often understood today solely in terms of the meeting of subjective worlds, and in terms of linguistic structures, that the raising of the question of happenedness, of objective reference, is a welcome move, and one which process intepreters will find congenial.

At the same time, a usual way of raising this question is to presuppose a sharp distinction between fact and value, so that the interpreter is thought to be working back through layers of attributed value and meaning to some originally neutral "facts" that lie behind the tradition. This separation between fact and value is part of our modern heritage, which process thought intends to rethink. From the process point of view, there are no neutral "facts." All events are laden with value intrisically; they have value to themselves and to the network of events within which they come into being.

Thus the interpreter is indeed, as linguistically-oriented thinkers point out to us, involved in a web of meaning and value from the beginning—but this network of meanings is not self-contained. This network arises from interactions with the value-laden events in its past, and interpretation as an event contributes to the values and meanings of the future. Thus, interpretation does deal with the communication of meanings in a changed cultural situation. Meanings are established in networks of meanings so that a change of one term will affect the whole set or network. But this network does not only apply to meaning, leaving the facts untouched. The events themselves are value-laden, and any interpretation that we give them is as well.

We do indeed want to know what happened. Like many other types of philosophical theology, process thought, when it is discussing the probability that a given event did or did not take place, would want to find criteria that could be shared by as wide a public as possible. But process thought would firmly reject the assumption that the separation of fact and value provides adequate public presupposition for discourse. That is precisely what has to be challenged.

Some process interpreters would identify a fixed point, either an essence or a particular biblical formulation or a proclamation derived from the biblical presentation, as the basic point of comparison for our present response to the text. Others would test the nature of the transformation that the text elicits in us: is it the creative transformation that God is continually working, or is it to be reconsidered because it is not in harmony with this criterion?

In a believing community, interpretation is a shared enterprise, not an individual one, and the specific historical setting may demand that creative fidelity to a particular faith embody strong and central elements of *preservation*. Thus, creative transformation does not always mean changing the formulations of the faith that have been inherited.

In reading a text, we encounter a bundle of proposals or, in technical process language, "propositions." A proposal or proposition brings together a concrete datum of experience with a possibility; it suggests how something might be. Taken together, the propositions offered in our reading of a sustained passage from the Bible offer a proposed world. But this world is not simply derived from the Bible. The propositions that we encounter in reading the biblical text are not the same propositions that were suggested to the original readers or hearers, or that were in the mind (only partly consciously, of course) of the author. Each reading of a biblical text invokes a different group of propositions. So far, we are on Alter's ground. A part of the significance of scholarly work on the Bible is to test the degree of overlap of the propositions that we "hear" with those that we believe would have been heard by a reader or hearer in the formative time of the Scripture.

But from a process point of view there is no simple normativity in the original hearing of the scriptural word. The use of Scripture is not to replicate its original meaning, but to assure our foundation in the historical stream that flows from the foundation of our faith. It is not just that a reconstruction of what the text might have meant in biblical times is always hypothetical. More fundamentally, in process thinking we believe that God is continually at work in the process of creative transformation, so that the attempt to reactualize an earlier configuration of faithful belief and action would be constrictive of the present work of God. Although not all process thinkers would put it this way, for the type of process hermeneutics for which I speak, there is no fixed point in Scripture, no basic item that has to be held in the form in which Scripture and tradition bring it to us. Another way of stating this point would be to say that there is no such thing, in our experience, as a pure experience of Scripture. We always deal with Scripture-and-interpretation.[2]

Two things, accordingly, are to be said about the function of Scripture. On the one hand, it serves as access to the historical foundation of our faith. It is not possible to be human in a purely general way; we are historical beings, definitely located in the flow of a particular history. This history makes accessible to us a particular vision of reality which, we believe, does have universal implications, but which, because of the nature of our historical limitations, cannot be a purely universal vision. The theological norm is the creative transformation which we know by bringing together what we learn of creative transformation from the Bible with what we know of it in our present experience defined as broadly as possible.

On the other hand, process hermeneutics tries, at least, to think about the relation between Scripture and the interpreter in a way that is different from the usual effort to identify something fixed, some essence or some unchanging basis of historical facts in the Bible. Here, we turn to another aspect of process thought, its standard of valuation of experience. We bring a vision of the world to our reading of Scripture. In the Bible we find a different vision (or, to be more precise, a group of visions). Usually interpreters have believed that they had to choose between the biblical vision, in spite of the fact that it was hard to integrate into their modern experience, or the contemporary vision, which seemed not to be able to include some important elements of the biblical vision. This choice has been based on the assumption that one or the other is true. We would say that neither vision is true. Both are inadequate, although both hold elements of truth. We start with our own vision, because there is nowhere else to start, and we do not want to be forced into a heteronomous situation in which something is imposed on us in spite of its incoherence with our world. But we do not assume that our contemporary vision of the world is a fixed and finished entity. We hold together in contrast the biblical vision and our own, in the conviction that our own vision can be creatively transformed; indeed, the process may work both ways, in that we may be able to see unexpected things in the biblical text itself, as we hold it in contrast with our own.

II. The Question of Reference

However, a process hermeneutic will not consider only the question of how to enlarge the world as we imagine it by bringing it into creative interaction with the biblical world. As I noted earlier, the question of reference—not only the question of intended reference, which Sternberg insists on, but the question of our own judgment about the actual reference of the text, which traditional historical study raises—is important in the total vision of process hermeneutics. As Whitehead put it, "truth adds to interest." Process thinking would not simply apply criteria of truth that our present world brings to the text, however. It would make the effort to allow these also to be questioned and enlarged by interaction with the biblical text.

A central instance for Christian interpreters is the resurrection of Jesus. It is surely a case in which the two visions of reality, that of the contemporary person and that of the New Testament, are strongly in tension. Process interpreters bring these two worlds together in different ways.

For some process thinkers, the question of the bare historical testability of the resurrection of Jesus would be a wrong question, a confusion of categories. The resurrection is given in the Christian proclamation, they say, and cannot be encountered by procedures such as historiographical analysis. Others would bring the biblical and the contemporary world closer by pointing to evidence for parapsychological phenomena, which show that the harsh break between traditional nineteenth-century historiography and the occurrence of events like the appearances of the risen Jesus is produced by the narrowness of the "modern" vision of truth. John Cobb, in *Christ in a Pluralistic Age*, compares the interpretations of the resurrection by Willi Marxsen and Ulrich Wilckens. Marxsen takes it that Christ was raised into the kerygma; Wilckens, like Wolfhart Pannenberg, holds that the resurrection appearances were real events, and can be judged so on the basis of a historical method that is not restricted by our contemporary notions of what is possible. Cobb opts for a position similar to that of Wilckens and Pannenberg rather than that of Marxsen.[3] My own thinking holds that the visual content of the resurrection appearances was composed of elements available in the memories of the disciples— they did not actually see Jesus—but that these visions served as the vehicle for a real and new communication between God and the disciples, and that the image of Jesus as the Christ, which came out of the whole encounter with Jesus, provided and still provides an authentic way of knowing the living God.[4]

I believe that it would be correct to say that in Jewish interpretations of the scriptures, a similar variety in the interpretations of foundational events can be found. It would be worth exploring the similarities and differences in a further discussion some time.

In closing, I note that this particular topic has uncovered something of the unexpectedness that a process hermeneutic attempts to be on the alert for, and the challenge of novelty in the midst of the preservation of tradition. A similar tension between the text and the reader can be seen in the issues that feminists raise for all serious readers of the Scriptures. Feminist readings of the Bible do indeed recover overlooked elements in that story. But it would be fruitless to try to find either in the Hebrew Scriptures or in the New Testament the full recognition of mutuality between women and men that feminists call for. Once we have become sensitized to this claim, our reading of the Bible is changed, and we see in it both its shortcomings and its suggestions leading toward a new type of liberation that the Bible itself does not fully present.

Notes

1. Meir Sternberg, *The Poetics of Biblical Narrative: Ideological Literature and the Drama of Reading* (Bloomington: Indiana University Press, 1985), 23–35, commenting on Robert Alter, *The Art of Biblical Narrative* (New York: Basic Books, 1981).

2. See David J. Lull, "What Is Process Hermeneutics?", *Process Studies* 13 (1983), 194.

3. John B. Cobb, Jr., *Christ in a Pluralistic Age* (Philadelphia: Westminster, 1971), chapter 15.

4. See further the discussion in William A. Beardslee, "What Is It About? Reference in New Testament Literary Criticism," in Edgar V. McKnight and Elizabeth Struthers Malbon, *The New Literary Criticism of the New Testament* (Valley Forge: Trinity Press International, 1994), 367–86.

Chapter 16

Living Torah:
A Response to William Beardslee

Nahum Ward

For most of my adult life I have wrestled with Torah. On the one hand, I recognize in the Torah a sacred Source that has had great power in the life of my people. On the other hand, I wrestle to find Torah's power within my own life.

I have often experienced this ambivalent relationship with Torah within the congregation during the Sabbath service. At the height of the service, as the congregation sings, "From out of Zion goes forth Torah, the word of God from Jerusalem," I remove the Torah from the ark and face the congregation. I feel the excitement in the sanctuary as we sing, "Praised be the One Who in holiness has given the Torah to His people, Israel." And then I walk through the sanctuary with the Torah. People move toward the aisles. They extend their hands to kiss the Torah, to connect to the Source. As I witness the people reaching to touch Torah, I am moved by the power of the moment.

I. Desire for Connection to the Sacred

When I reflect on the emotional response that the Torah evokes, I find myself asking why people who reach to touch Torah so rarely read Torah. Why do people who are moved by Torah's presence so rarely inquire into its teachings?

The answer is not hard to find. Many of us reach to touch Torah because we want a sense of connection to the sacred, to the Source. In the midst of the service, the power of the communal ritual can move us beyond the limitations of our rational thinking. For the moment we encounter a truly sacred object. Unfortunately, as soon as we step away from the power of this moment, the limitations of our worldview take hold. We realize, once again, that the Torah is not God's word. The Torah may be wise, as much literature is wise, but it is not divine.

This ambivalent relationship with Torah is a phenomenon of the last two centuries. Until modern times, the predominant Jewish worldview held that Torah was *devar Adonai*, the word of God. Approximately two hundred years ago, liberal thinkers introduced historical consciousness to biblical interpretation. This historical consciousness inevitably called into question the divine authority of the Torah.

In the modern world, accordingly, we seem to be left with two choices. We either read the Torah with mental blinders and assert that the words of Torah are literally the words of God, or we learn from the critical insights of our day and give up the sense of an Ineffable Presence behind the text.

Fundamentalist readers of Scripture have chosen the former and have paid for that choice in the narrowness and rigidity of their worldview. Liberals, like myself, have chosen the latter approach. We have reaped the reward of open and inquiring minds, but we have also paid a price. The Torah no longer carries the power of the word of God coming alive in our lives. The traditional Jewish passion for Torah is lost for most liberal Jews.

Can Torah once again be for us a place where we come into intimate contact with the divine? Can we bring our modern historical consciousness to Torah without squeezing the sense of divine revelation from the text? Those are crucial questions for contemporary Jews.

Professor Beardslee asserts that process thought provides an understanding of the nature of sacred texts that allows us both our modern consciousness and our traditional reverence. The key to his argument is his understanding of the nature of an event and of the "happenedness of the events narrated in a tradition."

We can best understand Beardslee's approach by examining a specific biblical event. For this purpose, I've chosen the giving of the Ten Commandments at Mt. Sinai. The Torah tells us that God gave Moses two tablets of stone containing the Ten Commandments. Did a literal revelation of God's word happen or not? If we think the event happened, then we had better make camp with the fundamentalists and affirm the words of Torah as literally the word of God. If a literal revelation did not occur, we are free to understand Torah and its teachings in a manner that conforms to our current worldview.

Beardslee, however, presents a third alternative. He suggests that a process understanding of the nature of an event allows historically conscious people to affirm the happenedness of a biblical event. In our case, one could affirm that Moses met God on the mountaintop. However, in process thought, the reader is not limited to a literal understanding of the text. From a process perspective, the biblical account of the event is only one possible interpretation of what actually happened. Because the nature of the event at Sinai, as recounted in the Torah, is defined both by the divine presence and by Moses, the divine revelation at Sinai itself is still open to our interpretation. If a modern person could be transported to Mt. Sinai during the revelation, that person's experience and Moses' experience would differ from one another. Given the enormity of the event, we could imagine that Moses could have heard God talking. All of Moses' prior experience prepared him for an encounter of this kind. The modern person would bring a radically different life-experience and thereby would experience a very different event: most probably no voice, maybe only, if even this, the terror of the divine Presence.

I find Beardslee's approach helpful. We moderns are so often triumphant in our perception of reality that we discount any experience radically different from our own. Following a process approach, we can affirm that Moses could have experienced the revelation as described in the Torah. However, the biblical account is only one possible interpretation. We are not limited to the literal meaning of the text. We can continue our inquiry into the nature of God's presence behind the text and in our lives. Once liberal Jews can affirm the reality of Moses' encounter with God, the Torah regains its power as a sacred Source. When one approaches the stories as accounts of actual encounters, however embellished in the retelling, then God's Presence stands behind the account. The event moves beyond story and becomes mystery. How are we to understand, in our own terms, the mystery of Moses' meeting with God? In the case of mystery, our lack of understanding ceases to be an impediment and becomes an incentive to delve deeper. That is the shift we want to make, from Torah as story to Torah as mystery, continually revealing truth.

II. Sacred Texts and Creative Tension

This approach to sacred texts allows us to affirm that events that are inconceivable within our own experience could indeed have happened. But the question remains: *Did* these events happen? It is not enough to suggest that an event *could* have happened. We are seeking God's presence behind the events recounted in the Torah. We want to know if the text offers us accounts of actual revelatory experiences, actual encounters with the holy. What can we find in the text that suggests that an event not only could have happened but *did* happen?

Beardslee offers an answer to this question. He suggests that we "test the nature of the transformation that the text elicits in us: is it the creative transformation that God is continually working, or is it to be reconsidered because it is not in harmony with this criterion?" I understand this to mean: Does this text move within our experience as we know the Divine Presence to move in our life?

This criterion is certainly not an objective standard for determining the historicity of a biblical event. And I agree that we should not be looking for an objective standard. When we read Torah, our ultimate goal is not objective proof that an event actually happened. Rather, we seek to experience God's presence in the encounter described in the text. Hence, we seek not an external, objective knowing, but rather an internal, subjective sensing. And Beardslee offers us a viable subjective standard: Does our meeting with this text have transformative power in the way that we know God to be transformative within our lives?

Assessing the transformative power of a text offers a powerful criterion. After all, the Torah is about transformation. In the Torah we read about encounters in which the Divine challenges humans to transform their lives. The God of the Torah is forever breaking into the human scene to shatter old forms and to offer a new form, a higher covenant. This God opens avenues of liberation, which move people past prior limitations and enable them to make a new covenant on a more expanded ground. This is the God whom the patriarchs and matriarchs knew, the God of Exodus, the God of the Wilderness and the Promised Land, the God of the prophets and psalmists. This transformative power is the God many people seek in coming to the sacred text.

We come to Torah asking that the Divine help us to break through those forms that bind us and to embrace a larger mode of living. The Torah serves as a transforming power in our lives by confronting us with a reality that breaks into and challenges our own. Like our ancestor Jacob who awoke from a dream with his eyes open to a larger reality, one can emerge from an encounter with the text affirming, "God is in this place and I did not know it."

In modern times we have diminished the transforming power of Torah by dismissing elements in the Torah that do not conform to our contemporary worldview. In so doing, we have eviscerated the Torah's power to disrupt the established patterns of our lives. If the Torah must make sense within our current worldview, how can Torah function to challenge the limitation and narrow places of this view?

The process approach to Torah allows us to preserve the creative tension betweeen the biblical vision and our own worldview. As Beardslee writes, "We do not assume that our contemporary vision of the world is a fixed and finished entity. We hold together in contrast the biblical vision and our own, in the conviction that our vision can be creatively transformed."

This approach, which embraces conflict and tension, is not foreign to Rabbinic hermeneutics. One classic Rabbinic method of interpretation was to affirm both the happenedness of an event and some problem in the text when viewed from a contemporary perspective. The ensuing tension served as a springboard for a new teaching.

It is worth emphasizing that the classic Rabbinic interpreters did not limit themselves to a literal understanding of the text. Liberal readers can find solid support for nonliteral approaches to Torah within traditional Rabbinic commentaries. The Rabbis understood that every text speaks on at least four levels. They accepted the truth of the simplist, most literal level of the text, which they called *pshat*. But they also understood that the literal account only touched the surface of what happened. The *pshat* of any text contained countless *remezim*, hints, of details and meanings that are not to be found in the literal account. And these *remezim* can open up into entire expositions, *midrashim*, worlds unimagined in the simple *pshat*-level description. At the deepest level, every text also contained a mystical or secret teaching. The Rabbis knew that the literal words of the Torah were both true and not the full truth. Every letter of the Torah opened up a gateway to the profound mystery at the center of life.

Of course, the Rabbis did not use process thought to arrive at their understanding of a text. Their worldview more easily accommodated apparent contradictions in the understanding of a text. For contemporary people, who approach a text with a modern sense of history and of "objective reality," process thought can be useful in understanding that the "events" recounted in the Torah both could have happened and are still open to our interpretation.

III. Torah Study as Transformative

Beardslee's approach opens the events of the Torah to modern interpretation. But I believe that we must go much further. When we study Torah, we are not after interpretation, we are after *revelation*. By this I mean that we want Torah to reveal to us that which is normally hidden, the sacred presence manifesting within our life experience. So we must ask, how can Torah speak at this deep level of life experience?

I have found that revelation is possible to the extent that students bring their full selves to the encounter with the text. If Torah study is only a mental exercise, then the student may receive new insights, but not revelation. Revelation requires that the student come fully present in heart, mind, body, and soul. In this sacred study, a conversation opens between the text and the entire life experience, and especially the deepest concerns of the reader. As we saw in the Rabbinic method, the student engages the text around some point of conflict, tension, or heightened interest. A dynamic dialogue ensues. Something fresh and new emerges—a new revelation.

This kind of dialogue requires significant openness, vulnerability, and trust on the part of the reader. The reader is being asked to permit a real meeting between the most profound depths of the self and an ancient text. As modern people, we are not naturally inclined to such an encounter. We cherish our freedom and are understandably wary of opening ourselves to a text that purports to be God's word. How do we support people in opening their lives to a meaningful encounter with the text? This is a crucial question for serious students of Torah.

I have discovered two keys to creating an atmosphere of openness. The first is to support students of Torah in validating the authority of their own life experience. Each student comes to the text with a wealth of personal "lived-in" knowledge about life. In the study, the authority of one's life experience must be held in balance with the authority of the text. All too often, we either give up our authority too easily or fail to open ourselves to the transforming authority of true teaching. The value in this process comes from holding the authority of one's life experience and the authority of the sacred text in creative tension.

The second key is community. I have found that a safe, supportive, non-judgmental community of fellow students helps to create an atmosphere that fosters openness and risk-taking.

The meeting with Torah takes place most effectively in the context of community for an additional reason as well. Torah addresses the community. The dialogue between the reader and the text is unbalanced if the reader stands alone. The dialogue takes place between communities—the ongoing community that received and recorded the revelation, and the community that encounters the revelation as handed down by tradition. Each individual within the community will understand Torah from within the uniqueness of his or her individual life experience. But each individual comes to this understanding from within the context of the study community.

A third requirement for a deep encounter with Torah is imagination. In modern life we have been taught to devalue our imagination as idle fantasy. This arbitrary limitation on our tools of comprehension is a peculiarly modern phenomenon. The Rabbis understood that the imagination is a tool of deep knowing. They used their imagination in interpreting a text and confidently held that these new teachings, these *midrashim*, were also given to Moses by God at Mt. Sinai. In our day we *study* Midrash. I suggest that each student in search of the living Torah needs to *do* Midrash. We need to bring our own imagination and creativity to the text. We need to find deep within ourselves the stories, images, songs, and dances that the sacred text evokes. We cannot afford to leave the arts solely to the trained artists among us. For millennia humankind probed the depths of awareness through imagination. The creative arts have always been vessels of the sacred. We need to use these sacred vessels, the imagination and the creative arts, to bring forth the truths of Torah.

In my experience, Torah does not seem to carry transformative power when people simply read Torah. Torah truly speaks deeply and transformatively when students are invited into a deep dialogue with the text. This deep dialogue with the text seems to follow a certain process. First, people open their lives to a dialogue with Torah. Second, people work through the tension that rises out of this dialogue. Third, people bring their own imaginative creativity to the wrestling with Torah. Fourth, this process takes place in the context of a study community that embraces these values. When these four elements are present, I have been repeatedly amazed by the power and the vitality of the dialogue between life and text.

Too often our study of Torah falls flat because it is too safe, lacking in conflict, vulnerability, imagination, and communal risk-taking. Those who wish to transmit living Torah are challenged to bring together communities of students that can support this kind of living, creative process.

Chapter 17

Hylotheism:
A Theology of Pure Process

Alvin J. Reines

The "theological question," the primary question confronting the person pursuing theology, is: "What existent—if any—shall I refer to by the term God?"[1] Preliminary to this exposition of hylotheism, my answer to the theological question, two observations are in order. The first describes the general approach I take to the theological inquiry, which is polydox;[2] the other sets forth the requirement of evidence in my response to the theological question.

I. The Polydox Approach to Theology

The polydox approach to theology can be summarized by three propositions.

(1) The essential proposition is that every person possesses an ultimate moral right to determine for himself his[3] answer to the theological question, namely, his God-view.[4] Underlying this proposition is the judgment that no person possesses evidence for some particular God-view so convincing that all other persons find themselves compelled to assent to it. The ultimate reason for this, I believe, is that every answer to the theological question is given over an abyss, the void surrounding the human psyche that encloses it within its finity and separates it unalterably from certain knowledge. All theologies, consequently, are born of human subjectivity; no absolute objective standard exists by which to establish

that one rather than another of the answers to the theological question is irrefragably true.

(2) Every person is a unique individual. This proposition, although not inherent in the essential logic of polydoxy, is in perfect accord with it. The primary basis for accepting this proposition is psychological and biological research, particularly the study of evolution.[5] Rejected by this proposition is the view that all humans share an essence (as asserted by such thinkers as Aristotle and Maimonides), and owing to this common essence all human minds function alike, so that what appears to be true or real to one right-thinking person will so appear to all other right-thinking members of the human species.

(3) Where fundamental theological disagreements exist, disputation between the disagreeing parties is futile. It makes no sense when theological differences are ultimate to contend over which answer to the theological question, or God-view, is the correct one. God-views are subjective expressions of a unique, individual consciousness; when they differ basically, there is no objective way to decide among or resolve them. One can only state one's reasons for accepting one God-view and rejecting others. In a polydoxy, unlike orthodoxies,[6] there is no difficulty in accepting the diversity of God-views that result from this proposition, because every polydoxian affirms the ultimate moral right of all persons to hold the God-views they choose.

II. The Requirement of Evidence

Whether to require evidence as a condition for believing a God-view to be true and, if required, the kind of evidence necessary, are decisions each person makes for himself. Owing to my conception of the finity of the human mind, I believe these decisions are made subjectively and arbitrarily. I have chosen to require evidence as a condition for acceptance of a God-view. The kind of evidence I have decided upon is empirical evidence. In point of fact, the evidence I employ for verifying a God-view is no different from that which I require for establishing the reality of any extramental existent, or that required by the physical sciences to validate their theories. To my mind, there is no reason why verification of a God-view should enjoy privileged epistemological status.

By empirical evidence, I mean a sensum (plural: sensa).[7] A sensum, as defined here,[8] is a datum that appears to immediate awareness as a presentation of one of the five senses. I accept no experiences other than sensa as sources of information regarding the existence of entities in the extramental world (among which is a real God), and no propositions other than those verified by sensa as true of the extramental world.[9] All data other than sensa that appear to immediate awareness I take as sources of information regarding intramental entities that are reducible in their entirety to events within the psyche. Such an intramental datum is designated a selfum (plural: selfa).[10] Selfa constitute the evidence upon which statements relating to one's intramental life are based. Sensa and selfa exist only as long as they are present to awareness. As such, they are the only actual entities that are experienced and will, therefore, be referred to as *being*. What is past is not being and does not exist. That which is termed the *past* exists only as a memory in a selfum.

I will use the expression *misinterpreted selfum* to refer to a selfum that, in my view, has mistakenly been understood as a datum providing information regarding extramental reality.[11] It goes without saying that my designation of an experience as a misinterpreted selfum is a subjective evaluation based upon the decision that only my sensa constitute evidence regarding the not-self. Thus my judgment that a person who claims to have seen an angel has in fact experienced a misinterpreted selfum is based upon my having no sensum relating to such an entity. Similarly, I believe to be a misinterpreted selfum the experience of those who profess a meta-sensum apprehension of a divine presence, because I hold that only sensa relate to extramental reality.[12] I do not believe that theological differences based upon disagreements over whether an experience is a misinterpreted selfum or truly related to extramental reality can be argued. It is true that one can present evidence against the consistency of an ostensible misinterpreted selfum with other experiences, but proof that the datum of some other person's immediate awareness is a misinterpreted selfum cannot be brought.

What is the basis for genuine belief in one God-view and for rejection of another? The only authentic response I know to this question is that the one God-view is considered true and the other false.[13] Although this response would seem to be implicit in the foregoing discussion, I bring it up to underscore this principle: the fact that I am a Jew is in no way relevant to which God-view I accept as true. Authentic belief in a God-view is not created by the merely external circumstance that one happens to be born of parents who chance to be members of a particular religious community; authentic belief is not inherited. Genuine assent to a God-view comes from conviction born of a person's individual truth–process regardless of the beliefs of others. The long theological history of the Jews bears out that this has indeed been the course taken by Jewish religious thinkers. One need only look to the diverse theologies of Ecclesiastes, Maimonides, Spinoza, and Buber to see that this is so.[14] Hence, whether the God–views of Jews in the past or present agree with my theology is irrelevant to my belief; all that is germane is that the evidence for the theology creates within me the conviction of its truth. The corollary of this position is that all one has to do to convert me to his or her theology is to present evidence for it superior to that which exists for my own.

III. God, the Enduring Possibility of Being

We come then to hylotheism, the theology whose truth I find convincing. I find it convincing not only because the evidence for it justifies its acceptance, but equally important because of the subjective nature or lack of objective evidence for other God-views. Hylotheism is established by evidence that requires the minimum number of assumptions necessary for objective knowledge, the same assumptions in fact postulated by the physical sciences for scientific knowledge.[15] Hylotheism should, accordingly, be chosen over other God-views by the application of Occam's razor, the philosophic and scientific principle that entities should not be multiplied unnecessarily. That is, the simplest of competing theories (those requiring the least number of assumptions) are to be preferred over those that are more complex (require more assumptions). Once gratuitous, superfluous assumptions are allowed into the theological enterprise, the principle that evidence is a necessary condition for acceptance of a God-view is lost. On what basis, then, will rational choices among God-views be possible? If a God-view is validated by assumptions without limit, then any and all God-views are established as true simply by assuming them to be true, no matter that not a shred of evidence can be brought to substantiate them.[16]

As understood by this hylotheist, the reason generally that theologians violate the principle of Occam's razor in their God-views is a need to predicate of the godhead the following three attributes that the application of Occam's razor to the theological evidence would deny: personhood; omniperfection; and the absolute power to overcome nothingness.[17] Why do theologians personify, overstate the perfection of, and overvalue the power of the godhead to overcome nothingness? The answer is evident: confronted by the angst of finity, many humans find it unbearable to be alone in the universe without a personal, omniperfect deity who has absolute mastery over nothingness.[18] The

question then arises: If no objective evidence exists for the omniperfection and overvaluing of deity, whence do such attributes arise? Their
source, I believe, is unconscious projection of parental imagoes onto
extramental reality.[19] Those whose theologies personify and overvalue
the godhead's power to prevail over nothingness project the parental
imagoes in thinly-disguised fashion; those who eliminate personhood,
but retain the deity's absolute mastery over nothingness, project
parental imagoes in a more subtle way.

Hylotheism can be formulated in rather succinct fashion. It was
stated earlier that the test I require a definition of God or God-view
to meet is empirical verifiability.[20] If there are empirical consequences
of the definition, then the proposition "God exists" will be true, and
if there are not, the proposition will be meaningless or false. The
definition I propose, the hylotheistic God–concept, is this: "God is the
enduring possibility of being."[21] By "being" is meant selfa or sensa.
Inasmuch as being is analyzable without remainder into selfa and
sensa, the existence of God is verified whenever selfa or sensa can
both be experienced, and the existence of God is disproved when,
under equivalent conditions of personal normalcy, selfa are experienced and sensa no longer are. God is disproved as the enduring
possibility of being rather than as the enduring possibility of sense–
experience alone because the person—that is, the continuing self-
consciousness that is constructed out of the memory of a selfum—is
evidently dependent upon the external world (sensa and the unobservables verified by sensa), and, from the annihilation of the external
world, the inexorable annihilation of the person can be inferred.

Two classes of existence, each with its distinctive nature, can
thus be distinguished: the possible and the actual. Possible existence
suffers the defect that it lacks actuality. As possibility, it is not being—
namely, it is neither a selfum nor a sensum. Yet, if the divine existence
is to be lasting in duration, it can accomplish this only as possibility.
For the actually existent, as verified by experience, is always limited;
indeed, nothing unlimited can be imagined, let alone conceived. To
be actual, therefore, is to be finite. While the finity of every actuality
is present in all the spheres of its existence, it is temporal finity that
provides the definitive boundary. The actual is finite in time because,
as an actuality, its power of existence is finite and it is destined,
therefore, as an individual, for annihilation. Being, thus, breeds
nothingness; in fact, *nothing* has no meaning except in relation to
being. Accordingly, if God is to be lasting in duration, the divine
existence must forgo actuality for possibility. God, consequently, is

enduring in time, but possesses only possible existence, whereas being is finite in duration, but possesses actual existence.

Metaphorically speaking, existence as the act of overcoming nothingness is never fully successful in its effort and lays down conditions, therefore, on all that would possess it. As a consequence, nothingness is never entirely overcome. Actual existents (being) temporarily overcome nothingness at the cost of future and total annihilation. God overcomes nothingness by incorporating it into the divine existence; God is thereby emptied of actuality and must forever remain possibility. The godhead, so to speak, is a compromise between being and nothingness. The ground of being overcomes nothingness to exist as the enduring possibility of being, but, in this uneasy victory, defect is assimilated into the godhead.

The status of God's existence as the enduring possibility of being leads to a further consequence: God cannot exist without the world. God has no meaning without being; being cannot arise without God. God's existence is not absolute; the enduring possibility of being exists as a correlative of being. The world was not created by a God who arbitrarily willed it so; rather the world exists because the divine existence is unconditionally dependent upon it. Of creation *ex nihilo*, we have no evidence. In experience, God coexists with finites in a process of continuous interaction. In this process, as we are justified in concluding from the regular and orderly character of natural causal sequence, the possibility of future being is derived from present being. So to speak, the existence of God resides in every present moment of being and is realized in every future moment. In this sense: God is the ground of being and being is the ground of God.

A further consequence of God's nature as possibility is the relation that obtains between the godhead and humankind. In hylotheism, where the godhead is subject to the conditions exacted by existence, it is the nature of actual entities, by reason of the finity or encompassing boundary that is intrinsic to their existence, to be cut off from the ground of their being. To be actual is to be alone. To be finite is to be severed from the enduring.

As a consequence, the relation between the godhead and humankind is one of muted communication. There exists, accordingly, no infallible revelation or other certain knowledge, nor can there be such knowledge, because humankind, necessarily and substantially separated from the ground of being, has no sure relation to this ground. Equally, the omniperfect providence of theistic absolutism, with its messiahs and eschatologies of everlasting life, has no place in a world where the enduring exists only as possibility and every actual existent is always finite. And yet, although the godhead can be the ground only of finite entities, humans are not powerless. The possibilities that constitute the godhead can be affected by humankind. Because the divine possibilities reside in actual existence, altering actual existents in the present correspondingly alters the nature of the possibilities of future being. Every ontal decision that helps resolve the conflict of finitude increases the possibility of meaningful being in the future,[22] every social decision that decreases injustice and poverty increases the possibility of pleasurable being in the future; every scientific discovery becomes a possibility for betterment in the future. If humans shape the present to contain the possibilities of good, the godhead conserves the possibilities for future realization.

This relation of action and passion between humankind and the godhead can be construed figuratively as a covenant, an ethics of hypothetical necessity: "If the human person acts, then God reacts," and, "As the human person acts, so God reacts." The covenant of hylotheism between humankind and the godhead is analogous to the covenant between Israel and the god Yahveh as taught by the preexilic prophets.

In the words of the prophet Amos:

> Seek good, and not evil, that ye may live;
> And the Lord, the God of hosts,
> Will be with you, as ye say.
> Hate the evil, and love the good,
> And establish justice in the gate.[23]

This covenant, in which the human person must do the good to receive the good, is to be sharply distinguished from covenants with deity in which a person is required to perform some act irrelevant to the good, ritualistic or otherwise, after which God miraculously produces the good.

IV. The Coherence of Hylotheism

A commonplace in our society is that various religious communities and even individuals claim ownership of the word *God* (or its equivalent). The word God, they declare, must be used in the sense they define it, any other meaning given to it is illicit. Generally, those who claim such ownership are theistic absolutists, although, paradoxically enough, there are those who reject theistic absolutism who nevertheless maintain vigorously that this is the only proper meaning for the word God.[24] For whatever intriguing psychological reasons, the latter have a need to insist that the word God must mean that which they do not believe. Viewed from the perspective of the history of theology, however, any claim to ownership of the word God by some religious community or individual is absurd. The word God has been employed over the millennia in a rich variety of senses. In this respect, the word God behaves as does all language, changing or multiplying its meanings as the humans who use it change their understandings of the world and their attitudes toward it.[25] Still, it may help to clarify hylotheism if I describe briefly my use of the term. By "God" I mean the metaphysical cause or ground of being and/or the processes of being. The primary importance of the human search for an understanding of the ground of being is to acquire the knowledge necessary to attain soteria, that is, ultimate meaningful existence.[26] The fundamental problem that humans must resolve to achieve soteria is the conflict of finitude inherent in human existence, namely, the conflict between the individual's infinite conation and his awareness of finity. Failure to resolve the conflict of finitude results in asoteria, the utter annihilation of meaningful existence; partial failure to resolve the conflict produces dyssoteria, a borderland psychic state between soteria and asoteria.[27] Belief in one category of God-views provides for a resolution of the conflict of finitude by the decision that through God's grace, despite appearances, humans are ultimately infinite; another category of God-views requires the decision that humans are ineluctably finite. Theistic absolutism belongs to the former category; hylotheism and process theologies generally belong to the latter.[28]

It is evident that hylotheism represents a God-view that gives no comfort to those whose psyches are dominated by infinite conation and require, therefore, assurance of personal infinite and invulnerable existence to attain soteria. Even for those who are capable of resigning themselves to finite existence and the consequent acceptance of the ultimate finality of death, hylotheism is an austere and demanding God-view. Why then should one accept it? For the reason given earlier for accepting any God-view: the conviction that it is true. The primary or direct evidence for the truth of hylotheism has already been presented; I now wish to offer corroborative evidence for its truth. The corroborative evidence consists in the coherence of hylotheism with the following five fundamental facts of existence: the existence of dysteleological surds; existence only through destruction; evolution; death; and the value-death of the universe. Additional fundamental facts certainly could be enumerated; the ones I have chosen represent major instances of the "hard" facts that confront theology.

In speaking of the coherence of hylotheism with the fundamental facts of existence, I am employing the term *coherence* as defined by E. S. Brightman:

> [A]ccording to the criterion of coherence, a proposition is to be treated as true if (1) it is self-consistent, (2) it is consistent with all the known facts of experience, (3) it is consistent with all other propositions held as true by the mind that is applying this criterion, (4) it establishes explanatory and interpretative relations between various parts of experience, (5) those relations include all known aspects of experience and all known problems about experience in its details and as a whole. It is to be noted that coherence is more than consistency; the latter is absence of contradiction, whereas the former requires the presence of the empirical relations mentioned under points (4) and (5); thus consistency is necessary to coherence, but consistency is not sufficient.[29]

A distinction is to be drawn between Brightman's use of coherence and mine. For Brightman coherence is employed as the primary method of verification. My primary method is empirical verification, with coherence providing only ancillary evidence.

The coherence of hylotheism with the fundamental facts of existence enumerated above derives from three principles that are inherent in this God-view: the actuality principle; the equivalence principle; and the process-time principle.

(1) **The actuality principle:** This principle explains why there is being or actual existence, namely, the universe. The history of philosophical and theological cosmology is replete with reasons for the existence of the universe. This is appropriate, because a cosmology would seem rather incomplete without offering an answer to the ancient question: Why existence, why not nothingness? The answer of hylotheism to this question is that the godhead, the enduring possibility of being, requires actual existence for its own existence. Inasmuch as possibilities reside in being, without being there would be no possibilities and the godhead would cease to exist. Being is thus an instrument of the godhead's existence. In sum, the actuality principle states that being

or the universe exists only because the godhead's existence requires it.

(2) **The equivalence principle:** According to hylotheism, all actualities or instances of being are of equivalent worth to the godhead. This worth is that they enable the continuation of the divine existence, as described earlier. Any and every occurrence of being performs this function, so that to deity no actuality is of greater value than any other.

(3) **The process-time principle:** More intriguing and certainly more fundamental to the Greek philosophers than the question of "Why being, why not nothingness?" was "Why becoming?"; that is, why does process or change occur? The answer necessitated by hylotheism is that the power of deity to prevail over nothingness is limited to the point where it is only capable of being the ground of being of actualities that survive ephemerally. Or, in other words, the kind of being for which the possibilities that constitute the enduring possibility of being are a potentiality is being limited in duration. Process, therefore, is the result of an impuissance of deity so great that eternally enduring, immutable being cannot be sustained. Without entering into a discussion of the various philosophers and theologians who hold that process is either an instrument of or coherent with divine perfection, the view of hylotheism is that process results from divine imperfection, the godhead's inability to attain an assured and lasting dominance over nonexistence. Moreover, it is evident that for hylotheism deity in its entirety is in continuous process. The possibilities that constitute the godhead are continually realized in being, and the possibilities that emerge from being are new.

a. Accordingly, hylotheism differs from the theologies that are generally referred to as *process theologies*. These are hybrids rather than pure process theologies. The reason is that they characterize deity as static or immutable in part and dynamic or mutable in part. This view contrasts with hylotheism, which is a pure process theology inasmuch as deity is conceived of as entirely and always becoming—the possibilities constituting the godhead are continually going out of existence and new possibilities are continually arising.

b.   Hylotheism also differs from those process philosophies that equate process with progress—that is, they conceive of the divine process as a cosmic becoming leading assuredly, albeit gradually, to universal betterment and the increase of human good. In hylotheism, process is not progress; process has no necessary relation to progress. Process occurs because it must, the existential need and impuissance of the godhead require it. Because process serves only deity's need, any direction that process takes accomplishes this service, with the result that human good or evil can result from it.

c.   Similarly, the existential need of deity requires time, the movement of present to future. As already observed, the possibilities that make up the godhead are transient. The godhead would therefore go out of existence if there were no time. The possibilities of a particular present perish, and only the emergence into existence of new possibilities gives duration to the godhead. In sum, the process-time principle is that process and time entail neither human progress nor regress; either may occur as the consequence of a process-time which is solely an instrument for satisfying the existential need of the finite godhead.

We proceed now to the fundamental facts of existence for which the foredescribed principles, in particular, and hylotheism, in general, provide an explanation that meets the test of coherence.

(1)   **The existence of dysteleological surds.** A dysteleological surd is defined as a kind of evil that by any reasonable standard from the human standpoint is inherently and irreducibly evil, containing within itself no principle of development or improvement. An evil that is a dysteleological surd serves in absolutely no sense as an instrumental good; it is not expressible in terms of good (as retribution or otherwise) no matter what operations are performed upon it.[30] The concept of the dysteleological surd is fundamental to theological inquiry. A theology stands or falls depending upon whether it can give a credible account for the occurrence of dysteleological surds.[31] Instances of dysteleological surds can be enumerated without end, but two examples suffice to illustrate the concept: the Holocaust, and a child born with AIDS who lives a life of sickness and dies in infancy. As these

examples underscore, it is not the quantity of an evil that determines its nature as a dysteleological surd, but its quality: no purpose other than evil is served.

Hylotheism provides this explanation for dysteleological surds. The nature of the possibilities that constitute the godhead is determined ultimately by that which is necessary for the godhead to overcome nothingness and, thereby, exist as the ground of being or actualities. The nature of the actualities that exist is in turn determined by the possibilities of the ground of being from which they are realized. The possibilities required by the godhead to prevail over nothingness are of such a nature that actualities that are dysteleological surds arise from them. As the actuality principle states, the purpose of actual existence is to provide for the existential need of deity, and dysteleological surds as actualities serve this end. Thus, dysteleological surds exemplify the equivalence principle. No matter how dysteleological surds may horrify humans, the worth of an actual existent, dysteleological surd or otherwise, for deity is the same: it provides for the continued existence of the godhead. Figuratively described, prevailing over nothingness exacts from deity the price of dysteleological surds.

(2) **Existence only through destruction.** Existence through destruction is clearly exemplified by the fact that all living beings, other than non-carnivorous plants, must kill other living beings in order to exist. It may well be argued that the fact of "existence only through destruction" extends even further to include non-carnivorous plants and inanimate objects. For it has been demonstrated by the natural sciences that non-carnivorous plants and inanimate systems from subatomic particles to galaxies must by incorporation destroy either the structures or the integrity (that is, the independent or pure condition) of other entities in order to exist. What is the reason for a poverty of existence so great that existence only through destruction of other entities is a pervasive characteristic of the universe? Certainly it should be understood as an evil—if not a dysteleological surd—that the universe is constructed this way.[32] Given the principles of hylotheism, existence only through destruction by virtue of the poverty of existence flows inexorably. The quantity of possible existence is limited by the ability of the godhead to prevail over nothingness. Consequently, the quantity of

existence available to actualities is also limited with the result that, to exist, one actuality must take existence from another by destroying it.[33]

(3) **Evolution.** This is the theory that the various species of flora and fauna have their origin only in other pre-existing species and that the distinguishable differences are due to modifications in successive generations. The theological problem evolution poses is most evident in respect of the human species. The question is: Why has humankind (Homo sapiens) come into existence through evolution, inasmuch as the evidence is patent that this mode of origination is the primary cause of most, if not all, basic and pervasive human problems? It is difficult to conceive of traits that are base and destructive in the nature of human beings that do not result from the fact of their having evolved from non-rational ancestors, which, lacking reason, were forced to rely for survival on predatory aggression, ruthless competitiveness, domination over other members of their species, selfish territoriality, indiscriminate and unrestrained sexuality, and other impulses that in humans produce persistent and fundamental problems, personal and social. In my view, the most profound and destructive problem bequeathed to humans by evolution is the intra-psychic conflicts we suffer between reason, on the one hand, and desires and emotions inherited from non-rational ancestors, on the other. Such intra-psychic conflicts for the most part remain unresolved by human beings and result in widespread dyssoteria or asoteria. For the sake of argument, let us hypothesize that a rational craftsman or demiurge had the task of creating *de novo* a being endowed with reason. Would the demiurge have built into his rational creature's structure the instinctual desires and emotions that are necessary for the survival of a non-rational creature, but that are not only unnecessary for the survival of the rational creature but also destructive to its existence and to the quality of its life? The hylotheistic understanding of human emergence through evolution, no matter how flawed the process and product, is that all possibilities of the godhead, as stated earlier, reside in actualities, and, we may add, only in actualities that are qualified for them, that is, can contain them as potentialities. Actualities, therefore, determine and limit the kind of possibilities that can exist. That is to say, the possibilities that constitute the

enduring possibility of being overcome nothingness, but
these possibilities are determined not only by the conditions
required to prevail over nonexistence but also by the actualities in which they must reside. Consequently, Homo
sapiens possesses primitive and rationally unnecessary
desires and emotions because the only kind of actuality in
which the possibility for a rational actuality could reside was
one that required primitive instincts to survive owing to the
conditions of its evolution—and so backward to the beginning of the universe.

(4) **Death.** The ultimate cause of death is set forth by the
process-time principle already discussed, which explains that
the only actualities for which the possibility of existence
is present in the godhead are those that are finite in duration.
Death, therefore, human and otherwise, is fully coherent
with hylotheism, which entails as inherent in the godhead
a profound impuissance in supporting being. When deity is
believed to possess the assured power to overcome nothingness there is a manifest incoherence between the power of
eternality in deity and the finity of humans and all other
entities for whose reality there is credible evidence. The
question is: Why is there a God who can prevail over nothingness at will, while humans and all other actualities are
destined for death? The traditional theological answers given
to this question have been extravagantly convoluted and
often deplorable. Take the answer widespread in religions of
the Western world derived from the story of Adam and Eve
in Genesis. Humans undergo death because Adam and Eve
sinned in the Garden of Eden by disobeying the god Yahveh's
commandment not to eat of the tree of knowledge of good
and evil. Among the punishments for this sin imposed by
Yahveh was that Adam and Eve, who before their disobe-
dience had been immortal, must now undergo death and, in
addition, their descendants would as well be programmed
for death. Certainly such a theological explanation of the
reason for death is unfortunate, adding to the anguish and
pain of illness and impending death a burden of sin and guilt
for which perishing is the penalty. In hylotheism, the reason
for death is the finity of God, not the sinfulness of humans.

An additional observation provides further insight into the
implications of hylotheism for human death. From the stand-

point of hylotheism, humans can be viewed as undergoing two kinds of death: death-in-life and death-of-life. Because the actual existence of a human in its entirety consists of a single selfum or sensum,[34] and each endures only instants in time, humans are continually going out of existence or perishing. This form of perishing is called death-in-life—for new selfa emerge linked by memory to the selfa and sensa that have perished. Death, as ordinarily understood, is the cessation of a perished selfum and sensum series that can be linked together by a presently existing selfum recollecting the series. This is death-of-life. The importance of the concept of death-in-life is that it provides an explanation and validation for a recurrent ontal angst or fear of seeming nothingness that many persons experience throughout their lives.[35] Present on the fringes of consciousness in every selfum or sensum experience is awareness of its imminent death.

(5) **Value-death of the universe.** "The value-death of the universe" means that the universe (the totality of actualities) ceases to be or contain anything that can reasonably be considered of worth. The value-death of the universe does not require its annihilation, although annihilation, of course, entails value-death. Philosophical theologies (as distinguished from theologies based on supernaturalism), which I consider process theologies to be, cannot disregard scientific theories and the evidence upon which these theories are based. Scientific cosmological theories, although they may differ on points not germane to this discussion, generally agree that at some time in the future the universe will undergo value-death. There are at present several cosmological theories that have proponents in the scientific community. Three of them bear mentioning here: the open universe theory; the closed universe theory; and the no-boundary universe theory. Each predicts the value-death of the universe.

a.   *The open universe theory.* This theory, which is substantiated by the evidence presently known, predominates among scientists. The theory states that the universe began at a big–bang singularity. The universe is expanding and will continue to do so indefinitely, and at an infinite time in the future it will approach zero density. The stars and all other cosmic entities will radiate away their energy.

The end will be universal darkness at a temperature of approximately three degrees above absolute zero. Clearly, there would be nothing of worth in existence at this time; it is a state of value-death of the universe.[36]

b. *The closed universe theory.* This theory agrees with the open universe theory that the universe began at a big–bang singularity. It disagrees, however, that the universe will expand to a point of universal darkness. Rather, at a certain point, the universe will stop expanding and begin a collapse that will end at a big–crunch singularity. Nothing of worth could exist in such a state and the value-death of the universe will have occurred.[37] The point is to be emphasized that no human knowledge is possible regarding a singularity or what might take place after a big–crunch singularity. Postulating that something of value will arise from or after the big–crunch singularity is pure fantasy and unacceptable to philosophical theology. Moreover, evidence for the closed universe theory does not at present exist.

c. *No-boundary universe theory.* This theory has been proposed by Stephen Hawking, and is admitted to be inadequate by its author. It is, however, of interest. The theory is best presented in Hawking's own words:

> On the other hand, the quantum theory of gravity has opened up a new possibility, in which there would be no boundary to space-time and so there would be no need to specify the behavior at the boundary. There would be no edge of space-time at which one would have to appeal to God or some new law to set the boundary conditions for space-time. One could say: "The boundary condition of the universe is that it has no boundary." The universe would be completely self-contained and not affected by anything outside itself. It would neither be created nor destroyed. It would just BE.[38]

I include the no-boundary universe theory to point out that, even though it requires no big-crunch singularity, which certainly brings the value-death of the universe, it still entails value-death. (One should bear in mind that the no-boundary universe theory is at this time not theoretically satisfactory, besides being devoid of observational verification. For, according to the no-boundary universe theory, the universe expands and contracts. Value-death takes place at some point in both the contracting and expansion phases. Hawking writes:

Conditions in the contracting phase would not be suitable for the existence of intelligent beings. . . .The inflation in the early stages of the universe, which the no boundary proposal predicts, means that the universe must be expanding at very close to the critical rate at which it would just avoid recollapse, and so will not recollapse for a very long time. By then all the stars will have burned out and the protons and neutrons in them will probably have decayed into light particles and radiation. The universe would be in a state of almost complete disorder.[39]

The coherence of the value-death of the universe with hylotheism is evident when it is related to the three principles inherent in hylotheism enumerated earlier: the actuality principle; the equivalence principle; and the process-time principle. According to the actuality principle, the universe exists not for its own sake, but because the existence of deity requires it. Moreover, according to the equivalence principle, no matter what the condition of the universe, it serves deity's need for existence since any actualities will do. From these two principles, it follows that a universe that has undergone value-death is equal in divine worth to a universe that is rich in value. The universe does not exist to fulfill some ideal and esteemed purpose of its own. It possesses no ultimate and intrinsic value. Its sole function is to be an instrument of the godhead's existence.

That the universe should at some point in time undergo value-death is, based on the process-time principle, a reasonable expectation, albeit not a necessary conclusion. Process, it states, is not progress; process results from a divine impuissance so limiting that the godhead cannot be the ground of lasting, unchanging being. That the process should therefore result at some future time in the value-death of the universe flows naturally from the very reason process occurs. In reality, has not the impuissance of the godhead already resulted in a universe that is for the most part value-dead? So far as present knowledge of the universe reveals, whatever in existence can reasonably be considered valuable is to be found on or in association with the planet earth. Nothing that is known about the remainder of the universe reveals anything of value. What intrinsic good is possessed by the myriad of clusters that populate space? Is there value in these lifeless aggregations of super-galaxies, galaxies, and stars? Is there any purpose they serve unless, as hylotheism maintains, they are necessary for the existence of the godhead?

V. Critique of Christian Process Theologies

Hylotheism, to be sure, is a process theology. Still it differs from other systems of process theology. In the critique of various other process theologies that follows, I have one primary purpose in mind, to show why I accept hylotheism and reject the other theologies. It is not my intention to enter into a theological disputation because, as I stated at the outset when discussing the polydox approach to theology, I consider theological disputation to be ultimately futile.

My critique begins with questioning the objectivity of Christian process philosophy. As I have stated, the fact that I am a Jew plays no part in my decision about the truth of a God-view. I believe that an analysis of my presentation of hylotheism will bear this out, especially because no Jew (or to my knowledge, anyone else) has ever put forth this concept of God.

Do Christian process theologians behave in the same way? Are their Christological beliefs based entirely on evidence or on some form of Christian presupposition or beginning point? I am not sure. David Griffin, for example, makes statements such as these:

All [a Christian theologian's] reflection must be rooted in a distinctively Christian perspective.

. . .every conceptualized understanding of reality is based upon some nonrational starting point. This starting point can be termed a "vision of reality."

The vision of reality common to a tradition can be called its "faith."

The one whom we call a theologian is more consciously aware of his indebtedness to his tradition for his own faith perspective. And because of this he will give explicit attention to those events which are central to his community's perspective.

Accordingly, . . . the Christian revelatory content is understood as the Christian vision of reality. . . . The theologian, in beginning with revelation, is not subjecting his thought to some heteronomous authority, but is simply reflecting upon reality in terms of the way he himself *sees* reality.[40]

Three questions come to mind here. First, have Christian process theologians chosen the process philosophy of A. N. Whitehead and Charles Hartshorne as their natural, rational *weltanschauung* because their Christian "vision of reality" is metaphorically congenial with it, rather than on the basis of its inherent truth? Second, if process philosophy were to be proved wrong or lacking adequate evidence, is the Christian "vision of reality" proved false? (In other words, is there justification for Christian process theologians believing in Christianity, other than the truth of process philosophy, and, if so, what would this justification be, and what would the *concrete* beliefs of this Christianity be?) Third, if a person accepts the process philosophy of Whitehead and Hartshorne, does that person still have to accept Jesus Christ as God's decisive revelation, or as revelation at all, in order to attain the highest stage of religious belief and salvation?

The answer to the question whether Christian process theologians are biased in their philosophical thinking by beginning with a Christological perspective may be arguable, but it certainly does seem to be the case that process theologians and philosophers begin with an unwarranted, and, in this writer's opinion, incorrect assumption regarding the nature of religion. I will cite two examples of this, one from David Ray Griffin, the other from Hartshorne.

Griffin's notion of religion comes as an explanation of a passage from Whitehead:

> The assumption behind Whitehead's statement, and basic to the present essay, is that man is a religious being in the sense that he wants to be in harmony with the ultimately real, self-existent, eternal, sacred—that which is divine. . . . It is because of this feature of man's nature that his emotions, attitudes, intentions, and actions will, in the long run, be brought into line with his deepest beliefs about deity.[41]

The assumption that the human person is a "religious being" as defined by Griffin clearly serves his theological viewpoint. If it is the case that all humans have an inherent and fundamental need to be in harmony with a deity (which from the description fits particularly well with the kind Griffin adheres to), then without belief in and harmonizing with such a deity humans cannot attain soteria. But is this in fact the case? Why should the assumption be made that humans are inherently "religious beings" in Griffin's sense when we can query or observe them with respect to their needs and desires?

In my own experience, I have found a considerable number of persons, including myself, who have no inherent desire to be in harmony with a deity, and certainly no inherent need for belief in and harmonizing with a deity in order to attain soteria. If they do believe in a deity, they do so because there is convincing evidence that compels assent to its existence.

Hartshorne presents a view of religion that makes all persons need a personal God, in this case, panentheistic, for their very sanity:

> Only man, among this earth's inhabitants, is a "religious animal." This suggests that consciousness, in the sense requiring language..., is part of the definition of worship. To worship is to do something consciously. To do what? That which all sentient individuals must do, at least unconsciously, so far as they are sane and not in at least a mild neurosis or psychosis [sic]. Worship is the *integrating* of all one's thoughts and purposes, all valuations and meanings, all perceptions and conceptions.... [T]he conscious wholeness of the individual is correlative to an inclusive wholeness in the world of which the individual is aware, and this wholeness is deity....God is the wholeness of the world, correlative to the wholeness of every sound individual dealing with the world.[42]

The objection to Hartshorne's view of the religious nature of the human person is simply stated. He declares that humans who do not worship a panentheistic deity are neither integrated, sound, nor sane without presenting an iota of evidence for this assertion. Yet such an assertion is open to verification by observation. One need simply explore the matter for oneself or study humans by means of the social or psychological sciences. Based upon my own experience, and upon the evidence of qualified observers, I must conclude that Hartshorne's assertion is false. There are clearly many persons, nonpanentheists and nontheists, who are integrated, sound, and sane. Accordingly, the view that the human race needs panentheism or theism for sanity or soteria must be firmly rejected.

We come now to the God-concept of nonhylotheistic process theology, panentheism. To state very briefly the attributes of God according to Hartshorne's view of panentheism, I will quote this summary he provides. God, he says, is:

E   Eternal—in some...aspects of his reality devoid of change, whether as birth, death, increase, or decrease

T Temporal—in some. . . aspects capable of change, at least in
   the form of increase of some kind
C Conscious, self-aware
K Knowing the world or universe, omniscient
W World-inclusive, having all things as constituents[43]

As I stated earlier, I require empirical evidence to accept the
extramental existence of any not-self entity, including God. Hartshorne
argues with great firmness that there cannot be empirical proof for
the existence of an entity corresponding to his God-concept.[44] It being
the case that there is no empirical proof for panentheism, I reject it
summarily along with the many other concepts of God that have been
proposed but for which there is no empirical evidence.

This is not to say that I have not examined proofs of various kinds
that Hartshorne has put forth for panentheism, and I would find them
unconvincing even if I were not committed to empirical verifiability
as the test of truth. Permit me to present an example of what I mean
by examining one proof Hartshorne gives, and which he apparently
considers fundamental, because he says it "sums up all the others."
I quote:

> The first is what I call the religious or "global" proof (because
> in a fashion it sums up all the others). It is not the usual argu-
> ment from religious experience taken as a mere fact. It is an
> argument from the rational necessity of religious experience and
> of God as its adequate referent. If an individual must have
> integrity in order to exist as an individual, and if the conscious
> form of integrity is worship, then while an individual may live
> by unconscious integrity, or may to some extent lack integrity,
> he cannot consciously and rationally choose to do either of these.
> Hence there is something irrational in choosing not to believe
> in God. There seems no other way than the theistic[45] to conceive
> the objective correlate of personal integrity.[46]

The defect in this purported proof has to do with a point made
earlier. This is that the proposition that human individuals can attain
personality integration (what Hartshorne apparently means by
"integrity") only through belief in a panentheistic deity is observa-
tionally false. There are many nonpanentheists who are integrated
personalities. (I will not address the question whether authentic
personality integration can ever be achieved through belief in panentheism or any extramental entity. My view is that it cannot.) Accord-

ingly, since one of the premises of this proof that Hartshorne offers is false, the proof is refuted.

So far as Whitehead's concept of God (as distinguished from Hartshorne's) is concerned, I can find no proof for it that he offers. For this reason, I see no alternative but to reject it. Yet inasmuch as one of his notions with respect to deity plays a basic role generally in nonhylotheistic process theology, I should like to comment upon it. This is the idea that God is incarnate in the human person (and indeed in the world).

The explanation of incarnation is to be found in Whitehead's view that all entities or actual occasions are constituted of prehensions of past entities and other actual occasions. Reduced to simple terms, this means that every entity is made up of every other entity with which it enters into relation. Nothing is a substance—namely, that which exists in and through itself, or, in other words, nothing is alone. Every entity, according to Whitehead, has a relation with God; therefore, every entity consists in part of God. Thus God is incarnate in the world and in the human person. Whitehead's concept of incarnation is related to his view that it is not the case that the extramental world is apprehended only through the five senses (or sensa). There are other ways through which the extramental world can be apprehended, such as prehension, the nature of which Whitehead leaves unacceptably vague.

Although Whitehead offers no proof for his concepts of God, incarnation, and prehension, I am of the opinion that he based these concepts on experiences he had. These experiences, however, I believe were selfa experiences, and his theological concepts were misinterpreted selfa. To my understanding, a deity who is prehended and incarnate is a product of the unconscious that comes to consciousness in a disguised and misleading form. More serious than this theological error, however, is that the notion that humans are constituted of God and other entities reveals, I believe, a faulty phenomenology of the human person and conceals a cold, harsh truth. This is that every person is a finite being bounded by the limits of his existence within which he is alone. Experientially, this is evident. Each person's cancer is his own; each person's schizophrenia is his own; and each person dies his own death, alone.

Certainly, among the least satisfactory areas of nonhylotheistic process theology is the casuistic and unsatisfactory way in which it deals with the problem of evil. The following statements by Hartshorne may be employed as a basis for analyzing the difficulty:

But any evil is also in some degree a misfortune, and in my opinion the theological "problem of evil" is quite misconceived if it is seen as that of justifying particular evils. Evils are to be avoided where possible; where not, to be mitigated or utilized for good in whatever way possible—but never, for heaven's sake never, to be metaphysically justified. . . .Thus not even the nastiest or most conceivable unhelpful evil could have anything to do with the nonexistence of God. Risk of evil and opportunity for good are two aspects of just one thing, multiple freedom; and that one thing is also the ground of all meaning and all existence. This is the sole but sufficient reason for evil as such and in general, while as for particular evils, by definition they have no ultimate reason. They are nonrational.

For creationist or neoclassical metaphysics deity must be the supreme or unsurpassable form of creative freedom. But "supreme" or unsurpassable form cannot be the only possible form. In creationist metaphysics, all concrete reality is in principle creative. But then what happens is never, as it stands, simply attributable to "the" creator, but only to deity *and* the creatures together. Reality is always in part self-created, causa sui, creativity being in this philosophy the supreme transcendental. All creatures have creativity above zero, all are creators.[47]

We can disregard Hartshorne's interdiction against justifying evil metaphysically inasmuch as he promptly proceeds to do just that. We can also grant for argument's sake the rather fanciful notion that entities such as atoms, molecules, and viruses possess creative freedom. Let us proceed to the substantive point. This is that evil is the result of deity not being the only entity in the universe that possesses freedom, indeed, creative freedom; all entities possess creative freedom. Accordingly, evil is the result of "multiple freedom," all the different entities in the universe exercising creative freedom. (We can also disregard Hartshorne's contradictory statement that particular evils have no reason after he had already said they do, namely, that they are the result of some entity's exercising its creative freedom.) Consequently, poliomyelitis is to be attributed to the poliovirus exercising its freedom, and the Holocaust, to Adolf Hitler exercising his freedom.

But is this an adequate explanation of evil according to the attributes of the panentheistic God as set forth by nonhylotheistic process theology? Panentheism maintains that deity is the unsurpassable. This means, among other things, that deity is unsurpassable in love, knowledge, and power (albeit not omnipotent). Now, can we not all agree that if there were a human person who loved humankind, and possessed the requisite knowledge and power, that person would put an end to poliomyelitis by producing a means for immunization, and would prevent the Holocaust by keeping Hitler from committing his atrocities? In fact, is not this precisely what happened? People of an altruistic will, when they possessed the knowledge and power, did produce a vaccine to prevent poliomyelitis and did stop Hitler from continuing with the Holocaust. Now, if humans with their quite limited and defective capacities for love, knowledge, and power were able to prevent poliomyelitis and bring an end to Hitler's atrocities, why did not the unsurpassable deity of panentheism do this before the evils occurred? Why must we wait for human persons using natural powers and procedures to cure the ills of the world when there is an unsurpassable panentheistic deity in existence? Moreover, it is no answer to say that such entities as the polio virus and Hitler are producing their evil by the exercise of their freedom, for reasonable and humane human persons possessed of a loving will can agree that there are entities so destructive that they should not be permitted to put into effect their freedom, because their use of freedom produces only abysmal evil. I see no explanation in panentheism for the deity unsurpassable in love, knowledge, and power not having rid the world of evils with which even very limited humans have done away.[48]

Before proceeding to a discussion of a distinctly Christological use of process theology, I wish to raise one more difficulty that I find with it. This objection is based upon what I see to be the *weltanschauung* implied by contemporary cosmology. I will begin with excerpts from Hartshorne and Griffin that express the general process theology view:

> Though we do not forever continue to serve God, our temporary service is everlasting in a sense which I find deeply satisfying: whatever enters the treasury of divine life is at once where moths cannot corrupt and thieves cannot break through nor steal. And we can in this life be aware of ourselves as already immortal elements in deity, and so by Love we participate now in our immortality. The triumph over death as our triumph is now, not in a magical future. But apart from God is not the triumph with death?
>
> Rationality as such requires that there be an aim which it is rational to pursue in spite of the mortality of nondivine indi-

viduals and species of individuals. But only deity provides a clear meaning for immortality. And only an all-loving Deity whom all may love can provide nondivine individuals, even though vicariously, with permanent achievement for their effort.[49]

God's aim is for the entities in the world constantly to experience greater value. The prerequisite for greater value is greater complexity, for as a greater variety of data can be synthesized into a harmonious unity, a greater intensity of feeling is possible. A few of the most important thresholds in the ascending complexity of finite existence were life, the psyche, and consciousness. These novel possibilities were able to emerge out of an extremely complex ordering of molecules; and a psyche, especially one with consciousness, could only emerge out of an extremely complex order among the living cells. Hence the fact that the direction of the evolutionary process is toward ever-increasing complexity is illuminated by the idea that God's aim is toward higher types of values being experienced by his creatures.[50]

Thus the panentheistic deity—if one can accept with joy the finality of one's own death—provides us with an optimistic view of the direction of the universe and its future. But is this in truth the direction of the universe? Because science is employed by process theology as a basis for its claims, it is to science that we must turn to see the direction in which the universe is actually moving. Briefly stated, the direction of the universe is toward the complete annihilation of everything reasonable humankind holds valuable. The following quotation epitomizes my earlier discussion of the view of contemporary scientific cosmology.

> We do not know for sure whether the universe is open or closed. . . . If the universe [is open and] expands forever, the stars, one by one will collapse into white dwarfs, neutron stars, and black holes (or some other form of superdense state). The white dwarfs will cool into black dwarfs. The pulsars will radiate away their energy, and run down. The end will be universal darkness.

> If, as many would prefer on philosophical grounds, the universe stops expanding and collapses, perhaps to rebound into a new universe as part of a cycle without beginning or end, the prospects for anyone alive at the time of collapse are no more appealing.[51]

Thus the direction of the universe is toward extinction of everything that reasonable human beings hold valuable: either in an eternal lifeless cold and darkness (as the evidence now indicates), or in the annihilation of a big–crunch singularity that is followed by a new beginning, a senseless cycle in which whatever is valuable is always doomed to ultimate and inevitable destruction. I find the optimistic view of God and the universe set forth by process theology to be incoherent with the destiny of the universe as presently conceived by scientific cosmology. Where do we see "permanent achievement" for human effort; where do we see God's aim "toward higher types of values being experienced by his creatures"?

I should like to repeat my earlier statement as we approach the subject of a Christological process theology. This is that I present my views of other theological positions not to criticize them, but to explain why I do not accept them. The critical question in process Christianity appears not to be whether Jesus is God, but whether Jesus is God's supreme or decisive revelation. Because process Christianity is dependent upon the truth of process theology generally, and I have already explained why I reject this view philosophically, it follows that I reject the notion that Jesus is God's supreme revelation, or a revelation of God at all. Nevertheless, I should like to touch upon some difficulties I find inherent in the concept of revelation as process Christians seem to conceive it.

Primarily, I do not understand how process Christologists can call Jesus God's supreme or decisive revelation when they apparently have invented on their own what they believe about God and Jesus inasmuch as their beliefs about either do not appear in the New Testament. Plainly, process Christologists reject both the inerrancy of the New Testament and the truth of the theology in it that they take to represent Jesus' beliefs. I confess I cannot express the point better than Griffin himself does:

> A fourth difficulty involves bringing "Jesus" and "truth" together. For if Jesus is to be appropriately received as the decisive revelation about God, then he must somehow be understandable as having expressed the basic truth about God. But we have become increasingly aware of the tremendous gulf separating us from the first century, and of the fact that Jesus himself shared first-century conceptions that we must consider mythological and false. The attempt to pick out those sayings which are less obviously objectionable as constituting the real "kernel" of his message will not work, for Jesus' message as a whole presupposed

a mythological view of reality. How then can we see him as expressing the basic truth about reality?[52]

Griffin's answer, to say the least, is unconvincing. His explanation is that there are two parts to revelation, the subjective and the objective. The subjective part is that an event constitutes a revelation only if a person receives it as revelation. Admittedly, such subjective reception is unacceptable for convincing any critical thinker that it is a revelation from God, inasmuch as we have innumerable conflicting claims of subjective revelation ranging from the prophets of the major religions to psychotics in institutions. Consequently, according to process Christology, there must be an objective part to revelation. This apparently means that Jesus was God's supreme act of self-expression, and is therefore properly taken as revelation by someone who experiences Jesus' revelation subjectively as God's decisive revelation. But what did God express through Jesus that constituted God's supreme act of self-expression? I can only conclude that it was process theology. But what makes the objective part objective? Clearly enough it cannot be the New Testament, for the New Testament cannot provide evidence of an objective revelation for three reasons. One is that, according to process theology, the New Testament in not inerrant, so that we have no way of knowing what is true in it and what is not. Another is that Jesus' own theology in the New Testament is dismissed as mythological. The third is that process theology appears nowhere in the New Testament. Accordingly, where does the supposedly objective part of the revelation come from? Does it not come from the process theologian's subjective metaphysical speculation? Consequently, taking Jesus as God's supreme and decisive revelation would seem to be entirely subjective revelation after all.

I must emphasize my belief that the process Christologists have not taken sufficiently seriously the consequences of denying the inerrancy of the New Testament. How else can we explain these lines of Griffin:

In summary, then, the Christian belief that Jesus is God's decisive revelation can be understood to be a real possibility in terms of the following conceptualization. Partly because of the content of the divine aims given to Jesus during his active ministry, and party because of Jesus' conformance to these aims, the vision of reality expressed through his sayings and actions is the supreme expression of God's character, purpose, and mode of agency, and is therefore appropriately apprehended as the decisive revelation of the same. The finality of this expression is due to the fact that at least at decisive moments Jesus identified himself with the divine aims for him, so that he provided no hindrance to the expression of the divine Logos other than that which is inherent in human nature as such.[53]

Now once the New Testament is declared fallible, and explicitly stated to contain errors, how in truth can we say anything in it is true? On what basis can one speak of "divine aims given to Jesus," of "sayings and actions" of Jesus, of Jesus at "decisive moments" identifying himself with divine aims? Indeed, on what basis can we say Jesus ever existed at all; if one part (and for process Christologists there are actually many parts) of the New Testament is said to be false, by what evidence do we say any part is true?

VI. Epilogue

The essential concept of all process theologies is that substantial change takes place in the godhead either in whole or in part. I believe that this is a profound truth and of great significance for humankind. For to the degree that the godhead changes, so does the nature of human beings change, bringing into existence new conditions and requirements for the attainment of soteria. Process theology thus has a vital message for humankind, and my hope is that process theologians through dialogue among themselves and with other theologians will disseminate its truths far and wide.

Notes

1.   Or by its equivalents: "godhead"; "deity"; "ground of being"; and the like.

2.   See A. J. Reines, *Polydoxy: Explorations in a Philosophy of Liberal Religion* (Buffalo: Prometheus Books, 1987), 14–29.

3.   Unfortunately, there is no singular pronoun in English for persons that does not have a sexual gender. I regret this.

4.   A God-view also includes the view of a person who states that he knows of no existent to which he refers by the term "God."

5.   R. Lewin, *Human Evolution: An Illustrated Introduction* (New York: W. H. Freeman, 1984), 4–10.

6. In orthodox religions, such as Orthodox Judaism and Roman Catholicism, only one God-view is permissible; other God-views are considered heretical.

7. Sensum and sensa are also commonly referred to as sense-datum and sense-data.

8. The term *sensum* has more than one meaning among philosophers.

9. Without entering into the complications of the point, the existence of extramental entities can be established directly by sensa, or, in the case of unobservables (subject to strict rules), indirectly by sensa.

10. "Selfum" and "selfa" are also referred to as "self-datum" and "self-data."

11. Misinterpreted selfa include phenomena commonly referred to as illusions, delusions, and hallucinations.

12. A meta-sensum apprehension is an apprehension ostensibly relating to extramental reality attained by means of a datum present to awareness that is not experienced as coming through the senses.

13. There are, of course, other responses to this question, but I do not consider them authentic. An example of an unauthentic response is belief in a God-view not because one is convinced it is true, but because one finds it comforting or thinks it to be required in order to be loyal to one's religious community.

14. In the long theological history of the Jews, as the intellectual, political, economic, and social conditions under which they lived changed, new Jewish theologies have been created to meet the demands of the new knowledge that the changed conditions produced or made available. The fundamental reason for this theological dynamism is the function of the name "Jew" as an ontal symbol; see A. J. Reines, *Polydoxy*, 166–68, and 52n.53.

15. An assumption is a statement or proposition accepted as true without evidence. An example of an assumption is the validity of memory. The reason the validity of memory must be assumed is that it cannot be proved without employing memory, and without memory, there can be no knowledge.

16. A tragic consequence of allowing any and all God-views to be validated by assumptions alone is that some God-views urge their adherents to persecute or murder those who believe other than they do.

17. The third attribute can be understood as included in the second.

18. I claim no originality for this analysis; Maimonides, Spinoza, and Freud, among countless others, have given it.

19. Freud is the one who most convincingly presented this view. See, *The Future of an Illusion*, Vol. XXI of *The Standard Edition of the Complete*

Psychological Works of Sigmund Freud, 17–19 and elsewhere (London: Hogarth Press & Institute of Psychoanalysis, 1961).

20.   It is of interest to note that empirical verification is the test of truth required by the Pentateuch and the Bible generally.

21.   The term *hylotheism* in rare and obsolete usage has been employed to refer to the doctrine that God and the material universe are one. In this usage, the prefix *hylo* (from the Greek hyle) means matter understood as "corporeality" or "extension." The primary meaning of *hyle* in Aristotle (who coined its philosophic meaning) is "potentiality" or "possibility of being." It is by reason of this meaning that I have given the name "hylotheism" to the concept of God as the "enduring possibility of being."

The concept of the ground of being, or godhead, as consisting of the possibility of being is consistent with quantum theory. John Wheeler, for example, states:

> Quantum phenomena are neither waves nor particles but are intrinsically undefined until the moment they are measured. In a sense, the British philosopher Bishop Berkeley was right when he asserted two centuries ago that "to be is to be perceived" (*Scientific American* [July 1992], 97).

Stated in hylotheistic terms: Before being sensed, quanta exist in a state of possibility; only after perception do they become actual entities or being. Hence, in hylotheism, quanta prior to being sensed are part of the enduring possibility of being or deity; upon observation they become being, and because all being is finite, so quanta upon attaining actuality are destined for death.

22.   For a discussion of "ontal decision" see A. J. Reines, *Polydoxy*, 63–66. It should be borne in mind, however, that, owing to the limitations of the godhead, the possibilities for meaningful being are always limited.

23.   Amos 5:14–15.

24.   Freud's earlier pronouncements on the word "God" are a notable example; later he used the term "God" himself. See my "Freud's Concepts of Reality and God," *Hebrew Union College Annual* LXXI (1990), 254.

25.   For example, the term *atom* literally means "indivisible," and this was its original technical meaning as used by the philosophers Leucippus and Democritus. Scientists have since divided or split what they call the atom, but nevertheless have retained the name.

26.   See A. J. Reines, *Polydoxy*, 63, for further explanation of the term *soteria*.

27.   Ibid., 61–63.

28. Not that all process theologians deny a personal afterlife; E. S. Brightman, for one, argues that there is individual immortality. See, *A Philosophy of Religion* (New York: Prentice-Hall, 1940), 400–04.

29. Ibid., 128.

30. I have somewhat modified E. S. Brightman's definition of a dysteleological surd, but the language is almost entirely his (ibid., 245–46).

31. For example, the concept of theistic absolutism, which predicates of deity the attributes (among others) of omniscience, omnipotence, omnibenevolence, and providence is contradicted by the occurrence of dysteleological surds and would for this reason be rejected.

32. Animal rights groups and many vegetarians display great sensitivity on this point.

33. I consider the notion of a theistic or panentheistic God with surplus existence to dispense to be incoherent with the fact of existence only through destruction.

34. Actual existence or being consists only of a selfum and/or a sensum, which exists in a momentary present.

35. Ontal angst is to be distinguished from fear or anxiety that appears causeless to consciousness but, in fact, has causes repressed in the unconscious. The latter can be effectively dealt with by psychoanalysis, whereas ontal angst cannot. Ontal angst is overcome only by an ontal decision that resolves the conflict of finitude.

36. Steven Weinberg, *The First Three Minutes* (New York: Basic Books, 1977).

37. Owen Gingerich, *Cosmology + 1* (San Francisco: W. H. Freeman, 1977), 16ff. For an excellent summary of the present status of scientific cosmology, see C. S. Powell, "The Golden Age of Cosmology," *Scientific American*, July 1992: 17–22. Powell discusses the significant new evidence for the big-bang theory of the origin of the universe. He also examines the search for "dark matter" which must exist if the closed universe theory is to be substantiated. To this date, evidence of dark matter has not been discovered. Hylotheism is consistent with either the open or closed cosmological theories. In both theories, the universe and the godhead are in continuous process, as hylotheism maintains. The only difference between the two theories so far as hylotheism is concerned is this: If the open universe theory—which present evidence substantiates—is correct, and all that this universe will come to is a state of darkness at approximately three degrees above absolute zero, the impuissance of deity, namely, the enduring possibility of being, might conceivably be considered greater than if the universe exists in a continuing process of proceeding from big bang to big crunch and back

again. For such repeated expansion (or inflation) and contraction could be deemed a more positive process than the onetime movement of the universe from big bang to eternal darkness. I do not see much difference between the two theories so far as one's being a more positive process than the other is concerned. In the case of the open universe theory, value–death comes to the universe once; in the case of the closed universe theory (conjecturing that future universes produced will be like the present one), value–death will occur repeatedly for all eternity. In both the open and closed theories of the universe, the fundamental impuissance of deity as conceived by hylotheism is the same: the inability of the godhead to maintain a stable universe in which values fashioned in the past and those to be created in the future are preserved in a process of progress. Value-death comes to everything.

38.   Stephen W. Hawking, *A Brief History of Time* (Toronto and New York: Bantam Books, 1988), 136.

39.   Ibid., 151.

40.   David R. Griffin, *A Process Christology* (Philadelphia: Westminster Press, 1973; Lanham, Md.: University Press of America, 1991), 153ff.

41.   Ibid., 16–17. For my part, I do not believe that Whitehead meant the passage in the way Griffin interprets it.

42.   Charles Hartshorne, *A Natural Theology for Our Time* (La Salle: Open Court, 1967), 4–6.

43.   Charles Hartshorne and William L. Reese, *Philosophers Speak of God* (Chicago: University of Chicago Press, 1953), 16.

44.   Hartshorne, *A Natural Theology*, 66–67.

45.   I.e., panentheistic. Hartshorne at times refers to panentheism as theism. Theism, however, does not in normative usage refer to a deity who is world-inclusive.

46.   Hartshorne, *A Natural Theology*, 45–46.

47.   Ibid., 80–82; see also 58–59.

48.   Indeed, if humans can do away with evils that deity cannot, does this not mean that humans exercising their freedom surpass the deity in this regard? If so, deity is not the unsurpassable in all ways.

49.   Hartshorne, *A Natural Theology*, 56.

50.   David R. Griffin, *op. cit.*, 185. Process theologians and philosophers, notably Samuel Alexander and A. N. Whitehead, as well as philosophic systems such as absolute idealism and dialectical materialism, have assumed without further analysis the equation of complexification with higher value. I believe this equation to be an error. The prime example of complexification

is the human person. The question is: Did the evolutionary process produce higher value in the universe by the emergence of the human person? The answer, of course, is determined by the criterion employed to measure higher value. The criterion I use is: that which furthers the well-being of the earth (which includes its atmosphere) and all life on earth. By this criterion, the emergence of humankind through the evolutionary process has been the greatest and most calamitous disvalue produced in earth's history. No species has destroyed more of the earth, more of the earth's species of living creatures, more members of its own species, and has suffered, apparently, more anguish, particularly from inherent defects and conflicts of its psychic structure. Complexification does not mean higher value, just as process does not mean progress.

51. Walter Sullivan, *Black Holes* (New York: Warner Books, 1983), 267–68.

52. David R. Griffin, *A Process Christology*, 227.

53. Ibid., 231–32.

Chapter 18

Modern and Postmodern Liberal Theology: A Response to Alvin Reines

David Ray Griffin

In his enunciation of his own position, and in his criticisms of (Whiteheadian) process theology, Alvin Reines presents us with what I call a *modern liberal theology*. I will begin my response by indicating the meanings I give to the terms "liberal" and "modern" and how the theology of Reines exemplifies these meanings. Sometimes in theological circles these two terms are used interchangeably. They are, however, distinguished in my own usage.

I. Liberalism and Modernism

For me, the term *liberal* refers primarily to a theological method and only secondarily to substantive doctrines insofar as they are presupposed by the liberal method. Negatively, liberal theology rejects an authoritarian approach, according to which the question of what one should believe today is settled by reference to what was believed in the past, in scripture and tradition, and/or by what some authoritative interpreter of the tradition pronounces. In this sense, Reines' method, which he takes to be implied by the philosophy of Reform Judaism, is clearly liberal. Presuming that all humanly produced beliefs are fallible, including those of scripture and of any "prophets," he rejects all authoritarianism.[1] He also, like process theologians, rejects the substantive doctrine that had provided the crucial presupposition of the belief in an infallible revelation, namely, theistic absolutism, with its ideas of creation *ex nihilo* and of perfect provi-

289

dence.[2] Positively, liberal theology says that a central concern of theology is to discover and articulate truth, and that the generally accepted criteria of experience and reason are to be employed. That is, a theological position is to be tested in terms of its self-consistency and its adequacy to the facts of experience. The previous beliefs of one's tradition determine at most whether or not one's theological position can be called, say, "Jewish" or "Christian"; reference to these beliefs cannot settle the question of truth. I add the words "at most" because the "polydoxy" of Reform Judaism, as understood by Reines, does not make the beliefs of previous Judaism even partially normative for the Jewishness of Reform Judaism. This difference between Reines and Christian process theologians is not unrelated (as pointed out later in Section V) to the difference between modern and postmodern liberalism, to which I now turn.

By "modern" or "modernist" theology, I mean that form of liberalism that accepts certain distinctive beliefs or presuppositions of the worldview that has been dominant in the modern West, for which the ideas of men such as Galileo, Descartes, Boyle, Newton, Locke, and Hume, and more recently Darwin and Freud, have been formative. These distinctive beliefs are of two basic sorts, epistemological and ontological. *Epistemologically,* modern thought has had a sensationist theory of perception, insisting that our only experience and, hence, knowledge of the world beyond ourselves comes through our physical senses. Perception, except for self-perception, is exhausted by sense-perception. *Ontologically,* modernity has been radically individualistic, seeing the world as composed of substances that are essentially unrelated to each other. That is, their relations to other things are purely external to them, rather than being internal to (constitutive of) them. Each thing is thought to be what it is independently of its relations to other things. As Descartes put it, a substance is "that which requires nothing but itself in order to exist." Or in Newton's language, matter is "solid, massy, hard, impenetrable."

This individualistic ontology and the sensationist epistemology are mutually supportive; they are, in fact, two sides of the same coin. Sensationism supports and exemplifies radical individualism by saying that we have no awareness of other things except through our senses. This means that things without sensory organs have no awareness of other things at all. And it usually means that the only relation perceiving beings have to a perceived thing is a sense-datum that somehow "represents" the perceived thing; the perceived thing does not in any way enter into the perceiver so as to be constitutive of his or her essence. The mysterious relationship of "representing" is the only qualification of a world of essentially autonomous substances.

Rabbi Levi Olan said that Reform Judaism was created by people who accepted this worldview. He did not think, however, that Reform Judaism is essentially tied to this modern worldview, and he called for the development of a *postmodern* theology. He pointed to three issues that would be central in a movement from a modern to a postmodern theology:

(1)   It would involve moving beyond not only the classical view of God as a supernatural, omnipotent being, but also beyond the scientistic secularism that resulted from its collapse.[3] The postmodern view would see reality as a unified whole, understood as a personal, relational, purposive Holy One who guides (without determining) our free choices among alternative possibilities.[4] Among other things, Olan pointed out, this relational view of God is implicit in the notion of covenant.

(2)   The move to a postmodern theology would involve moving beyond the sensationist form of the empiricist epistemology, seeing instead with Whitehead that awareness "begins with a non-sensuous perception—a mode of awareness more basic than sensation."[5]

(3)   It would involve moving beyond the materialistic individualism of modern thought to the view that makes relational processes or events primary.[6]

In Olan's thought, as in my own, these moves are connected with overcoming the limitations in the liberationist project of modernity, especially the notion of liberation through competition among egoistic individuals and the idea that the liberation of one group can be achieved apart from the liberation of all.[7] I will not discuss this feature of the postmodern vision in this essay, however, but only those ontological and epistemological issues that are central to Reines' essay.

Reines can be seen to exemplify just those features of modernity lifted up by Olan. In rejecting theistic supernaturalism, Reines has developed a worldview that is substantively indistinguishable from scientistic secularism. He continues to use the word "God," to be sure, but the meaning of the word has virtually nothing in common with widely accepted meanings. His deity not only is not perfect, purposive, personal, or providential; it is not even actual. If to believe in God were, as Reines proposes, to believe in the enduring possibility of being, so that "the existence of God is verified whenever selfa and sensa can both be experienced" (249), then virtually everyone generally considered an atheist could be said to believe in God. As will be seen later, furthermore, Reines turns to the natural and human sciences to answer theological and metaphysical questions.

The following two sections show that the sensationist epistemology and individualistic ontology of modernity are central to Reines' own position and to his criticisms of process theology. In the fourth section, I examine Reines' critique of process theology's treatment of the problem of evil. In the final section, I examine the legitimacy of Reines' continued use of God-language, especially in relation to values.

II. Sensationism and God

Reines' basic reason for rejecting the process concept of God (and virtually every other concept of God) is his acceptance of the sensationist epistemology. While he accepts "selfa," or internal apprehensions, as evidence for statements about his own internal life, he accepts nothing but sensa as evidence for the extramental world. "Empirical" is equated with "sensory." No propositions about the extramental world are acceptable, Reines says, unless they are verified by evidence from the five senses, and he explicitly connects this criterion to statements about God (256–57). His basic reason for rejecting the idea of God as an actual being who acts providentially in the world, therefore, seems to be that sensory experience provides no evidence of such a being. He believes that the idea of such a being, like all ideas about the extramental world that are not derived from the external senses, must have originated within the human person, either from conscious or unconscious parts of the psyche. Insofar as such ideas are thought to have been derived from experiences, they are "misinterpreted selfa" (257, 276). In Freudian language, they are "projections of the unconscious."[8]

Because Reines' rejection of any concept of God as an actual being is an *a priori* rejection, based upon his epistemological starting point, it is appropriate to ask how adequate that starting point is. Reines apparently wants to forbid this examination, claiming that what a person considers to be evidence is a purely subjective choice, about which dispute is futile (256). That claim, however, is surely extreme. In the first place, although Reines says that it does not make sense to argue about which God–concept is the correct one (256), he does not hesitate later to refer to the "theological error" of those who think that their concept of God originates in experiences of a reality beyond themselves (276). Furthermore, and more important, Reines' sensationist position is self-refuting, because he affirms various types of propositions that are not verified by sensa "as true of the extramental world."

One example is provided by his references to the "external" or "extramental" world (256, 259). As has been shown by Hume and Santayana, among others, sensa by themselves provide no evidence of an external world. One who rigorously limits her or his information to these sensa must be a positivist or phenomenalist. Reines, nevertheless, clearly believes that there is an external world. He refers, for example, to "the direction in which the universe is actually moving" (279), and he presupposes that other people exist who may read his essay. The affirmation of "other minds" has been one of the chief problems of modern philosophy, given its sensationist bias. How does Reines, on the basis of selfa and sensa alone, affirm the truth of these propositions about other selves and a world in general beyond his own experience? Does not his practice show that he is presupposing some evidence, based upon something other than sensory experience alone, about the world beyond his own experience?

Another example is provided by his references to the past, as in "Jews in the past" (258). George Santayana in *Scepticism and Animal Faith* has demonstrated that the Humean, sensationist epistemology leads not merely to solipsism, according to which the self supposedly knows of no actualities beyond itself, but more strictly to "solipsism of the present moment," in which the present self cannot even know that there has been a past. The sensa derived from our five senses, such as colored shapes, do not by themselves tell us that there has been a past. Whitehead refers to the perception of sense-data as "perception in the mode of presentational immediacy." Through this mode of perception by itself we only know that we are *presently* experiencing certain colored shapes, scents, sounds, and so on, *not that this present experience is continuous with past experiences.*

It might be thought that the reality of the past would be grounded in selfa—namely, those selfa commonly called "memories." I would know that there had been a past because I would "remember" my previous experiences of it. This is true, but for Reines to give this answer would be doubly problematic. In the first place, we have already seen that sensationism leads to solipsism, so that by hypothesis Reines' memories would provide evidence only of his own past existence, not of the past existence of an actual world in which he was located. In the second place, he says: "Sensa and selfa exist only as long as they are present to consciousness." That would seem to mean that his past experiences no longer exist; as such they could not be known. At the very least, Reines' view seems to involve the Humean replacement of the notion of an enduring, substantialist self with that of momentary experiences that are not only discrete but separable. Reines says that the "continuing self-consciousness" is "constructed out of the memory of a selfum" (259). Affirming the reality of past momentary experiences seems to involve an affirmation of "extramental" actualities, that is, actualities beyond one's present experiences. Reines is, therefore, affirming the reality of extramental actualities that are not known through his sensory experiences. He does not doubt their reality. Is not some form of nonsensuous perception, accordingly, being presupposed? That is, is that which we call "memory" not an example of nonsensuous perception?

Reines, however, expressly rejects Whitehead's idea that there is a nonsensory way, called "prehension," of apprehending the extramental world on the grounds that Whitehead offers no "proof" for this idea. What more proof could be wanted, I ask, than the fact that we all in practice presuppose, and cannot help but presuppose, all sorts of things about the world that cannot be known about the world by sensory perception alone? Whitehead, in fact, holds that the "metaphysical rule of evidence" is "that we must bow to those presumptions, which, in despite of criticism, we still employ for the regulation of our lives."[9] In other words, philosophy's "ultimate appeal" must be "to the general consciousness of what in practice we experience."[10] When our metaphysics does not include some inevitable presupposition of practice, we cannot (with Hume) rest content with an appeal to "practice" to supplement our metaphysics; we must revise the metaphysics.[11] In applying this point to epistemology, Whitehead makes a criticism that would seem to apply to Reines' procedure:

> No philosopher really holds that this [perception of sensa] is the sole source of information . . . . But the general procedure of modern philosophical "criticism" is to tie down opponents strictly to the front door of presentational immediacy [i.e., sense-data] as the sole source of information, while one's own philosophy makes its escape by a back door veiled under the ordinary usages of language.[12]

The past, the external world, and other selves are not the only things affirmed by Reines that do not pass his own sensationist criterion of criticism. He also speaks of the existence of "possibilities." Here he is similar to Whiteheadian theologians in speaking of two major classes of existence: "the possible and the actual" (259). He clearly means that these possibilities are not simply projections of one's own experience. Rather, they exist beyond one's own experience; they belong to the "extramental world." A possibility, however, is not something that we see, smell, taste, hear, or touch: We cannot confirm the existence of possibilities through evidence derived from our five senses. As Reines himself says, a possibility "is neither a selfum nor a sensum" (259). This is one reason why sensationist philosophies are usually deterministic; they can provide no ground for speaking of "counter-factuals," of what might have, but did not, happen.

This difficulty seems especially problematic for Reines, because he says that "possibilities. . .constitute the godhead" (261) and defines God as "the enduring possibility of being" (259).[13] Because the existence of possibilities cannot be verified through sensory experience, Reines' criterion of meaningful talk about the world beyond one's own immediate experience seems to render his own concept of God meaningless.

Reines' sensationism undercuts his own attempt to talk about God in yet another way. He claims that to be actual is to be finite *in all respects*, hence, *temporally* finite (259). Accordingly, process theology's notion of God as an actuality who exists eternally (and therefore necessarily), and who endures everlastingly, must be false. Reines thereby rejects one of the fundamental notions of process theism, that our lives have permanent meaning because they make a permanent contribution to the everlasting individual, God. But what is his basis for claiming that to be actual is to be finite in time? It goes back to his epistemology:

> For the actually existent, as verified by experience, is always limited; indeed, nothing unlimited can be imagined, let alone conceived. (259)

In saying that nothing unlimited can be experienced, Reines means, I take it, "experienced as unlimited." He, therefore, rejects the idea of an actuality that is unlimited in any respect (such as temporally), because he has committed himself to accept "no propositions other than those verified by sensa as true of the extramental world" (257). He fails to note, however, that the idea that "the actually existent is always limited" is equally unverifiable by sensory experience. As Reines' predecessor Hume pointed out, none of us witnessed the coming of our world into being. It is equally true that there is no sensory basis for saying that the universe will come to an end in every sense, that its actuality will dry up altogether. By his own criterion, accordingly, Reines cannot claim that to be an actual individual is necessarily to be temporally limited. Insofar as the universe can be thought of as an individual, it may have existed forever, and it may continue to exist forever. (This supposition is compatible with the idea that the history of the universe consists of various cosmic epochs, and that our present epoch originated perhaps some twelve to twenty billion years ago.) Reines' commitment to accept "no propositions other than those verified by sensa as true of the extra-mental world" leaves him unable to say anything, positive or negative, about such a supposition. It, thereby, leaves him with no basis for his own preferred view of God as the enduring possibility of being, because his justification for this view is primarily that only possibility, not actuality, can endure forever.

Perhaps even more important to Reines than his doctrine of God is his concern for truth. He insists (along with process theologians) that the theological task is not exhausted by hermeneutics: "the purpose of theology is truth." A religion should be accepted not because it is Jewish (or Christian), but "because it is true."[14]

What, however, is the status of truth? It is not an actuality: An actual event or thing is just what it is; it does not make sense to call it either true or false. Truth, rather, must be a type of possibility, namely, a possible relationship between a proposition and an actuality. (The proposition can either correspond to the actuality or not.) Because possibilities are not the sorts of things that can be experienced through the senses, however, Reines' sensationist epistemology should forbid him from speaking of ideal possibilities, such as truth. This same point would apply to other ideals, such as beauty and justice.

The point of this discussion is not that Reines should quit speaking of the past, the external world, other selves, ideals, and possibilities. The point is that, to have a position that is not self-refuting, he needs to enlarge his epistemology so as to allow for the knowledge of things beyond his immediate experience, both actual and ideal, that are not perceivable through the senses. That is, he needs to allow for nonsensory perception. Of course, once he explicitly acknowledges the reality of this type of perception, which allows (among other things) his own talk of God as a possibility to be meaningful, he has thereby removed his primary basis for rejecting talk of God as an actuality. One of his fundamental bases for rejecting process theology's doctrine of God is, accordingly, removed.

III. Individualism and God

Closely related to the sensationist epistemology of modern thought has been its ontology of atomic individualism. A widespread

Renaissance idea was that every actuality is a microcosm, in some sense including the macrocosm within itself. Each thing was internally related to (constituted by) its relations to everything else. This premodern ontology of internal or constitutive relationships was replaced in the modern period by a doctrine of substances with purely external relationships. This new ontology implied, in epistemology, the "way of ideas," according to which the mind does not directly perceive and, hence, somehow include other things, but is merely aware of its own ideas, which at best can be hoped to "represent" something beyond themselves. The sensationistic solipsism discussed earlier is, accordingly, merely the epistemological aspect of the ontology of radical individualism, according to which each creature, be it an atom or a soul, is only externally related to every other. As Leibniz put it, every monad is windowless, having no openings for influence from other monads; its representations are generated purely from within. The only exception to this doctrine of mutually external relationships, in the early stage of the modern period, involved God. Descartes acknowledged that every finite substance required its relation to God in order to exist; the representations enjoyed by Leibniz's monads corresponded with the external world because God had pre-programmed them thus to correspond. In later modernity, this constitutive relationship to God was dropped; everything was said to be radically isolated from everything else.

Reines affirms this bleak vision of modernity. "To be actual is to be alone" (260). This boundary between each actuality and the rest of the world is explicitly said to separate it from God: "it is the nature of actual entities, by reason of the finity or encompassing boundary that is intrinsic to their existence, to be cut off from the ground of their being" (260).

Whitehead, by contrast, rejects this modern view. With his doctrine of "prehension," which is a nonsensory grasping of aspects of other things into an experiential unity, he develops a postmodern version of the idea that each thing is a microcosm. Each actual entity is constituted by its relationships to all other things, including God. Through this prehensive unification, previous actual occasions and God are incarnate in each present occasion of experience. Reines, however, in line with his modern vision, finds this notion false, saying:

> [T]he notion that humans are constituted of God and other entities reveals. . . a faulty phenomenology of the human person and conceals a cold, harsh truth. This is that every person is a finite being bounded by the limits of his existence within which he is alone. (276)

As this statement makes clear, Reines does not counter Whitehead's ontology simply by saying that he prefers his own; he claims that an *accurate* "phenomenology of the human person" supports his view. Let us look further at his experiential support. He continues: "Experientially, this is evident. Each person's cancer is his own" (276). The general point he means this phenomenological account to undermine is Whitehead's idea that all "actual occasions are constituted of prehensions of . . . other actual occasions," so that "(n)othing is a substance . . . or, in other words, nothing is alone" (276). What, however, is one experiencing when one has cancer? Precisely the pain and general debilitation derivative from the fact that one's experience is significantly constituted by one's relation to the cancerous cells of one's body. Besides memory, it is this direct, unmediated, nonsensory relation we have to our own bodily parts that Whitehead uses as his chief example of "prehension." If our minds were Cartesian substances, not internally constituted by their relationships to our bodies—that is, if we were truly alone—the cancerous state of our bodies would cause us no distress.

Reines' radical individualism, accordingly, is refuted by his own example. He could fail to see this because of an ambiguity in the notion of the "external world." In ordinary language, this phrase is often taken to refer to *the world beyond one's own body*. Given that meaning, the fact that an accurate "phenomenology of the human person" shows us to be intimately related to our bodies, and radically constituted by our awareness of them, would not contradict the doctrine that we are radically alone. However, in Reines' thought, and in that of modern philosophy in general, the "external world" has to mean the *extramental world*, that is, anything beyond one's immediate experience. One's own body is as much part of the "external world" as the pen with which one's hand writes. In fact, it is impossible to say exactly where one's body ends and the rest of the external world begins (for example, when an oxygen molecule that enters the lungs and then the blood stream becomes part of one's body, or when urine or a scab ceases to be part of one's body). The fact that our present experience is internally related to and, hence, constituted by its body, and that the line of demarcation between the body and the rest of the world is arbitrary, shows the inadequacy of Reines' phenomenology. It fits his ontology but not the facts. Whitehead's more adequate phenomenology supports his (Whitehead's) ontology, in which each experience is constituted by its appropriating relationship to other experiences, including the all-inclusive experience of the universe.

Reines' rejection of process theology's doctrine of God is based, in part, upon another dictum of the modern world that follows from its sensationism and atomic individualism. As Stephen Toulmin has emphasized in calling for the move to a postmodern worldview, the modern worldview has been based upon the assumption that all knowledge worthy of the name is to be derived from the various special sciences. There is no integrating knowledge to be derived from "natural theology" or "metaphysics."[15] This assumption is reflected in Reines' rejection of process theology's twofold doctrine that "the direction of the evolutionary process toward ever-increasing complexity" is explainable in terms of God's aim "toward higher types of values" and that our realization of values constitutes a "permanent achievement" (280). In rejecting this twofold view, Reines says: "it is to science we must turn to see the direction in which the universe is actually moving." The true direction thus revealed is said to be toward "the complete annihilation of everything reasonable humankind holds valuable" (279).

In his argument Reines confuses two issues. One issue is whether the present order of the universe will eventually fade away. That it will is central to the cosmology of process theologians. We assume not only that all the stars will die out, but that even electrons and protons are transient forms of existence. They all belong only to the "present cosmic epoch." Whether or not the inevitable end of this epoch means that there will be no "permanent achievement" is, however, a distinct issue. It depends upon whether there is any everlasting, receptive individual. The fact that Reines thinks he can counter the *metaphysical* doctrine that an everlasting individual exists with statements from physical scientists shows how fully he has imbibed the modern assumption identified by Toulmin.[16]

The other issue in Reines' discussion is the question of whether, within our present cosmic epoch, it is meaningful to say that there has been a direction to the evolutionary process. Evolutionary theorists committed to the positivism of modern thought have tried valiantly to deny that there has been any direction, especially any direction that could be called "progressive," but, as John Greene has shown, they have failed.[17] In any case, the fact that the present order of the universe will eventually decay (on which Reines and process theologians agree) says nothing about whether there is a discernable direction to the evolutionary process within our cosmic epoch thus far. The virtually undeniable fact that there has been such a direction cries out for an explanation. We process theologians believe that our doctrine of God provides a more satisfactory explanation than the scientistic view that the evolutionary order results solely from "chance and necessity." As Levi Olan has said:

> That there has been an evolutionary movement from the simple to the complex is undeniable. It is no more to be explained by chance than by coercive power. The existence of a power directing this process over billions of years, a power "introducing richer possibilities of order for the world to actualize," is inescapable.[18]

IV. Power and Evil

Thus far, I have looked at Reines' criticisms of process theology that are based upon his modern presuppositions. I have suggested that the cogency of these criticisms is undermined by the fact that the modern assumptions are less adequate than the postmodern assumptions of process theology. Reines, however, makes several criticisms of process theology that cannot be so classified. Most of these are based on simple misunderstandings, and will therefore, be discussed in a note, not in the text.[19] It is necessary, however, to look at his discussion of process theology's solution to the problem of evil.

As indicated earlier, Reines and process theologians are united in the rejection of supernaturalistic theism. We agree that theologies based on the idea of creation out of absolute nothingness, and the correlative notion of divine providence, cannot provide a satisfactory solution to the problem of evil. We agree that God can only offer those possibilities in the present that the actualizations of the past have made really possible (261).[20] We agree that God cannot unilaterally prevent evil, and that the possibility of evil is inherent in the idea of a world, so that the only choice is between a world with the possibility for evil and no world at all (or, more precisely, *no significant world*, because there must, process theologians maintain, be *some* realm of finite being).

In spite of all this agreement, however, Reines finds the process solution unsatisfactory. The crucial difference between his doctrine of God and that of process theologians is that the latter not only speak of God as an actual being but even ascribe perfection to God, regarding God as unsurpassable in love, knowledge, and power. Reines criticizes the process theodicy as part of his attempt to show that the only viable doctrine of God regards God as radically imperfect. This imperfection must extend not only to God's power but also to the mode of the divine existence, which is defective in lacking actuality (260).[21]

Whereas part of Reines' criticism of the process theodicy consists in charges of inconsistency, which are based on misunderstandings,[22] his main criticism is that a God unsurpassable in love, knowledge, and power should be able unilaterally to prevent evils such as polio and the Nazi Holocaust. He says:

> Now, if humans with their quite limited and defective capacities for love, knowledge, and power were able to prevent poliomyelitis and bring an end to Hitler's atrocities, why did not the unsurpassable deity of panentheism do this before the evils occurred? . . . Moreover, it is no answer to say that such entities as the polio virus and Hitler are producing their evil by the exercise of their freedom, for reasonable and humane human persons possessed of a loving will can agree that there are entities so destructive that they should not be permitted to put into effect their freedom. (278)

This is a question to which process theologians have responded, at length, in many places,[23] including my own essay earlier in this volume. The essence of the answer is that God's power is essentially evocative, or persuasive. It is *not* to be thought of by analogy with the kind of coercive power we can exert on other physical things (including human bodies) by means of our physical bodies. Reines' criticism presupposes that if God is actual and has "unsurpassable power," God must have this kind of coercive power raised to the nth degree. Process theologians are accustomed to criticisms based upon that misunderstanding from supernaturalists. It is somewhat surprising to receive it from Reines, however, given the fact that he himself thinks of God's influence on the world in terms of possibilities offered for realization (260). He evidently believes that there is no alternative between theistic absolutism and his own doctrine that God is a mere possibility. Levi Olan knew otherwise. He rejected as fully as does Reines the view of God as an omnipotent supernatural being who can unilaterally "either cause a holocaust or prevent it."[24] Yet he regarded God as an actual, personal, purposive being who influences the world.

> The idea of an omnipotent being possessing both coercive and unlimited power is disabused in history. Power, however, need not be coercive; it can be persuasive and unlimited. God creates by persuading the world to create itself.[25]

As Olan saw, the postmodern worldview moves us beyond a forced choice between supernaturalism and atheism.

V. God, Values, and God-Language

Two final issues to examine are the relation between God and values and the related question of the legitimacy of theistic language. In thinking of God as the all-inclusive individual, as the soul of the universe who gives it its unity, process theology portrays God as having a twofold relation to values.

On the one hand, *God as primordial* is the primordial orderer and locus of all values and the agent by which previously unrealized potential values can have efficacy in the world. This idea is especially important for the question of the possibility of novelty in an evolving universe. By the ontological principle that nonactual entities can exist (or "subsist") only in actual entities and that only actual entities can act, it is necessary to posit an actuality that transcends the realm of finite achievement. This is necessary to explain how potential values that have not been realized in the past can exist at all, and how they can exert any pressure on finite events to actualize them. (This is part of process theology's argument for God's existence, alluded to earlier.) God as primordial to the world is the source of novel values, which lure the world forward to, for example, more inclusive realizations of beauty, truth, and goodness.

On the other hand, *God as consequent* to the world is the locus in which the values selectively actualized in the world are preserved everlastingly. Whitehead evidently first arrived at this notion of the "consequent nature of God" through rational inference from the ontological principle. That is, if only *actual* entities can act, then the functions of ordering and presenting possible values cannot be performed by an abstract principle (the principle of "limitation" or "concretion" of which he had spoken in Chapters 10 and 11 of *Science and the Modern World*). God must be an actuality. To be an *actual* entity, furthermore, is to embody creativity, which involves a receptive unification of many into one, as well as an outgoing influence of this unity upon a subsequent multiplicity. The idea that God acts on the world by presenting it with possibilities requires, therefore, the supposition that the world acts back on God.[26] In his later thought, Whitehead evidently came to regard this belief in a receptive and conserving side of the divine reality as grounded not simply in rational inference, but also in more immediate intuition.[27] In any case, it was his doctrine that God is an everlasting actuality, with a receptive as well as an outgoing dimension, that allowed him to conceptualize the haunting intuition that "the immediate facts of present action pass into permanent significance for the Universe."[28]

Reines also speaks in this twofold way about God's relation to value. On the one hand, he speaks of God, understood as the possibility of being, as thereby the ground of being. On the other hand, he says that God "conserves" value that has been realized. More generally, Reines speaks of "interaction" between God and finite actualities and of a "relation of action and passion between humankind and the godhead" (260, 261). In Reines' thought, however, God is not an actuality, or even a quasi-actuality, but a mere possibility. How is it meaningful, even metaphorically, to use theistic language, implying action and response, to refer to a mere set of possibilities? Possibilities conceived by themselves, in abstraction from actualities entertaining or actualizing them, can neither initiate anything nor be affected. To speak of divine "action" and "passion," as if God were an active and receptive agent distinct from the possibilities themselves, is very misleading language. It disguises how far the notion of God as mere possibility departs from the notion of God as personal agent that gives the word "God" its meaning in biblically-based traditions.

The fact that Reines continues to use this language suggests that he is not as free from the Jewish tradition as he implies. He considers it a cause for reproach that some Christian process theologians confess that they do not begin with a purely neutral natural theology but from a vision of reality that conditions the way they perceive and weigh evidence. By contrast, he says: "the fact that I am a Jew is in no way relevant to which God-view I accept as true" (257). Whether or not this is true, it seems that the fact that he is a Jew *is* relevant to the God-*language* he employs. Would someone not standing in a biblically-rooted tradition be inclined to use the word "God" for a set of possibilities, and to attribute "action," "passion," and "conservation" to it?

I suspect, however, that there is something deeper going on here than mere accommodation to tradition by stretching language beyond legitimate lengths. I suspect that at some level Reines shares the intuition that the world process involves some kind of agency beyond that of the multiplicity of finite agents. For one thing, without this the emergence of novelty would be unintelligible. With regard to the possibilities that can be offered for realization in the future, Reines says that "the possibility of future being is derived from present being" (260). If that were taken strictly, then nothing could be realized in the future that had not already been realized in the past, so that the evolutionary and historical processes would involve no real novelty, but mere reshuffling. The other way to interpret Reines' statement is that the realization of certain possibilities in the present determines which previously unactualized possibilities within the realm of abstract possibility will be *real* possibilities for actualization in the future. However, this allowance of possibilities that transcend past realization requires, it seems, an actuality transcending the realm of finite actualization in which these unactualized possibilities can subsist and by which they can be presented as lures for actualization. Also, Reines' language of "passion" and "conservation" possibly suggests an intuition, which his own explicit conceptuality also denies, that there is an actuality beyond the multiplicity of finites that is somehow affected by what they do.

If there is any merit to these speculations (which I am emboldened to make in part by Reines' own speculations about the unconscious processes going on in other theologians [259]),[29] then it would seem that there would be two major obstacles to an explicit conceptualization by Reines of these intuitions. First, there is his apparent acceptance of the position of theistic absolutists, that an omnipresent actual being would have to have the kind of power they have attributed to God, which is the kind of power that produces an intolerable problem of evil and sanctions an authoritarian theology. Second, there is his apparent acceptance of the modern worldview, with its individualistic ontology and sensationist epistemology. This acceptance makes it difficult to take seriously a postmodern worldview, even though this worldview points to an understanding of deity that performs the roles Reines' own language about God seems to presuppose while ruling out the kind of divine power posited by the absolutist understanding of divine actuality. Overcoming these two obstacles would allow Reines' position not only to be more self-consistent, but also to stand in greater continuity with his Jewish tradition and thereby be more capable of reforming those traditional views that need reformation, such as the supernaturalistic view of covenant.

As recent historical studies have shown, the relation between these two obstacles to a naturalistic theism is not adventitious.[30] The modern worldview was in part created to prevent the entertainment of any conception of deity except that of a wholly transcendent, omnipotent, supernatural being. It has worked all too well. Modern men and women have, by and large, thought that supernaturalism and atheism were the only choices, both of which lead to tragic consequences. To move beyond these limited options, we need to reject both traditional theism and the modern worldview. I can only hope that Levi Olan is right, that God at this moment of history is not only Creator but also "Liberator from the modern to the postmodern world."[31]

Notes

1. Alvin J. Reines, "God and Jewish Theology" (henceforth GJT), *Contemporary Reform Jewish Thought*, Bernard Martin, ed. (Chicago: Quadrangle Books, 1968), 62–87, esp. 65, 68, 76.

2. The page numbers here and henceforth in the text refer to Reines' "Hylotheism: A Theology of Pure Process," which procedes this essay. On the present point, see also GJT 62–63, 83, 84.

3. Levi A. Olan, "The Prophetic Faith in a Secular Age," reprinted in this volume, 25–34, esp. 25, 27, 28; "Reform Judaism in a Post-Modern World," *Journal of Reform Judaism* 28/1 (Winter, 1981), 1–14, esp. 4, 5.

4. Olan, "Prophetic Faith," 28, 29–32; "Reform Judaism," 4, 14.

5. "Prophetic Faith," 27.

6. Ibid., 27, 29–30; "Reform Judaism," 4.

7. "Reform Judaism," 8.

8. GJT 79.

9. A. N. Whitehead, *Process and Reality*, Corrected Edition, David Ray Griffin and Donald W. Sherburne, eds. (New York: Free Press, 1978), 151.

10. Ibid., 17.

11. Ibid., 13.

12. Ibid., 174.

13. GJT 83.

14. GJT 85, 86.

15. See the last chapter of Toulmin's *Return to Cosmology* (Berkeley: University of California, 1982), "The Future of Cosmology: Postmodern Science and Natural Religion."

16. The extremity of Reines' scientism is revealed in an assertion in a previous version of his essay, that "deity can conceivably go out of existence, and with it all being, if the evidence of an empirical, that is, scientific cosmology, required this." What might this mean? The "empirical" criterion

presumably involves possible experiences that would verify the assertion. What possible experience could verify the assertion that all possibility had disappeared? Furthermore, it is hard to see how Reines can avoid the *metaphysical* assertion that "the possibility of being" (which he calls God) exists necessarily. He rejects the notion that the actual world came into being *ex nihilo*. Actuality and its correlative possibility must, therefore, have existed eternally. Are not the eternal and the necessary convertible? Once we recognize the necessity for at least one nonempirical or metaphysical assertion, there is no reason to exclude the possibility of others. Our theology need not be *based entirely* on scientific or empirical statements in order to be *in accord* with the best science of the day.

17. John C. Greene, *Science, Ideology, and Worldview* (Berkeley: University of California Press, 1981), ch. 6.

18. Olan, "Prophetic Faith," 30.

19. Reines' criticism of my discussion of the objective and subjective poles of a revelatory event is based on confusion. For one thing, he misunderstands the distinction between the two poles. The main confusion, however, is thinking that I said that the content of the objective part of God's self-revelation in Jesus consists of process theology. In the book in question, I devoted an entire chapter to the distinction between a pre-conceptual "vision of reality" (with which I identified the objective part of God's self-revelation in Jesus) and a philosophical conceptuality (such as that of process theology). Reines even quoted a passage in which I had stated that "the Christian revelatory content is understood as the Christian vision of reality" (272). With regard to my early discussion of Jesus as the "supreme incarnation" and "decisive revelation" of God, which Reines discusses (280–81), see note 9, page 123, above.

One of Reines' criticisms of Hartshorne is that the latter's claim, that people who do not worship an inclusive deity cannot be sane and sound, is empirically false. Here, Reines takes Hartshorne to be speaking of *conscious* belief and worship, whereas Hartshorne's statements quoted by Reines (274, 275) spoke of worshipping God "at least unconsciously" and said that individuals "may live by unconscious integrity."

Reines furthermore objects to the philosophical theology of Whitehead and Hartshorne on the grounds that they do not offer any proof for their doctrines of God. His statement about Hartshorne's denial of the possibility of "empirical proofs," however, reflects a failure to appreciate the precise (Popperian) sense in which Hartshorne uses the term *empirical*. He does not mean that there are no proofs or arguments based on experience, but only that there are no proofs based on purely empirical (meaning "contingent") features of the world. With regard to Whitehead, it is true that he does not set out one or more formal proofs in the way that Hartshorne does. However, his entire philosophy can be considered an argument for the reality of God (understood in a particular way), in that his worldview has a God-shaped hole in it. In particular, the world as he portrays it requires God as the locus and orderer of pure possibilities, as the basic source of order and novelty in the actual world, and as the necessary presupposition of our conviction that transitory experiences have permanent significance.

20. See also GJT 84.

21. See also GJT 81.

22. Reines charges Hartshorne with saying that we should not justify evil metaphysically and then doing it. Reines fails to see that the statement by Hartshorne that he cites (277) distinguishes between providing a metaphysical justification for the possibility of evil as such, which needs to be done, and justifying *particular* evils, which cannot be done and should not be attempted. Reines also claims that Hartshorne contradictorily says that "particular evils have no reason" but then says that they do, being the result of some entity's exercising its creative freedom. However, Hartshorne's statement was that particular evils have no *ultimate* reason. His point is that, because there is creative freedom at every level of the world, no particular evil is necessitated by either the existence or the will of God.

23. David Ray Griffin, *God, Power, and Evil: A Process Theodicy* (Philadelphia: Westminster Press, 1976; Lanham, Md.: University Press of America, 1991), 275–310; "Creation out of Chaos and the Problem of Evil," *Encountering Evil: Live Options in Theodicy*, Stephen T. Davis, ed. (Atlanta: John Knox, 1981), 101–17, plus responses to critiques, 128–36; *Evil Revisited: Responses and Reconsiderations* (Albany: State University of New York, 1991); John B. Cobb, Jr., and David Ray Griffin, *Process Theology: An Introductory Exposition* (Philadelphia: Westminster, 1976), 69–75; John B. Cobb, Jr., *God and the World* (Philadelphia: Westminster, 1969), chapter 4; Charles Hartshorne, *Omnipotence and Other Theological Mistakes* (Albany: State University of New York, 1984); "A New Look at the Problem of Evil," *Current Philosophical Issues: Essays in Honor of Curt John Ducasse*, F. C. Dommeyer, ed. (Indianapolis: Charles C. Thomas, 1966), 201–12.

24. Olan, "Prophetic Faith," 28.

25. Ibid., 30.

26. See A. N. Whitehead, *Religion in the Making* (Cleveland: World Publishing Co., 1960), 64–65, 85, 95.

27. See A. N. Whitehead, *Modes of Thought* (New York: Free Press, 1968), 110, 116–17, 119–20, and the discussion in Cobb and Griffin, *Process Theology*, 120–23.

28. Whitehead, "Immortality," Paul A. Schilpp, ed., *The Philosophy of Alfred North Whitehead* (New York: Tudor, 1951), 682–700, esp. 698.

29. See also GJT 78–79.

30.   Eugene M. Klaaren, *Religious Origins of Modern Science: Belief in Creation in Seventeenth-Century Thought* (Grand Rapids: Eerdmans, 1977); Margaret C. Jacob, *The Newtonians and the English Revolution 1689–1720* (Ithaca: Cornell University, 1976); J. R. Ravetz, "The Varieties of Scientific Experience," Arthur Peacocke, ed., *The Sciences and Theology in the Twentieth Century* (Notre Dame: University of Notre Dame, 1981). I have discussed this point in *God and Religion in the Postmodern World* (Albany: State University of New York Press, 1989).

31.   Olan, "Reform Judaism," 14.

Notes on Contributors

William A. Beardslee is author of *First Corinthians: A Commentary for Today, A House for Hope: A Study in Process and Biblical Thought,* and *Margins of Belonging: Essays on the New Testament and Theology,* and coauthor of *Varieties of Postmodern Theology.* He is Charles Howard Candler Professor of Religion, Emeritus, Emory University, and Director of the Process and Faith Program, Center for Process Studies, 1325 North College Avenue, Claremont, CA 91711.

John B. Cobb, Jr., is author of *For the Common Good: Redirecting the Economy Toward Community, the Environment, and a Sustainable Future, Christ in a Pluralistic Age, Beyond Dialogue: Toward a Mutual Transformation of Christianity and Buddhism, Can Christ Become Good News Again?* and numerous other books and articles. He is Ingraham Professor of Theology at the School of Theology at Claremont, Emeritus, Visiting Professor of Religion at Claremont Graduate School, and founding director of the Center for Process Studies, 1325 North College Avenue, Claremont, CA 91711.

David Ray Griffin, editor of the SUNY Series in Constructive Postmodern Thought, is author of *God, Power, and Evil, God and Religion in the Postmodern World,* and *Evil Revisited,* coauthor of *Process Theology: An Introductory Exposition, Founders of Constructive Postmodern Philosophy,* and *Primordial Truth and Postmodern Theology,* editor of *Physics and the Ultimate Significance of Time* and *The Reenchantment of Science,* and coeditor of the Corrected Edition of Whitehead's *Process and Reality.* He is Professor of Philosophy of Religion and Theology at the School of Theology at Claremont and Claremont Graduate School, and Executive Director of the Center for Process Studies, 1325 North College Avenue, Claremont, CA 91711.

Hans Jonas (deceased) was author of *Gnosticism, The Imperative of Responsibility: In Search of an Ethics for the Technological Age, The Phenomenon of Life: Toward a Philosophical Biology,* and numerous books in German. He was Alvin Johnson Professor of Philosophy, Emeritus, New School for Social Research, New York.

William E. Kaufman is the author of *Contemporary Jewish Philosophies, Journeys: An Introductory Guide to Jewish Mysticism,* and *The Case for God,* and coauthor of *A Question of Faith: An Atheist and a Rabbi Debate the Existence of God.* He is Adjunct Professor of Philosophy at Rhode Island College and Rabbi of Temple Beth El, 385 High Street, Fall River, MA 02720.

Lori Krafte-Jacobs is the author of *Feminism and Modern Jewish Theological Method* (forthcoming). She is currently pursuing a Juris Doctor degree at the University of Cincinnati College of Law. Her mailing address is 2216 Heather Hill Boulevard, Cincinnati, OH 45244.

Harold S. Kushner is author of *To Life: A Celebration of Jewish Being and Thinking, When Children Ask About God, When Bad Things Happen to Good People,* and *When All You've Ever Wanted Isn't Enough.* He is Rabbi Laureate of Temple Israel of Natick, 145 Hartford Street, Natick, MA 01760.

Anson Laytner is author of *Arguing with God: A Jewish Tradition* and *Wheels of Observance: A Growth Guide to the Jewish Holidays,* and editor of *Points East* (published by the Sino-Judaic Institute). A rabbi by training, he currently serves as Executive Director of the Multifaith AIDS Project of Seattle and is past president of the Interfaith Council of Washington. He may be contacted at his home address at 1200 17th Avenue East, Seattle, WA 98112.

Sandra B. Lubarsky is author of *Tolerance and Transformation: Jewish Approaches to Religious Pluralism.* She is Associate Professor of Religious Studies at Northern Arizona University, Flagstaff, AZ 86011.

Peter W. Ochs is author of *Reading Pragmatism: Charles Peirce's Pragmatic Writing,* and editor of *Understanding the Rabbinic Mind: Essays on the Hermeneutic of Max Kadushin* and *Postcritical Scriptural Interpretation: Essays in Jewish and Christian Hermeneutics.* He is Wallerstein Associate Professor of Jewish Studies at Drew University, Madison, NJ 07940.

Levi A. Olan (deceased) was the author of *Prophetic Faith and the Secular Age* and *Judaism and Immortality.* He served as rabbi of Temple

Emanu-El, Dallas, and as president of the Central Conference of American Rabbis.

Alvin J. Reines is author of *Maimonides and Abrabanel on Prophecy, Polydoxy: Explorations in a Philosophy of Liberal Religion,* and numerous articles. He is Chairman of the Board of the Institute of Creative Judaism and Professor of Jewish Philosophy, Hebrew Union College-Jewish Institute of Religion, Cincinnati, OH 45220.

Norbert M. Samuelson is author of *An Introduction to Modern Jewish Philosophy, The Exalted Faith of Abraham ibn Daud, The First Seven Days,* and *Judaism and the Doctrine of Creation,* editor of *Studies in Jewish Philosophy: Collected Essays of the Academy for Jewish Philosophy, 1980–1985,* and coeditor of *Proceedings of the Academy for Jewish Philosophy.* He is Professor of Religion at Temple University, Philadelphia, PA 19122.

Sol Tanenzapf is author of "Reasons for the Commandments" in Werblowsky and Wigoder, eds., *The Oxford Dictionary of the Jewish Religion* and "Social Ethics and Religion" in Donald MacNiven, ed., *Moral Expertise.* He is Associate Professor of Religious Studies at York University, 4700 Keele Street, North York, Ontario, Canada M3J 1P3.

Nahum Ward, a congregational rabbi who teaches and writes about Jewish spirituality, is author of "Judaism in the Planetary Era" and "Keeping Eco-Kosher." His mailing address is Temple Beth Shalom, 205 E. Barcelona, Santa Fe, NM 87501.

Clark M. Williamson is the author of *A Guest in the House of Israel, Has God Rejected His People?,* and *When Jews and Christians Meet: A Guide for Christian Preaching and Teaching,* coauthor of *The Teaching Minister, A Credible and Timely Word: Process Theology and Preaching,* and *Interpreting Difficult Texts: Anti-Judaism and Christian Preaching* and editor of *The Church and the Jewish People* and *A Mutual Witness: Toward Critical Solidarity Between Jews and Christians.* He is editor of *Encounter* and Indiana Professor of Christian Thought at Christian Theological Seminary, 1000 West 42nd Street, Indianapolis, IN 46208.

This series is published under the auspices of the Center for Process Studies, a research organization affiliated with the School of Theology at Claremont and Claremont University Center and Graduate School.

Founded in 1973 by John B. Cobb, Jr., and David Ray Griffin, the four Co-Directors now also include Mary Elizabeth Moore and Marjorie Suchocki. The Center encourages research and reflection upon the process philosophy of Alfred North Whitehead, Charles Hartshorne, and related thinkers, and upon the application and testing of this viewpoint in all areas of thought and practice. The Center sponsors conferences, welcomes visiting scholars to use its library, and publishes a scholarly journal, *Process Studies*, and a newsletter, *Process Perspectives*. Located at 1325 North College Avenue, Claremont, CA 91711, it gratefully accepts (tax-deductible) contributions to support its work.

Index

Lewis and Clark College - Watzek Library

3 5209 00636 5445